THE MACARTHUR NEW TESTAMENT COMMENTARY

2 TIMOTHY

John MacArthur Jr.

MOODY PRESS/CHICAGO

ISBN: 0-8024-0757-9

1 3 5 7 9 10 8 6 4 2

Printed in the United States of America

To Steve Camp,
whose zeal for what is divinely true
knits our souls and gives us a
depth of friendship belonging to
those with such a passion

Contents

Preface

It continues to be a rewarding divine communion for me to preach expositionally through the New Testament. My goal is always to have deep fellowship with the Lord in the understanding of His Word and out of that experience to explain to His people what a passage means. In the words of Nehemiah 8:8, I strive "to give the sense" of it so they may truly hear God speak and, in so doing, may respond to Him.

Obviously, God's people need to understand Him, which demands knowing His Word of truth (2 Tim. 2:15) and allowing that Word to dwell in us richly (Col. 3:16). The dominant thrust of my ministry, therefore, is to help make God's living Word alive to His people. It is a refreshing adventure.

This New Testament commentary series reflects this objective of explaining and applying Scripture. Some commentaries are primarily linguistic, others are mostly theological, and some are mainly homiletical. This one is basically explanatory, or expository. It is not linguistically technical, but deals with linguistics when this seems helpful to proper interpretation. It is not theologically expansive, but focuses on the major doctrines in each text and on how they relate to the whole of Scripture. It is not primarily homiletical, though each unit of thought is generally treated as one chapter, with a clear outline and logical flow of thought. Most truths are illustrated and applied with other Scripture. After establishing the context of a passage, I have tried to follow closely the writer's development and reasoning.

My prayer is that each reader will fully understand what the Holy Spirit is saying through this part of His Word, so that His revelation may lodge in the minds of believers and bring greater obedience and faithfulness—to the glory of our great God.

Introduction

AUTHORSHIP

Some critics question Paul's authorship of this second letter, arguing that, in such an intimate message, he would not have bothered to emphasize his apostleship, which Timothy would never have questioned. But Paul mentions many truths in this epistle that Timothy already knew and firmly believed. He confirmed his apostleship in writing in order to strengthen and encourage his beleaguered and sometimes fainthearted young friend and to undergird the authority of Timothy's leadership and teaching.

This letter has been called Paul's last will and testament. He knew that the time of his departure was near (4:6), that his earthly ministry and life were soon to end.

BACKGROUND

A few years earlier (A.D. 64), Nero had ordered the torching of his own capital city of Rome, which burned furiously for six days and nights. Not only the wooden shacks of the poor but also the stone mansions of the rich, the massive public buildings, and the magnificent pagan temples and shrines were gutted. The Roman historian Tacitus wrote, "But all human efforts, all the lavish gifts of the emperor and the propitiations of the gods did not banish the sinister belief that the conflagration was the result of an order by Nero. Consequently, to get rid of the report, Nero fastened the guilt and inflicted the most tortures on a class hated for their abominations, called Christians by the populace."

During Paul's first incarceration in Rome, he was under house arrest. Within those confines, he apparently was free to have visitors and to preach and teach (Acts 28:30–31). But by the time of this epistle, some five or six years later (A.D. 66), he was in chains (2 Tim. 1:16), languishing in a Roman prison and treated as a criminal (2:9)—with little light to read or write by, no sanitation, and no prospect of relief except by death. Whereas in his first imprisonment he had a measure of comfort and was granted some freedom, he was now confined in a dank and perhaps crowded dungeon. It is remarkable that, in addition to witnessing to his fellow inmates, he was able to write letters.

Worse than that, however, he was tragically deserted by everyone in Asia Minor (1:15; 4:16) but Onesiphorus (1:16), and only Luke was with him (4:11). The apostle freely forgave the defectors, saying, "May it not be counted against them" (4:16), but their cowardly ingratitude must have brought him great pain and disappointment. Like his Lord, he was forsaken by those he had served and loved the most. He had led many of them to the Lord and nurtured them not only as an apostle but as a spiritual father and friend.

The church at Ephesus had fallen still further into corrupt theology and ungodly behavior. Church leaders, including Timothy to some extent, were even weaker and less effective than when 1 Timothy was written. Heresy, apostasy, and even persecution had become more destructive.

That situation, as well as the abandonment by most of his friends, made Paul's longing to see Timothy particularly poignant, and he twice implores him to "make every effort to come" and see him soon (2 Tim. 4:9, 21).

MESSAGE

Paul was passing the mantle of ministry to his son in the faith and urged him to persevere in strength and faithfulness (2:1). He also understood that, despite Timothy's soundness in doctrine and personal godliness, he was prone to waver. He therefore reminded him that "God has not given us a spirit of timidity, but of power and love and discipline" and lovingly commanded him "not [to] be ashamed of the testimony of our Lord," to "retain the standard of sound words which you have heard from me, in the faith and love which are in Christ Jesus," to "guard, through the Holy Spirit who dwells in us, the treasure which has been entrusted to you," to "be diligent to present yourself approved to God as a workman who does not need to be ashamed, handling accurately the word of truth," to "flee from youthful lusts, and pursue righteousness, faith, love and peace," and to avoid being caught up in "foolish and ignorant speculations" (2 Tim. 2:7–8, 13–14; 4:15, 22–23).

Paul wanted Timothy to fully understand that he (Timothy), like the apostle himself, was under divine compulsion as a minister of Jesus Christ (cf. 1 Cor. 9:16). His final words to Timothy include few commendations but many admonitions, including some twenty-five imperatives of command—several of them just cited above. Nine of the imperatives are in chapter 4, by far the most personal section of the epistle. Paul wanted Timothy to understand that these were not merely suggestions from a loving friend and adviser but were divinely inspired commands from an apostle of the Lord Jesus Christ.

In its wider purpose, the epistle is a call for every believer to seek strength and pursue faithfulness in spiritual service.

Motivating a Spiritual Son

1

Paul, an apostle of Christ Jesus by the will of God, according to the promise of life in Christ Jesus, to Timothy, my beloved son: Grace, mercy and peace from God the Father and Christ Jesus our Lord.

I thank God, whom I serve with a clear conscience the way my forefathers did, as I constantly remember you in my prayers night and day, longing to see you, even as I recall your tears, so that I may be filled with joy. For I am mindful of the sincere faith within you, which first dwelt in your grandmother Lois, and your mother Eunice, and I am sure that it is in you as well. (1:1–5)

As mentioned in the Introduction, Paul's primary instruction to Timothy begins with verse 6 of chapter 1. The first five verses are motivational and constitute a beautiful and moving salutation to the apostle's **beloved son** in the faith. Yet even these very personal comments reflect principles pertinent not only to Paul's discipling of Timothy but also to Christian parents, Sunday school teachers, youth leaders, pastors, counselors, neighbors, and friends—to any believer who is helping another grow toward maturity in Jesus Christ and effectiveness in ministry.

These six implicit, but easily discernable, principles of motivation are: authority (1:1–2a), altruism (v. 2b), appreciation (v. 3a), appeal (v. 3b), affection (v. 4), and affirmation (v. 5).

AUTHORITY

Paul, an apostle of Christ Jesus by the will of God, according to the promise of life in Christ Jesus, to Timothy, my beloved son: (1:1–2a)

The first principle of godly and successful motivation is that of authority, as seen in the opening declaration by **Paul** that he was **an apostle of Christ Jesus.** As explained in the Introduction, Paul's apostleship already was well understood by Timothy. It is mentioned here by way of reminder that, despite their close and loving relationship, Paul ranked above Timothy in spiritual authority because he brought the Word of the Lord and was writing in that capacity.

Intimacy does not preclude authority. The relationship of love that parents have with their children does not preclude their authority over their children. A parent-child relationship of love without authority is doomed to tragedy for the entire family. No matter how cordial a working relationship may exist, a business cannot succeed if employees refuse to recognize and submit to the employer's authority over them.

Although they shared a deep friendship, Paul's loving salutation to Timothy carried the full weight of his apostleship. *Apostolos* (**apostle**) literally means one who is sent out, "a messenger," as it is sometimes translated (see, e.g., 2 Cor. 8:23; Phil. 2:25). But in the New Testament it more commonly carries the connotation of ambassador, a representative who carries with him the authority of the one he represents. It is used in that sense of the twelve disciples Jesus called during His earthly ministry (Luke 6:13; 9:10) and of Paul, whom Christ called from heaven after His ascension (see Acts 9:3–15; 22:6–14; 26:13–18). The Lord used the verb form of *Himself,* as "Jesus Christ whom Thou [the Father] hast sent [*apostellō*]" (John 17:3), and in the book of Hebrews Jesus is called "the Apostle and High Priest of our confession" (3:1).

As **an apostle of Jesus Christ,** Paul stood in the place of Christ and spoke the Word of Christ, and he did so **by the will of God** the Almighty Father. Paul writes Timothy not merely as a dear friend but as a divinely commissioned ambassador of God the Father and God the Son. He is not offering brotherly counsel but declaring divine truth with firm authority.

He does so according to, meaning "in conformity to," the gospel, here called **the promise of life in Christ Jesus.** Paul's calling to serve the will of God as a messenger of the Savior was to be discharged by proclaiming the saving good news that those who are dead in sin can find life **in Christ Jesus.** A favored phrase of Paul was **in Christ Jesus,** which signified his own and every believer's union with our Lord and Savior through participation in His death, resurrection, and eternal life. Jesus is Himself "the way, and the truth, and the life" (John 14:6), and He gives the divine **promise** that "whoever believes in Him should not perish, but have eternal life" (John 3:16) and "have it abundantly" (10:10). Those who claim that promise in faith can claim with Paul that Christ "*is* our life" (Col. 3:4, emphasis added).

Every worthy father deeply desires an unbreakable and rich relationship with his children. In the same way, Paul not only desired but experienced and expressed the intimacy of bonding love that he shared with **Timothy,** his **beloved son.** And just as this intimacy did not preclude authority, neither did authority preclude intimacy. As a loving spiritual father, Paul spoke with apostolic authority to his son in the faith. That authority gave Timothy a strong incentive for obedience.

ALTRUISM

Grace, mercy and peace from God the Father and Christ Jesus our Lord. (1:2b)

Although commonly expressed as a greeting, these were not just words but the expression of a genuine desire for God's best to be reality in the young preacher's life. Timothy was to be motivated by Paul's altruism, his unselfish concern for and devotion to the welfare of others. Like every believer, his young protégé was saved by divine **grace,** the unmerited favor of God's providing forgiveness and justification. The apostle wanted his son in the faith to continually live in divine **mercy,** the inexpressible blessing of deliverance from the misery that sin deserves and creates. He also wanted Timothy to continue in full **peace** of mind and heart, the inner tranquillity produced by divine grace and mercy. He wanted Timothy to have the best that **God the Father and Christ Jesus our Lord** offer to redeemed sinners: grace to cover sin, mercy to overrule misery, and peace to dominate life.

If we want to truly motivate other believers, we must, like Paul, have genuine, loving, and unqualified concern for their full spiritual blessing. In addition to their recognizing our authority under God, we want our brothers and sisters in Christ to know that they are loved by us without reservation. This, too, elicits response.

APPRECIATION

I thank God, whom I serve with a clear conscience the way my forefathers did, (1:3a)

A third principle of godly and successful motivation is appreciation. Not only was Paul a blessing to Timothy, but Timothy was a blessing to Paul. **I thank God** for you, the apostle assured him, saying in effect, "I am grateful for what **God** has done for me through you." While Paul was incarcerated in the dark, damp, dangerous, filthy, and stinking Roman prison, he nevertheless rejoiced that the Lord had given him the privilege of knowing and discipling Timothy. He was not bitter or resentful. He had no anger or hatred for those who placed him in prison or for the hardened and brutal criminals who were beside him. He did not lament the unjust and cruel execution he knew soon awaited him. His thoughts were on his sovereign **God** and on memories of his beloved son in the spirit, with whom he had spent so many blessed hours in mutual service of **God** and whom he likely would never see again in the flesh. Only the Lord could give such an unbelievably beautiful perspective!

To be appreciated, encouraged, and told that God has wonderful plans for them is a great motivation for young men and women who serve the Lord, and Paul's statement of appreciation for Timothy must have given that young servant of the Lord great confidence. Timothy knew Paul's words were not empty. First of all, he knew that Paul's integrity would not allow him to flatter. Timothy also was well aware that he and Paul had come to know each other intimately in their many years together. They had traveled together, eaten together, ministered together, and doubtless suffered together for the sake of the gospel. At the time this letter was written, Paul doubtless knew Timothy better than any other person.

The appreciation that Paul spoke from his own heart must therefore have profoundly touched Timothy and placed on him a great sense of responsibility to live up to the high expectations of his spiritual mentor. The young disciple knew that this dear friend and peerless saint in the cause of Christ was facing imminent death. Yet, even during his last painful and uncertain hours, he thanked God and held up before Him a young pastor who, although incomparably trained in the gospel, had yet to fully prove himself in the difficult areas of the Lord's service.

In the midst of unimaginable physical misery, Paul not only continued to praise God but did so with deep gratitude from a guiltless mind and heart. With full conviction and truthfulness he could testify, "**I serve** the Lord and continually stand before Him **with a clear conscience the way my forefathers did.**" *Latreō* (serve) was sometimes used of godly worship or even priestly service. Standing falsely accused by the Jewish leaders before Felix, the Roman governor in Caesarea, Paul said, "According to the Way which they call a sect I do serve [*latreuō*] the God of our fathers" (Acts 24:14). Speaking of true children of God, whether Jew or Gentile, Paul assured the Philippian believers: "We are the true circumcision, who worship [*latreuō*] in the Spirit of God and glory in Christ Jesus and put no confidence in the flesh" (Phil. 3:3).

As the aging apostle stood near death, he could testify that his **conscience** did not accuse or condemn him. His guilt was forgiven, and his devotion was undivided. "After careful self-examination," he said, in effect, "I can say with sincerity that, although I am not perfect, I am living in holiness before the Lord." He wanted Timothy to have no doubt that he endured his present physical afflictions, as he had countless others, because of his unswerving faithfulness to the Lord, not as a consequence of unfaithful, ungodly living.

Although even the most spiritual believer cannot know his own heart with complete certainty or understanding, it not only is possible but expected that, like Paul, every Christian have **a clear conscience.** This was a vital matter to Paul, who often refers to his conscience. When defending himself against the lying attacks he experienced in Corinth, he responded with an appeal to the highest human court, the conscience. His defense was: "For our proud confidence is this, the testimony of our conscience, that in holiness and godly sincerity, not in fleshly wisdom but in the grace of God, we have conducted ourselves in the world, and especially toward you" (2 Cor. 1:12; cf. Acts 23:1).

In his first letter to Timothy he wrote, "The goal of our instruction is love from a pure heart and a good conscience and a sincere faith" (1 Tim. 1:5), and we are to hold "to the mystery of the faith with a clear conscience" (3:9). In that same epistle he said that "the Spirit explicitly says that in later times some will fall away from the faith, paying attention to deceitful spirits and doctrines of demons, by means of the hypocrisy of liars seared in their own conscience as with a branding iron" (4:1–2). To continually reject God's truth causes the conscience to become progressively less sensitive to sin, as if covered with layers of unspiritual scar tissue. Paul's conscience was very clear and very sensitive, and he responded readily to its convicting voice.

Paul does not explain whom he meant by **forefathers,** but he obviously was speaking of godly men who had lived in former times. Unlike Timothy, Paul had no godly heritage from his immediate family. He had an impressive *religious* heritage, but he utterly discounted that as so much rubbish (Phil. 3:4–8). It therefore seems more probable that he was referring to the patriarchs, prophets, and other Old Testament saints. It is also possible that he had in mind the other apostles and the many other godly believers in the early church who preceded him in faith.

APPEAL

as I constantly remember you in my prayers night and day, (1:3b)

A fourth element of motivation was Paul's constant appeal to the Lord on Timothy's behalf. It is hard to imagine the strength and encouragement that Paul's intercession gave to his young friend as he ministered in Ephesus and other parts of Asia Minor without Paul's companionship.

The adverb *adialeiptōs* (**constantly**) refers to that which is unceasing, without interruption. We can be sure that Paul's saying **I constantly remember you** was not hyperbole. The apostle had used the same word in exhorting Thessalonian believers to "pray *without ceasing*" (1 Thess. 5:17, emphasis added), and he was himself accustomed to doing no less. He already had assured those believers of his unceasing prayers and concern for them (1:2–3). Using the same word, he assured the church at Rome that "God, whom I serve in my spirit in the preaching of the gospel of His Son, is my witness as to how *unceasingly* I make mention of you, always in my prayers" (Rom. 1:9–10, emphasis added). He gave similar assurance to believers in Corinth (1 Cor. 1:4), in Philippi (Phil. 1:3–4), in Colossae (Col. 1:3), and to his dear friend Philemon (Philem. 4).

Prayers is from *deēsis,* which in the New Testament always carries the idea of genuine entreaty and supplication before God. It was used by the angel who assured the godly father of John the Baptist, "Do not be afraid, Zacharias, for your petition [*deēsis*] has been heard, and your wife Elizabeth will bear you a son, and you will give him the name John" (Luke 1:13). Later in that gospel the word is used of the disciples of John the Baptist, who were said to "often fast and offer prayers" (5:33). It was used by Paul of his "prayer to God" for the salvation of his fellow Israelites (Rom. 10:1) and by James of "the effective prayer of a righteous man [which] can accomplish much" (James 5:16).

At first glance, the reference to **night and day** seems redundant and somewhat inappropriate. It seems redundant because, by definition, **constantly** means around-the-clock, and inappropriate because it is likely that Paul and his fellow prisoners could not distinguish one hour from another in that dungeon. But he doubtless used the phrase **night and day** in the way it is often used today, as a figure of speech expressing continuity. He simply wanted to reinforce his devotion to Timothy.

There is no better way to motivate other believers to consider their accountability to be faithful and to move their hearts in service of

Christ than to continually hold them up before the Lord in prayer—and to tell them of it.

AFFECTION

longing to see you, even as I recall your tears, so that I may be filled with joy. (1:4)

       A fifth principle for motivating other believers, especially those we may be discipling, is to love them and to express genuine affection for them. Paul greatly missed Timothy's companionship and was **longing to see** him. **Longing** is from *epipotheō*, a verb denoting intense desire or yearning for. Later in the letter he reflects the same aching desire, imploring Timothy, "Make every effort to come to me soon" (4:9), and "When you come bring the cloak which I left at Troas with Carpus . . . [and] make every effort to come before winter" (vv. 13, 21).

       I recall your tears, the apostle says, perhaps referring to their time of last parting, following a brief visit to Ephesus sometime after writing his first letter to Timothy and before he was arrested at Nicopolis and taken prisoner to Rome. Paul had a similar bond with the elders in Ephesus. When they came out to meet him on the beach near Miletus, "he knelt down and prayed with them all. And they began to weep aloud and embraced Paul, and repeatedly kissed him, grieving especially over the word which he had spoken, that they should see his face no more" (Acts 20:36–38).

       Although he doubtless realized he might never see Timothy again, even the remote prospect of such a reunion **filled** Paul **with joy.** Knowing the apostle's deep love and yearning to see him again surely filled Timothy with joy as well and inspired still greater commitment to follow in the footsteps of his beloved teacher and friend.

AFFIRMATION

For I am mindful of the sincere faith within you, which first dwelt in your grandmother Lois, and your mother Eunice, and I am sure that it is in you as well. (1:5)

       The final principle of motivation Paul alludes to is that of affirmation. In the two previous verses Paul mentions his remembering Timothy in prayer and recalling his tears. Now again he reflects on their intimate association, this time being **mindful of the sincere faith** within Timothy.

Anupokritos (**sincere**) is a compound word, composed of a negative prefix attached to *hupokritēs*, from which we get the obviously related English word *hypocrite.* Timothy's **faith** was completely genuine, unhypocritical, without pretense or deceit. In his previous letter to Timothy, Paul had written, "The goal of our instruction is love from a pure heart and a good conscience and a sincere [*anupokritos*] faith" (1 Tim. 1:5). In his second letter to the church at Corinth, Paul used the term to describe his *"genuine* love" (2 Cor. 6:6, emphasis added). Peter used it in his admonition to all believers scattered throughout the Roman Empire: "Since you have in obedience to the truth purified your souls for a *sincere* love of the brethren, fervently love one another from the heart" (1 Peter 1:22, emphasis added). James used it as the final qualification of "the wisdom from above [which] is first pure, then peaceable, gentle, reasonable, full of mercy and good fruits, unwavering, *without hypocrisy"* (James 3:17, emphasis added).

Timothy had a heritage of **sincere faith within [him], which first dwelt in [his] grandmother Lois, and [his] mother Eunice.** The reference to **Lois and Eunice** suggests that Paul knew those women personally and perhaps was instrumental, along with Barnabas, in winning them to Christ during his first missionary journey, which had taken him through Timothy's home area of Galatia (see Acts 13:13–14:21). They probably were Jewish believers under the Old Covenant who immediately received Jesus as their Messiah, Savior, and Lord when they first heard the gospel from the lips of Paul. By the time of Paul's second journey, the women had led their grandson and son to the Lord, and he already had become "well spoken of by the brethren who were in Lystra and Iconium" (Acts 16:2). Timothy was Paul's indirect son in the faith who had come to belief through the witness of his **grandmother Lois** and his **mother Eunice,** who had been led to faith directly by the apostle. Through them, he had "from childhood . . . known the sacred writings which are able to give [him] the wisdom that leads to salvation through faith which is in Christ Jesus" (2 Tim. 3:15).

Some years ago I was involved in a discussion regarding the choice of a man to take up the leadership of a well-known Christian organization. In looking over the list of prospects, I commented that it was interesting that every one of those men had a godly pastor for a father. The Lord has, of course, raised up many faithful leaders, including Paul, from ungodly and even godless families. But a high percentage of the great men throughout church history have come from godly homes. Timothy's father was an unbelieving Gentile (Acts 16:3), but his mother and grandmother were believers of great godliness. Paul commends them for the immense influence for good they had on Timothy and for the **sincere faith** that the apostle was **sure** to be **in** Timothy as well.

Not Being Ashamed of Christ

2

And for this reason I remind you to kindle afresh the gift of God which is in you through the laying on of my hands. For God has not given us a spirit of timidity, but of power and love and discipline. Therefore do not be ashamed of the testimony of our Lord, or of me His prisoner; but join with me in suffering for the gospel according to the power of God, who has saved us, and called us with a holy calling, not according to our works, but according to His own purpose and grace which was granted us in Christ Jesus from all eternity, but now has been revealed by the appearing of our Savior Christ Jesus, who abolished death, and brought life and immortality to light through the gospel, for which I was appointed a preacher and an apostle and a teacher. For this reason I also suffer these things, but I am not ashamed; for I know whom I have believed and I am convinced that He is able to guard what I have entrusted to Him until that day. Retain the standard of sound words which you have heard from me, in the faith and love which are in Christ Jesus. Guard, through the Holy Spirit who dwells in us, the treasure which has been entrusted to you.

You are aware of the fact that all who are in Asia turned away from me, among whom are Phygelus and Hermogenes. The Lord grant mercy to the house of Onesiphorus for he often refreshed me, and was not ashamed of my chains; but when he was in Rome, he eagerly searched for me, and found me—the Lord grant to him to find mercy from the Lord on that day—and you know very well what services he rendered at Ephesus. (1:6–18)

During the Boxer Rebellion (1899–1900), extreme nationalist Chinese fomented a campaign of terror against officials of foreign governments, Christian missionaries, and even Chinese Christians. After they surrounded a certain mission station, they sealed all exits except one. They placed a cross in the dirt in front of the opened gate and told the missionaries and students that anyone who walked out and trampled the cross would be spared. According to reports, the first seven students who departed trampled the cross and were sent on their way. The eighth student, a young girl, approached the cross, knelt down, prayed for strength, carefully walked around the cross, and was immediately shot to death. The remaining 92 students, strengthened by that girl's courageous example, also walked around the cross to their deaths.

The second section of 2 Timothy 1:6–18 focuses on the believers' not being ashamed of Jesus Christ. Paul founds this appeal on the motivations for serving Christ he has presented in verses 1–5. Those six motivations were to generate in Timothy the pervasive attitude of not being ashamed of the Lord Jesus Christ, the underlying attitude that is indispensable for effective ministry in the kingdom. The positive expression of that attitude is courageous, unapologetic witness to and obedience of Him, no matter what the cost or consequences. It is the attitude that refuses to equivocate, vacillate, or compromise and that does not hesitate to be confrontational when necessary.

David expressed the attitude of courageous witness in these words: "I have proclaimed glad tidings of righteousness in the great congregation; behold, I will not restrain my lips, O Lord, Thou knowest. I have not hidden Thy righteousness within my heart; I have spoken of Thy faithfulness and Thy salvation; I have not concealed Thy lovingkindness and Thy truth from the great congregation" (Ps. 40:9–10). He would always speak for the Lord without restraint or reservation. Another psalmist declared, "My mouth shall tell of Thy righteousness, and of Thy salvation all day long; for I do not know the sum of them. I will come with the mighty deeds of the Lord God; I will make mention of Thy righteousness, Thine alone" (Ps. 71:15–16). Still another psalmist testified, "I will also speak of Thy testimonies before kings, and shall not be ashamed" (Ps. 119:46). Nothing could withstand the commitment of those saints to speak of God's grace and righteousness.

No matter how gifted a person may be, or how well trained, biblically literate, astute, or articulate, and no matter much opportunity or privilege he may have, if he lacks spiritual courage and commitment, he will not speak and act effectively for the Lord.

Paul is calling for a level of commitment that says, "I don't care what the world thinks, says, or does. I know what God has mandated for me to be and to do, and that is what I determine, by His power, to be and to do. Whatever the consequences, I will boldly stand for Christ." The apostle specifically mentions that theme three times in this passage (vv. 8, 12, 16), because it is the heart of his message to the young pastor Timothy. It is a call for him to have an uncompromising, unflinching commitment to proclaim Jesus Christ, regardless of the danger or difficulty.

As Christians, most of us must confess to being ashamed of the Lord at some time or another, afraid of what people might think and of how their opinions might affect our popularity in school, our social standing, or our success in business. Perhaps we were afraid they would wonder why our lifestyle is often inconsistent with our faith. Yet we must also confess that the risks we have faced were much less serious than those Timothy faced, which included physical persecution, imprisonment, and possible death.

The most familiar example in the New Testament of being ashamed of Christ is Peter's denial during Jesus' trial before the high priest Caiaphas and the Sanhedrin, the Jewish Council. All the disciples fled when Jesus was arrested in the Garden of Gethsemane (Matt. 26:56), but Peter returned and followed "Him at a distance as far as the courtyard of the high priest" (v. 58). While waiting there, he three times denied being Jesus' disciple or even knowing Him (vv. 70–74). As soon as a cock crowed, "Peter remembered the word which Jesus had said, 'Before a cock crows, you will deny Me three times.' And he went out and wept bitterly" (v. 75).

That vivid account makes Peter's denial an easy target for reproach. But, as mentioned above, every Christian knows that he, too, at times has been guilty of denying the Lord, though perhaps not as publicly or dramatically. The encouraging truth we gain from Peter's experience is that, just as we can be ashamed of the Lord as he was, we also can be forgiven and restored by the Lord as he was. When, after the resurrection, Peter three times affirmed love for Him, Jesus three times acknowledged that the love was genuine, although weak, and He charged Peter with care of His flock, the church (John 21:15–17). A few weeks later, during the feast of Pentecost, Peter fearlessly proclaimed before a great crowd in Jerusalem,

"Men of Israel, listen to these words: Jesus the Nazarene, a man attested to you by God with miracles and wonders and signs which God performed through Him in your midst, just as you yourselves know—this Man, delivered up by the predetermined plan and foreknowledge of God, you nailed to a cross by the hands of godless men and put Him to death. And God raised Him up again, putting an end to the agony of death, since it was impossible for Him to be held in its power." . . . And with many other words he solemnly testified and kept on exhorting them, saying, "Be saved from this perverse generation!" So then, those who had received his word were baptized; and there were added that day about three thousand souls. (Acts 2:22–24, 40–41)

Peter continued to preach the gospel in Jerusalem without compromise and without fear. Peter was brought before the very Council where his Lord was falsely charged and outside of which he had denied Him. But on this occasion Peter was a different man. When he was commanded to stop preaching, he declared with John, "Whether it is right in the sight of God to give heed to you rather than to God, you be the judge; for we cannot stop speaking what we have seen and heard" (Acts 4:19–20).

As with Peter, it is only when we move from shame and fear to ardent conviction and bold commitment that we become useful in the Lord's service.

It is possible that Timothy had become somewhat fearful or apathetic in his ministry. The difficulties and opposition he encountered at Ephesus, both from within and without the church there, may have taken a toll on his courage. His spiritual fire may have cooled. In this second letter to Timothy, Paul gives only one commendation, saying, "I am mindful of the sincere faith within you" (1:5). The remainder of the letter is devoted to exhortation. Although he does not accuse Timothy of sin, he gives many admonitions (see 1:8; 1:13; 2:1, 15, 22; 4:1–2, 4:5).

During His earthly ministry, Jesus made clear the cost of discipleship for those who are faithful and unashamed. "Everyone therefore who shall confess Me before men," He said, "I will also confess him before My Father who is in heaven" (Matt. 10:32). He then gives the sobering converse of that promise: "But whoever shall deny Me before men, I will also deny him before My Father who is in heaven" (v. 33). In Mark's account, Jesus spoke the same truth even more poignantly: "For whoever is ashamed of Me and My words in this adulterous and sinful generation, the Son of Man will also be ashamed of him when He comes in the glory of His Father with the holy angels" (Mark 8:38).

A person who refuses to openly proclaim Jesus Christ as Lord and Savior gives evidence that he does not belong to Christ, no matter what claim is made for being a Christian. True discipleship is costly. A nominal Christian who will not even "confess [Jesus] before men" surely will not pay the price that faithful, ongoing discipleship can incur. "He who loves father or mother more than Me is not worthy of Me," Jesus said, "and he who loves son or daughter more than Me is not worthy of Me. And he who does not take his cross and follow after Me is not worthy of Me. He who has found his life shall lose it, and he who has lost his life for My sake shall find it" (Matt. 10:37–39). The mark of a true follower of Christ is willingness to put his very life on the line. From the prospect of eternity, however, that is a small price. "For what does it profit a man to gain the whole world, and forfeit his soul?" Jesus asked rhetorically, "For what shall a man give in exchange for his soul?" (Mark 8:36–37).

The English word *martyr* translates the Greek *martur*, which simply means witness. But because so many early Christians paid for their witness with their lives, *martyr* eventually acquired that special meaning.

The cost of discipleship did not begin with New Testament saints. Countless saints under the Old Covenant, and even before the Old Covenant, willingly and gladly suffered because of their unswerving faith in the Lord. Consequently, "God is not ashamed to be called their God" (Heb. 11:16). Some "were tortured, not accepting their release, in order that they might obtain a better resurrection; and others experienced mockings and scourgings, yes, also chains and imprisonment. They were stoned, they were sawn in two, they were tempted, they were put to death with the sword; they went about in sheepskins, in goatskins, being destitute, afflicted, ill-treated (men of whom the world was not worthy), wandering in deserts and mountains and caves and holes in the ground" (11:35–38).

Like those saints, the great Reformer John Hus was not ashamed of his Lord and for it paid the ultimate physical price. In 1415, when he was a pastor in Prague, this "morning star of the Reformation," as he is often called, was arrested, condemned, and sentenced to burn at the stake for preaching the true gospel. As the flames engulfed his body, he quoted Psalm 25:2, praying, "O my God, in Thee I trust, do not let me be ashamed; do not let my enemies exult over me." He was not afraid of dying, only of being ashamed of his Master.

Even if they have not heard the gospel, all men are accountable before God, "because that which is known about God is evident within them; for God made it evident to them. For since the creation of the world His invisible attributes, His eternal power and divine nature, have been clearly seen, being understood through what has been made, so that they are without excuse" (Rom. 1:19–20). For those who have had the immeasurable blessing of hearing the way of salvation, of having "knowledge of the Lord and Savior Jesus Christ," yet refuse to trust in Him, "the last state has become worse for them than the first. For it would be better for them not to have known the way of righteousness, than having known it, to turn away from the holy commandment delivered to them" (2 Peter 2:21).

It is characteristic of the unsaved person to be ashamed of Christ, "because the mind set on the flesh is hostile toward God; for it does not subject itself to the law of God, for it is not even able to do so" (Rom. 8:7; cf. 5:10; Col. 2:21). Therefore, when a believer is ashamed of Christ he is acting like an unbeliever. The shame that marks the unbelieving soul should never mark a Christian, but tragically it sometimes does. The shame may be obvious and public or it may be subtle and private, but the Lord always knows of it and is grieved.

The writer of Hebrews reminds us that "it was fitting for Him, for whom are all things, and through whom are all things, in bringing many sons to glory, to perfect the author of their salvation through sufferings. For both He who sanctifies and those who are sanctified are all from one Father; for which reason He is not ashamed to call them brethren" (Heb. 2:10–11). Quoting the magnificent messianic Psalm 22, he reinforces that truth, saying, "I will proclaim Thy name to My brethren" (v. 12). The Lord redeemed us through His suffering, through which He became "sin on our behalf, that we might become the righteousness of God in Him" (2 Cor. 5:21). He "gave Himself for our sins, that He might deliver us out of this present evil age, according to the will of our God and Father" (Gal. 1:4).

A Christian's being ashamed of the Lord is caused by a shameless self-interest that is unwilling to pay the price of faithful discipleship. Throughout church history, the Lord's name has suffered reproach because of the sinfulness of His people. Yet, despite our many sins, including our shame of Him, the sinless and righteous Lord is not ashamed of us! He does not hesitate to call us brethren (cf. Heb. 2:11), even when we are ashamed to call Him Lord.

Speaking directly to Timothy, and indirectly to all believers, Paul sets forth eight means by which a Christian may guard against being ashamed of Christ. They are: renew your gift (1:6); consider your resources (v. 7); accept your suffering (v. 8a); remember your calling (vv. 8b–10); realize your duty (vv. 11–12a); trust your security (v. 12b); affirm your doctrine (vv. 13–14); and choose your associates (vv. 15–18).

RENEW YOUR GIFT

And for this reason I remind you to kindle afresh the gift of God which is in you through the laying on of my hands. (1:6)

As already mentioned, it seems likely that Timothy's fervor and devotion had cooled to some degree. Paul's first admonition, therefore, was for this young pastor to renew his divinely inspired commitment to proclaim and defend the gospel and to faithfully shepherd the believers God had entrusted to his care.

For this reason refers to the "sincere faith within" Timothy commended in the previous verse. The product of sincere faith is faithful service, and the heart of faithful service is ministering our gift unreservedly for the Lord, the gift which He distributes "to each one individually just as He wills" (1 Cor. 12:11). Apart from ministering our gift in the service of the Lord, our life on earth is worthless. Our sole purpose as Christians is to obey and serve the Lord through the gift with which He has uniquely blessed each of us, so that the body may be built up to be effective in evangelism.

Paul wanted to **remind** Timothy of something he already knew. *Anazpureō* (**to kindle afresh**) literally means "to keep the fire alive," to fan the embers into flame and not let them die out. It carries the same idea of constancy as does the apostle's declaration, "I die daily" (1 Cor. 15:31). We need to continually bury self-will in order to continually allow Christ's Holy Spirit to work His will through us. Just as every believer, like Paul, needs to wake up each day and bury self, every believer also needs each day to continually **kindle afresh the gift of God** he has received. The negative expression of that command is "Do not quench the Spirit" (1 Thess. 5:19). Under the Spirit's guidance, and in His power, we must regularly exercise **the gift** we have received from God, lest it atrophy from neglect and disuse.

Gift translates *charisma,* which denotes a specific expression of *charis* ("grace") and therefore carries the idea of a grace gift. It refers to the general categories of spiritual gifts that Paul explains in Romans 12 and 1 Corinthians 12. God sovereignly bestows these enablements on believers according to His own divine will, totally apart from any personal merit, qualification, or seeking. Therefore, "since we have gifts [*charismata,* plural of *charisma*] that differ according to the grace [*charis*] given to us," Paul admonished believers in Rome, "let each exercise them accordingly" (Rom. 12:6).

In the present passage, Paul uses the singular *charisma* in the same way as Peter does in his first letter: "As each one has received a special gift, employ it in serving one another, as good stewards of the manifold grace of God; . . . so that in all things God may be glorified through Jesus Christ, to whom belongs the glory and dominion forever and ever. Amen" (1 Peter 4:10–11). In both instances the apostles are speaking of each believer's unique spiritual giftedness, which may encompass several specific gifts.

A believer's divine giftedness is inseparable from his divine call-ing. At salvation, each Christian's grace gifts are bestowed on him uniquely to equip him to serve God in the specific area or areas of min-istry to which he has been called. The grace gifts are divine enable-ments for effective service of the Lord. Timothy's giftedness prepared him not only for preaching and teaching but also to "do the work of an evangelist, [in order to] fulfill your ministry" (2 Tim. 4:5).

That **gift of God** for preaching the Word already **is in you,** Paul reminded Timothy. It was received at salvation but had not come to full fruition; it was not being employed to the full extent of Timothy's calling and of the Spirit's power. In chapter 4 he explains explicitly what he means by **to kindle afresh the gift of God which is in you.** "Preach the word," he admonishes; "be ready in season and out of season; re-prove, rebuke, exhort, with great patience and instruction" (2 Tim. 4:2).

Through the laying on of my hands may mean that Paul laid his hands on Timothy at the time of his conversion, which corresponded to the time of receiving his unique spiritual giftedness. Or it may mean that Timothy's spiritual endowment was extraordinary, being received, or perhaps enhanced at a later time, **through the . . . hands** of the apostle, as well as through "the laying on of hands by the presbytery" (1 Tim. 4:14), and "in accordance with the prophecies previously made concerning you" (1 Tim. 1:18).

But Paul's basic admonition to Timothy, and to every believer, remains unchanged. Divine giftedness is to be continually rekindled, fanned into flame, in order that Christ may fully work out His will for us and through us. The very fact that we have giftedness from God de-mands its full and constant use. And the fact that every believer has a divinely bestowed gift means that every believer has a divinely equipped ministry.

Whatever specific gifts our giftedness may embrace, they are continually to be exercised in God's power for the extension of His king-dom, for the building of His church, and for the glory of His name. If a believer has the gift of prophecy, it should be exercised "according to the proportion of his faith; if service, in his serving; or he who teaches, in his teaching; or he who exhorts, in his exhortation; he who gives, with liberality; he who leads, with diligence; he who shows mercy, with cheerfulness" (Rom. 12:6–8). And in every case, he should not be "lag-ging behind in diligence, [but be] fervent in spirit, serving the Lord" (v. 11).

Although Timothy's gift was given to him by God through the Holy Spirit and placed within him, it could not become evident or begin to function until he was commissioned to minister. In a similar though not as unique a way, every believer must genuinely and unreservedly de-vote himself to serving the Lord in the energy of the Spirit before his giftedness can become truly evident or effective. When our heart's desire is to please the Lord, the Lord will guide us by that desire into the specific areas of service for which He has gifted us. The Lord does not mock His children. He lovingly bestows desires that correspond to His gifts.

When we begin to function in the area in which God has gifted us, our boldness in His service will grow, because we know we are doing what He has appointed and equipped us to do. Nothing gives a believer more courage and more protection from being ashamed of Christ than knowing he is in the Lord's will and is operating his gift in the power of the Holy Spirit.

CONSIDER YOUR RESOURCES

For God has not given us a spirit of timidity, but of power and love and discipline. (1:7)

A second means for guarding against being ashamed of Christ is to consider our divine resources. The Greek verb (*didōmi*) behind **has not given** is in the aorist active indicative tense, showing past completed action. **God** already has provided for us the resources.

The Lord may withhold special help until we have special need. Jesus told the Twelve, "When they deliver you up, do not become anxious about how or what you will speak; for it shall be given you in that hour what you are to speak. For it is not you who speak, but it is the Spirit of your Father who speaks in you" (Matt. 10:19–20). But God provided everything we need for everyday faithful living and service when we first believed.

From a negative perspective, we can be sure that any **spirit of timidity** we might have is not from God. Both testaments speak of a fitting and proper fear of God, in the sense of awe and reverence. But *deilia* is a timid, cowardly, shameful fear that is generated by weak, selfish character. The Lord is never responsible for our cowardice, our lack of confidence, or our being shameful of Him. The noun *deilia* (**timidity**) is used only here in the New Testament and, unlike the more common term for fear (*phobos*), carries a generally negative meaning.

The resources we have from our heavenly Father are **power and love and discipline.** When we are vacillating and apprehensive, we can be sure it is because our focus is on ourselves and our own human resources rather than on the Lord and His available divine resources.

Dunamis (**power**) denotes great force, or energy, and is the term from which we get *dynamic* and *dynamite*. It also carries the connotation of effective, productive energy, rather than that which is raw and unbridled. God provides us with His **power** in order for us to be effective in His service. Paul did not pray that believers in Ephesus might be *given* divine power but that they might be aware of the divine power they already possessed. "I pray that the eyes of your heart may be enlightened," he wrote, "so that you may know what is the hope of His calling, what are the riches of the glory of His inheritance in the saints, and what is the surpassing greatness of His power toward us who believe. These are in accordance with the working of the strength of His might which He brought about in Christ, when He raised Him from the dead, and seated Him at His right hand in the heavenly places" (Eph. 1:18–20). Through Christ we have the resource of God's own supernatural **power,** the very power He used to raise Christ from the dead.

Although Old Testament saints were not indwelt by the Holy Spirit in the same degree of fullness that New Testament believers are (cf. John 14:17), they did have the resource of God's Spirit providing divine help as they lived and served Him. They understood, as Zechariah declared to Zerubbabel, that their strength was not by human "'might nor . . . power, but by My Spirit,' says the Lord of hosts" (Zech. 4:6).

It is of utmost importance to understand that God does not provide His **power** for us to misappropriate for our own purposes. He provides His **power** to accomplish His purposes through us. When our trust is only in Him, and our desire is only to serve Him, He is both willing and "able to do exceeding abundantly beyond all that we ask or think, according to the power that works within us" (Eph. 3:20).

God also has given every believer the resource of His own divine **love,** which, like His power, we received at the time of our new birth. In his letter to the church at Rome, Paul exulted, "The love of God has been poured out within our hearts through the Holy Spirit who was given to us" (Rom. 5:5).

The love we have from God is *agapē,* the volitional and selfless love that desires and works for the best interests of the one loved. It is not emotional and conditional, as *philos* love often is, and has nothing in common with *erōs* love, which is sensual and selfish. The love we have from God is constant. It does not share the ebb and flow or the unpredictability of those other loves. It is a self-denying grace that says to others, in effect, "I will give myself away on your behalf." Directed back to God, from whom it came, it says, "I will give my life and everything I have to serve you." It is the believer's "love in the Spirit" (Col. 1:8), the divinely-bestowed love of the one who will "lay down his life for his friends" (John 15:13). It is the "sincere love of the brethren" by which we "fervently love one another from the heart" (1 Peter 1:22), the "perfect love [that] casts out fear" (1 John 4:18). It is the love that affirms without reservation or hesitation: "If we live, we live for the Lord, or if we die, we die for the Lord; therefore whether we live or die, we are the

Lord's" (Rom. 14:8). Above all, it is "the love of Christ which surpasses knowledge" (Eph. 3:19).

Our spiritual lives are measured accurately by our love. If our first love is for self, our life will center on seeking our own welfare, our own objectives, our own comfort and success. We will not sacrifice ourselves for others or even for the Lord. But if we love with the love God provides, our life will center on pleasing Him and on seeking the welfare of others, especially other Christians. Godly love is the first fruit of the Spirit, and it is manifested when we "live by the Spirit [and] . . . walk by the Spirit" (Gal. 5:22, 25).

Sōphronismos (**discipline**) has the literal meaning of a secure and sound mind, but it also carries the additional idea of a self-controlled, disciplined, and properly prioritized mind. God-given **discipline** allows believers to control every element of their lives, whether positive or negative. It allows them to experience success without becoming proud and to suffer failure without becoming bitter or hopeless. The disciplined life is the divinely ordered life, in which godly wisdom is applied to every situation.

In his letter to the church at Rome, Paul uses the verb form of the term, admonishing, "I say to every man among you not to think more highly of himself than he ought to think; but to think so as to have sound judgment [*sōphrone*], as God has allotted to each a measure of faith" (Rom. 12:3). In his first letter to Timothy (3:2) and in his letter to Titus (1:8; cf. 2:2), he used the adjective form to describe a key quality that should characterize overseers, namely, that of being prudent and sensible.

When we live by the godly **discipline** that our gracious Lord supplies, our priorities are placed in the right order, and every aspect of our lives is devoted to advancing the cause of Christ. Because of his Spirit-empowered discipline, Paul could say, "I run in such a way, as not without aim; I box in such a way, as not beating the air; but I buffet my body and make it my slave, lest possibly, after I have preached to others, I myself should be disqualified" (1 Cor. 9:26–27).

The great spiritual triumvirate of power, love, and discipline belong to every believer. These are not natural endowments. We are not born with them, and they cannot be learned in a classroom or developed from experience. They are not the result of heritage or environment or instruction. But all believers possess these marvelous, God-given endowments: **power,** to be effective in His service; **love,** to have the right attitude toward Him and others; and **discipline,** to focus and apply every part of our lives according to His will.

When those endowments are all present, marvelous results occur. No better statement affirming this reality can be found than in Paul's letter to the church at Ephesus, to whom he said,

For this reason, I bow my knees before the Father, from whom every family in heaven and on earth derives its name, that He would grant you, according to the riches of His glory, *to be strengthened with power through His Spirit* in the inner man; so that Christ may dwell in your hearts through faith; and that you, *being rooted and grounded in love,* may be able to comprehend with all the saints what is the breadth and length and height and depth, and to know the love of Christ which surpasses knowledge, that you may be filled up to all the fullness of God. Now to Him who is able to do exceeding abundantly beyond all that we ask or think, *according to the power that works within us,* to Him be the glory in the church and in Christ Jesus to all generations forever and ever. Amen. (Eph. 3:14–21; emphasis added)

ACCEPT YOUR SUFFERING

Therefore do not be ashamed of the testimony of our Lord, or of me His prisoner; but join with me in suffering for the gospel (1:8a)

A third means for guarding against being ashamed of Christ is accepting the consequences of being faithful. Consequently, Paul advised Timothy to prepare himself for misunderstanding, animosity, and rejection.

Therefore refers to the divinely bestowed gift and resources Paul has just mentioned in the two previous verses. "In light of those immeasurable blessings," the apostle was saying, "you have no reason to **be ashamed of the testimony of our Lord, or of [Paul] His prisoner.** Do not be afraid to name the name of Christ or to be known as my friend and fellow minister."

At the time this letter was written, probably in A.D. 66, being a Christian not only brought almost universal criticism but frequently persecution, imprisonment (as Paul was then experiencing), and even death. To be associated with the **Lord,** or with Paul, **His prisoner,** could be costly in the extreme. It is interesting and significant that the apostle did not consider himself primarily to be a **prisoner** of Rome but rather of Him, that is, of the **Lord** Jesus Christ, who had sovereign control of his life. He could say, "I bear on my body the brand-marks of Jesus" (Gal. 6:17).

But being a **prisoner** not only resulted *from* his being faithful to Christ but also resulted *in* the promotion of the cause of Christ. He told the church at Ephesus, "I, Paul, [am] the prisoner of Christ Jesus for the sake of you Gentiles" (Eph. 3:1). To believers at Philippi he said, "Now I want you to know, brethren, that my circumstances have turned out for the greater progress of the gospel, so that my imprisonment in the cause of Christ has become well known throughout the whole praetorian guard and to everyone else, and that most of the brethren, trusting in the Lord because of my imprisonment, have far more courage to speak the word of God without fear" (Phil. 1:12–14).

Paul would not ask Timothy to do what he would not. **Join with me,** he said, **in suffering for the gospel** (cf. 2:3). **Join with . . . in suffering** translates the single, compound Greek word *sunkakopatheō,* which here is an active imperative. Paul called on Timothy to share his own greatest desire, his supreme purpose in life: to "know [Christ], and the power of His resurrection and the fellowship of His sufferings, being conformed to His death" (Phil. 3:10).

It is important to note that Paul is speaking about **suffering for the gospel,** not about suffering punishment for our sinfulness. We should give "no cause for offense in anything, in order that the ministry be not discredited" (2 Cor. 6:3). "If you are reviled for the name of Christ, you are blessed, because the Spirit of glory and of God rests upon you," Peter explains. But "by no means let any of you suffer as a murderer, or thief, or evildoer, or a troublesome meddler" (1 Peter 4:14–15). Rather, "Let those also who suffer according to the will of God," Peter went on to say, "entrust their souls to a faithful Creator in doing what is right" (v. 19).

But when we live a godly, moral life before our family, our fellow students, our fellow workers, or our neighbors, we can expect hostility in some form or another, because their immorality and ungodliness will be more apparent by contrast. When we confront their sin and testify to their need for repentance and salvation, we will be resented.

Later in this letter, Paul echoes Jesus' promise that "in the world you have tribulation" (John 16:33), assuring Timothy that, "indeed, all who desire to live godly in Christ Jesus will be persecuted" (2 Tim. 3:12). **Suffering** is the inevitable cost of godly living.

But **suffering** for Christ is more a privilege than a sacrifice, more a blessing than an ordeal. "Even if I am being poured out as a drink offering upon the sacrifice and service of your faith," he told Philippian believers, "I rejoice and share my joy with you all" (Phil. 2:17). He could say with humble honesty, "In everything [we are] commending ourselves as servants of God, in much endurance, in afflictions, in hardships, in distresses, in beatings, in imprisonments, in tumults, in labors, in sleeplessness, in hunger, in purity, in knowledge, in patience, in kindness, in the Holy Spirit, in genuine love, in the word of truth, in the power of God; by the weapons of righteousness for the right hand and the left" (2 Cor. 6:4–7).

We should share that selfless attitude with Paul and with the apostles in Jerusalem, who "went on their way from the presence of the

[Jewish] Council, rejoicing that they had been considered worthy to suffer shame for His name" (Acts 5:41).

REMEMBER YOUR CALLING

according to the power of God, who has saved us, and called us with a holy calling, not according to our works, but according to His own purpose and grace which was granted us in Christ Jesus from all eternity, but now has been revealed by the appearing of our Savior Christ Jesus, who abolished death, and brought life and immortality to light through the gospel, (1:8b–10)

A fourth means for guarding against being ashamed of Christ is simply to remember our holy calling from our heavenly Father, who, as Paul has just declared, shares His divine power with His children.

These few verses are a study of soteriology, the doctrine of salvation, in miniature. The apostle was not, of course, teaching Timothy new truths, but simply reminding him of the cardinal, well-known truths of the gospel, truths that should motivate every believer to faithfulness, to courageous witness and living for Jesus Christ.

Remembering these truths and placing our confidence in the God who has given them enables us to "walk in a manner worthy of the Lord, to please Him in all respects, bearing fruit in every good work and increasing in the knowledge of God; strengthened with all power, according to His glorious might, for the attaining of all steadfastness and patience" (Col. 1:10–11).

Because of **the power of God,** we can say with Paul, "I can do all things through Him who strengthens me" (Phil. 4:13). We can testify with Peter that we "are protected by the power of God through faith for a salvation ready to be revealed in the last time" (1 Peter 1:5). The all-powerful **God who has saved us** has equally sufficient **power** to keep us. If we were "reconciled to God through the death of His Son, much more, having been reconciled, we shall be saved by His life" (Rom. 5:10).

God's **power** does not always manifest itself in our lives in obvious ways. When Paul had prayed three times that God would remove a certain affliction, "a thorn in the flesh, a messenger of Satan to buffet" him, God answered, "My grace is sufficient for you, for power is perfected in weakness" (2 Cor. 12:7–8). Without hesitation or disappointment, Paul replied, "Most gladly, therefore, I will rather boast about my weaknesses, that the power of Christ may dwell in me. Therefore I am well content with weaknesses, with insults, with distresses, with persecutions, with difficulties, for Christ's sake; for when I am weak, then I am strong" (vv. 9–10).

Our loving heavenly Father is both willing and "able to keep [us] from stumbling, and to make [us] stand in the presence of His glory blameless with great joy" (Jude 24). In light of that truth Paul prayed for believers at Ephesus, where he had ministered faithfully for a number of years: "[May God] grant you, according to the riches of His glory, to be strengthened with power through His Spirit in the inner man; so that Christ may dwell in your hearts through faith; and that you, being rooted and grounded in love, may be able to comprehend with all the saints what is the breadth and length and height and depth, and to know the love of Christ which surpasses knowledge, that you may be filled up to all the fullness of God" (Eph. 3:16–19).

God sovereignly designed salvation, and He sovereignly initiates, sustains, and completes salvation. He has forgiven us, justified us, and delivered us from sin and Satan, from death and hell. In every sense and in every tense—past, present, and future—God is our Savior.

That is a major theme in the pastoral letters. The Almighty is frequently called Savior (1 Tim. 1:1; 2:3; 4:10; Titus 1:3; 2:10; 3:4), as is Jesus (2 Tim. 1:10; Titus 1:4; 2:13; 3:6). Likewise, the saving work of God in Christ is presented together in several places (1 Tim. 2:3–6; 4:10; 2 Tim. 2:8–10; Titus 2:11–14; 3:4–7).

The God who has saved us also has **called us with,** or to, **a holy calling.** Paul is not speaking of God's calling unbelievers to repentance and salvation but of His effectual, saving call of believers, those who have been saved, to holy living and, ultimately, to eternal and perfect holiness (cf. 1 John 3:2).

Just as the Lord did not save us according to our works but by His grace, neither has He called us to live **according to our works, but according to His own purpose** (the plan) **and grace** (the means of operating the plan). Just as that inexplicable truth is the foundation of the saving gospel, so it also is the foundation of God's sustenance of those He has saved. He will keep all the elect until they reach glory. Jesus made clear that the divine purpose, working through divine grace, would reach complete fulfillment. He promised,

All that the Father gives Me shall come to Me, and the one who comes to Me I will certainly not cast out. For I have come down from heaven, not to do My own will, but the will of Him who sent Me. And this is the will of Him who sent Me, that of all that He has given Me I lose nothing, but raise it up on the last day. For this is the will of My Father, that everyone who beholds the Son and believes in Him, may have eternal life; and I Myself will raise him up on the last day. . . . No one can come to Me, unless the Father who sent Me draws him; and I will raise him up on the last day. (John 6:37–40, 44; cf. Phil. 1:6; Jude 24–25)

God "chose us in Him [Christ] before the foundation of the world, that we should be holy and blameless before Him" (Eph. 1:4; cf. 1 Peter 1:2), that is, that we should live **according to His own purpose and grace which was granted us in Christ Jesus from all eternity.** Our destiny was determined and sealed before the world began. Because we now belong to Christ, we can praise and thank our heavenly Father that He has loved us, just as He has loved His only Son, "before the foundation of the world" (John 17:24). He has chosen us and loved us "in accordance with the eternal purpose which He carried out in Christ Jesus our Lord" (Eph. 3:11).

But this divine plan **from all eternity** only **now has been revealed by the appearing of our Savior Christ Jesus, who abolished death, and brought life and immortality to light through the gospel.** Most often in the New Testament (see, e.g., 1 Tim. 6:14; 2 Tim. 4:1, 8; Titus 2:13), *epiphaneia* (**appearing**) refers to Christ's second coming. But here it obviously refers to His first coming, when He **abolished death.**

Katargeō (**abolish**) literally means to render inoperative. It is not that **death** no longer exists or that believers are promised escape from it, unless they are raptured. But for believers, **death** is no longer a threat, no longer an enemy, no longer the end. Quoting first from Isaiah 25:8 and then from Hosea 13:14, Paul exulted, "When this perishable will have put on the imperishable, and this mortal will have put on immortality, then will come about the saying that is written, 'Death is swallowed up in victory. O death, where is your victory? O death, where is your sting?'" (1 Cor. 15:54–55). "Since then the children share in flesh and blood," the writer of Hebrews explains, "He Himself [Christ] likewise also partook of the same, that through death He might render powerless him who had the power of death, that is, the devil" (Heb. 2:14).

More than simply abolishing death, at His first appearing Christ **brought life and immortality to light through the gospel.** It was not until the Son of God became incarnate in Jesus Christ that God chose to reveal the full truth about eternal **life and immortality.** Bringing them to light means making them known. That is our area of expertise. We know the immeasurable reality of eternal, immortal existence. That also is our joy and hope in Christ.

REALIZE YOUR DUTY

for which I was appointed a preacher and an apostle and a teacher. For this reason I also suffer these things, (1:11–12a)

To illustrate the next two means for guarding against being ashamed of Christ, Paul draws from his own life and ministry. The first of those two means is realizing one's duty, about which Paul had the strongest personal conviction. Using the same words (in the Greek text) as he had in his first letter (1 Tim. 2:7), Paul reminded Timothy, **I was appointed a preacher and an apostle.**

The Greek *egō* (I) is in the emphatic position, strengthening the meaning to "I myself." **Was appointed** refers, of course, to Paul's divine commission, which he dramatically received on the Damascus Road, after which the Lord informed Ananias, a faithful disciple in Damascus, that Paul "is a chosen instrument of Mine, to bear My name before the Gentiles and kings and the sons of Israel" (Acts 9:15). At least twice, Paul publicly testified to that calling, first on the steps of the Roman army barracks before a large crowd in Jerusalem (Acts 22:3–21) and, some years later, before the Roman governor Festus, King Agrippa, and his wife Bernice in Caesarea (Acts 26:2–23).

Saul, as Paul was known before his conversion, did not plan to become a Christian. When he first encountered Christ, he was the chief persecutor of the infant church (see Acts 8:1–9:2). Nor, after his conversion, was it his own plan, or any other human plan, for him to be a special ambassador for Jesus Christ. On the beach near Miletus, he reminded the elders from Ephesus that he had received his ministry solely "from the Lord Jesus, to testify solemnly of the gospel of the grace of God" (Acts 20:24; cf. Col. 1:25). In his first letter to the church at Corinth, he stated that truth in even stronger terms. "For if I preach the gospel, I have nothing to boast of," he said; "for I am under compulsion; for woe is me if I do not preach the gospel" (1 Cor. 9:16).

Paul first mentions his commission as **a preacher,** as a proclaimer, or herald, who officially and publicly announces a message on behalf of a ruler—in Paul's case, the Lord Jesus Christ. He also was commissioned as **an apostle** "of Christ Jesus by the will of God" (2 Tim. 1:1; cf. 1 Tim. 1:1) **and a teacher. Preacher** emphasizes his function in ministry, **apostle** emphasizes his authority, and **teacher** emphasizes his interpreting the message he authoritatively proclaimed.

It was **for this reason,** that is, his threefold divine calling, that he **also [had to] suffer these things,** a reference, in general, to his "suffering for the gospel according to the power of God" (v. 8) and, in particular, to his loneliness (1:4) and his "imprisonment as a criminal" (2:7; cf. 1:8). He suffered because he faithfully preached the fullness of the gospel of salvation, because he proclaimed that truth with divine authority, and because he interpreted that Word with divine insight. Very often, the price of devotion to divine duty is affliction by the world.

These things also applied to the long list of afflictions Paul mentions in his second letter to the church at Corinth, in which, "in foolishness," he boasted "according to the flesh" (2 Cor. 11:17–18). Speaking sarcastically about certain "false apostles, deceitful workers, disguising themselves as apostles of Christ, [who] disguise themselves as servants of righteousness" (vv. 14–15), he asked rhetorically,

> Are they servants of Christ? (I speak as if insane) I more so; in far more labors, in far more imprisonments, beaten times without number, often in danger of death. Five times I received from the Jews thirty-nine lashes. Three times I was beaten with rods, once I was stoned, three times I was shipwrecked, a night and a day I have spent in the deep. I have been on frequent journeys, in dangers from rivers, dangers from robbers, dangers from my countrymen, dangers from the Gentiles, dangers in the city, dangers in the wilderness, dangers on the sea, dangers among false brethren; I have been in labor and hardship, through many sleepless nights, in hunger and thirst, often without food, in cold and exposure. (vv. 23–27; cf. 6:4–10)

Faithful ministry in the Lord's service is always bittersweet. It brings suffering and joy, disappointment and gratitude. It is like the little book representing judgment that John took "out of the angel's hand and ate it, and it was in my mouth sweet as honey; and when I had eaten it, my stomach was made bitter" (Rev. 10:10).

But for Paul, as it should be for every believer, suffering was a small price to pay, because his joy always outweighed his suffering, and his satisfaction always outweighed his disappointments. "For to me, to live is Christ," he rejoiced, "and to die is gain" (Phil. 1:21). "Even if I am being poured out as a drink offering upon the sacrifice and service of your faith," he testified later in that letter, "I rejoice and share my joy with you all" (2:17). He gave similar testimony to believers at Colossae, saying, "Now I rejoice in my sufferings for your sake, and in my flesh I do my share on behalf of His body (which is the church) in filling up that which is lacking in Christ's afflictions" (Col. 1:24). The worst suffering we endure is not comparable to our future glory (Rom. 8:18).

Charles Spurgeon gave a vivid illustration of the overriding satisfaction that comes from selfless, godly service.

> A man shall carry a bucket of water on his head and be very tired with the burden; but that same man when he dives into the sea shall have a thousand buckets on his head without perceiving their weight, because he is in the element and it entirely surrounds him. The duties of holiness are very irksome to men who are not in the element of holiness; but when once those men are cast into the element of grace, then they bear ten times more, and feel no weight, but are refreshed thereby with joy unspeakable.

Duty can bring the deepest pain or the highest joy. Spiritual duty unfulfilled brings untold dissatisfaction, regret, and anguish, no matter how easy unfaithfulness may be. On the other hand, spiritual duty fulfilled brings untold satisfaction and happiness, whatever the cost of faithfulness. The Christian who is obedient to his duty under the Lord can say with Peter, "If anyone suffers as a Christian, let him not feel ashamed, but in that name let him glorify God" (1 Peter 4:16).

TRUST YOUR SECURITY

but I am not ashamed; for I know whom I have believed and I am convinced that He is able to guard what I have entrusted to Him until that day. (1:12b)

Summing up his previous testimony, and again using his own experience, Paul gives a sixth means for guarding against being ashamed of Christ: trusting in spiritual security.

Paul was **not ashamed** of his Lord, **for,** he says, **I know whom I have believed.** *Oida* (know) carries the idea of knowing with certainty. It is used frequently in the New Testament of God's own knowing and of man's knowing by direct revelation from God or by personal experience. In the Sermon on the Mount, Jesus used that verb in assuring His hearers, "Your Father knows what you need, before you ask Him" (Matt. 6:8). John repeatedly uses it of Jesus' knowledge. He records that "He Himself [Jesus] knew what He was intending to do" (John 6:6), and that "Jesus knew from the beginning who they were who did not believe, and who it was that would betray Him" (v. 64; cf. 8:14; 11:42; 13:11).

Whom refers either to God the Father (v. 8) or to Jesus Christ (vv. 9–10). In either case, the basic meaning is the same—Paul had first-hand, intimate, saving knowledge of God.

Pisteuō (**I have believed**) is in a perfect tense, indicating something that began in the past and has continuing results. As already pointed out, the object of Paul's certain knowledge was not a thing, or even God's truth, as important as that is, but rather God Himself. It was not Paul's divinely revealed theology, but the One who revealed to him that theology, in **whom** he **believed.** He was, in John's words, a spiritual father who had come to know the Eternal One (1 John 2:14).

I am convinced, he testifies, that **He [God] is able** [*dunatos,* lit., is powerful enough] **to guard what I have entrusted to Him.** *Phulassō* (to guard) was a military term used of a soldier on watch, who was accountable with his own life to protect that which was entrusted to his care. He was **convinced** not only by divine promises but also by God's constant faithfulness, already exhibited to him in such measure that he could testify from personal encounters and experience. He asked rhetorically,

> Who shall separate us from the love of Christ? Shall tribulation, or distress, or persecution, or famine, or nakedness, or peril, or sword? Just as it is written, "For Thy sake we are being put to death all day long; we were considered as sheep to be slaughtered." But in all these things we overwhelmingly conquer through Him who loved us. For I am convinced that neither death, nor life, nor angels, nor principalities, nor things present, nor things to come, nor powers, nor height, nor depth, nor any other created thing, shall be able to separate us from the love of God, which is in Christ Jesus our Lord. (Rom. 8:35–39)

Paul trusted his absolute security in God. He had been through years of relentless temptations, trials and testings, opportunities and hardships. He had seen the power of God at work again and again, both in him and around him. He had seen the Lord save and heal and protect and guide and encourage (cf. 2 Tim. 4:14–18). He had encountered Christ personally on the Damascus Road and had been "caught up into Paradise, and heard inexpressible words, which a man is not permitted to speak. . . . And because of the surpassing greatness of the revelations, for this reason, to keep me from exalting myself, there was given me a thorn in the flesh, a messenger of Satan to buffet me—to keep me from exalting myself!" (2 Cor. 12:4, 7).

His confidence did not come from a creed or a theological system or a denomination or an ordination. It came solely from a close, unbroken relationship with God, to whom he unreservedly gave his life, going about his divine mission with no concern for his own welfare, safety, or life. Without the least reservation, all of those things were **entrusted to Him until that day.** His only "ambition, whether at home or absent, [was] to be pleasing to Him" (2 Cor. 5:9).

Later in the letter Paul identifies **that day,** saying, "In the future there is laid up for me the crown of righteousness, which the Lord, the righteous Judge, will award to me on that day; and not only to me, but also to all who have loved His appearing" (2 Tim. 4:8). It is the day when believers will stand before the *bēma,* "the judgment seat of God" (Rom. 14:10), where "each man's work will become evident; for the day will show it, because it is to be revealed with fire; and the fire itself will test the quality of each man's work" (1 Cor. 3:13), in order "that each one may be recompensed for his deeds in the body, according to what he has done, whether good or bad" (2 Cor. 5:10).

Like Peter, Paul knew with perfect certainty that he was "protected by the power of God through faith for a [completed] salvation ready to be revealed in the last time" (1 Peter 1:5). He had utter confidence in Jesus' promise regarding His sheep: "I give eternal life to them, and they shall never perish; and no one shall snatch them out of My hand. My Father, who has given them to Me, is greater than all; and no one is able to snatch them out of the Father's hand" (John 10:28–29). When our life belongs to Jesus Christ, nothing in this world, not even all the demons in hell or Satan himself, can touch us!

AFFIRM YOUR DOCTRINE

Retain the standard of sound words which you have heard from me, in the faith and love which are in Christ Jesus. Guard, through the Holy Spirit who dwells in us, the treasure which has been entrusted to you. (1:13–14)

A seventh guard against being ashamed of Christ is affirming and holding onto right doctrine. Although our ultimate confidence is in Christ Himself, His truth is also of great importance. It is, in fact, absolutely required for faithful living as well as for certainty of our security. If we belong to Christ, we *will be* secure, but if we neglect His truth, our confidence in that security will wane. Many Christians, perhaps most, do not have the courage of their convictions simply because they have no clear convictions. Before you put your life on the line for what you believe, you must believe it.

During a radio interview some years ago, I said, "What is particularly tragic about the many scandals that plague evangelicalism today is the fact that so many churches, and so many individuals who call themselves Christian, have little concern for biblical truth and biblical standards of living. In the name of love, understanding, and peace within the church and with society, almost any theology is accepted, or at least not challenged, no matter how much it may contradict Scripture."

Much of the professing church is atheological, that is, without any significant theological convictions. Like the world around them, many people who go by the name of Christ believe that to hold and teach absolute doctrines is to be unloving, antagonistic, and even "unchristian." They fit Paul's description of those in the last days who "will not endure sound doctrine; but wanting to have their ears tickled, they will accumulate for themselves teachers in accordance to their own desires; and will turn away their ears from the truth, and will turn aside to myths" (2 Tim. 4:3–4). When you examine those today who deride doctrine, you discover they are also like those in the last days who Paul says "will be lovers of self, lovers of money, boastful, arrogant, revilers, disobedient to parents, ungrateful, unholy, unloving, irreconcilable, malicious gossips, without self-control, brutal, haters of good, treacherous, reckless, conceited, lovers of pleasure rather than lovers of God; holding to a form of godliness, although they have denied its power. . . . [They are] always learning and never able to come to the knowledge of the truth" (2 Tim. 3:2–5, 7). Sound doctrine leads to holy living, and the absence of it to unholy living.

Standard translates *hupotupōsis,* which was used of a writer's outline or an artist's rough sketch, which set the guidelines and standards for the finished work. The Christian's **standard** is God's Word, which encompasses the **sound words which you have heard from me [Paul],** an apostle of Jesus Christ. In Scripture we have God's own truth and standards, all we need or should want to have. It is the only divinely inspired, divinely revealed, absolute, unique, perfect, and sufficient truth. In it is found everything necessary for salvation and for living out the saved life. Later in this letter Paul commends Timothy, saying, "From childhood you have known the sacred writings which are able to give you the wisdom that leads to salvation through faith which is in Christ Jesus. All Scripture is inspired by God and profitable for teaching, for reproof, for correction, for training in righteousness; that the man of God may be adequate, equipped for every good work" (2 Tim. 3:15–17).

Courage in Christian ministry, as well as in Christian living in general, is not possible apart from strong biblical convictions. But Paul gives necessary balance to his counsel. Strong convictions are to be held and taught **in the faith and love which are in Christ Jesus.** When we defend God's Word in a self-righteous, unloving spirit, the resulting controversy and opposition are not caused wholly by the offense of the truth itself but also by the offensive and unspiritual way in which we proclaim it. We are to defend God's Word **in the faith,** that is, with the right attitude of confidence toward God; and we are to defend it in love, with the right attitude of kindness and compassion toward unbelievers and toward poorly taught and immature believers. "Speaking the truth in love, we are to grow up in all aspects into Him, who is the head, even Christ" (Eph. 4:15). Although we must not have a doubting or a dead orthodoxy, neither should we have a loveless, cold, and insensitive orthodoxy.

The Holy Spirit's indwelling all believers is a cardinal New Testament doctrine. Shortly before His crucifixion, Jesus promised the disciples, "I will ask the Father, and He will give you another Helper, that He may be with you forever; that is the Spirit of truth" (John 14:16–17). Immediately before His ascension He promised again, "You shall receive power when the Holy Spirit has come upon you; and you shall be My witnesses both in Jerusalem, and in all Judea and Samaria, and even to the remotest part of the earth" (Acts 1:8). "You are not in the flesh but in the Spirit, if indeed the Spirit of God dwells in you," Paul declared in his Roman letter. "But if anyone does not have the Spirit of Christ, he does not belong to Him" (Rom. 8:9). He rhetorically asked Corinthian believers, "Do you not know that you are a temple of God, and that the Spirit of God dwells in you?" (1 Cor. 3:16; cf. 6:19).

Therefore, just as God has power to guard what we have entrusted to Him (v. 12), He also gives *us* power to **guard, through the Holy Spirit who dwells in us, the treasure which** He has **entrusted to us.** Theologians would say this depicts both sides of our security, the keeping power of God and the Spirit-energized perseverance of the saints. At the close of the previous letter, Paul gave a similar command: "O Timothy, guard what has been entrusted to you," specifically warning him to avoid "worldly and empty chatter and the opposing arguments of what is falsely called 'knowledge'" (1 Tim. 6:20).

The deposit of our lives with God is secure. The question is, How secure is His deposit of truth with us? Christian colleges, seminaries, pastors, and other church leaders who deviate from Scripture, defecting to "a different gospel" and wanting "to distort the gospel of Christ" (Gal. 1:6–7), will face a dreadful day of reckoning before God. The most solemn responsibility that any believer has, especially those the Lord has called to be preachers and teachers, is to uphold and defend the integrity of His Word.

CHOOSE YOUR ASSOCIATES

You are aware of the fact that all who are in Asia turned away from me, among whom are Phygelus and Hermogenes. The Lord grant mercy to the house of Onesiphorus for he often refreshed me, and was not ashamed of my chains; but when he was in Rome, he eagerly searched for me, and found me—the Lord grant to him to find mercy from the Lord on that day—and you know very well what services he rendered at Ephesus. (1:15–18)

An eighth means for guarding against being ashamed of Christ is that of carefully choosing one's associates, a means which Paul here implies. In these four verses he contrasts fellow workers who were ashamed of the gospel with those who were not.

"Do not be deceived," he warned the church at Corinth; "Bad company corrupts good morals" (1 Cor. 15:33). If we associate with spiritually courageous Christians, our own courage will be strengthened. On the other hand, if we associate with those who are ashamed of Christ and His gospel, we will soon be tainted by that shame.

The first group Paul mentions included **all who are in Asia [who] turned away from** him. They were ashamed of Paul because they were ashamed of the gospel he preached and defended, and they became even more ashamed and fearful when he was imprisoned for the faith (cf. v. 8). Timothy **was aware of [that] fact,** because he had been pastoring for some years in Ephesus, a city in the Roman province of **Asia.** Once Paul was imprisoned, many of the men who had been with him, including **all who [were] in Asia,** were afraid of being found guilty by association. Because their first priority was self-preservation, they had nothing more to do with the apostle, who not only had ministered with them but to them.

To be rejected by the world is not pleasant, but to be deserted by fellow workers in the service of Christ is particularly painful. To have those you have spent your life spiritually nurturing turn away from you, and sometimes even against you, is heartbreaking in the extreme.

Paul had given himself without reservation to those men from Asia. Like the Galatian believers, they were Paul's spiritual children, with whom he would be in "labor until Christ [was] formed in" them (Gal. 4:19). It was no wonder that he expressed at the beginning of this second epistle his deep longing to see Timothy, one of the few who had not deserted him (2 Tim. 1:4).

Among the deserters were **Phygelus and Hermogenes,** about whom we know nothing but their cowardice. Because Paul says nothing more to identify them, we can assume they were known to Timothy. And because he bothers to name them specifically out of the many others, it seems likely that they were well known in Asia, that they were close to Paul, and that they were leaders who had shown promise. They probably would have been the last ones to be suspected of cowardice, ingratitude, and being ashamed of Christ and of Paul.

Although Paul no doubt continued to love those men who proved they did not love Him, his love would not allow him to hide their defection. "Those whom the Lord loves He disciplines, and He scourges every son whom He receives" (Heb. 12:6). Likewise, the Lord's people are to discipline those among them who are immoral and unfaithful. Even elders who "continue to sin" are to be rebuked "in the presence of all, so that the rest also may be fearful of sinning" (1 Tim. 5:20).

The second group Paul mentions stands in stark contrast to the group from Asia. Paul ended his rebuke of those men by naming names, and he begins this commendation also by naming a name. He prays, **The Lord grant mercy to [those in] the house of Onesiphorus,** who, like Phygelus and Hermogenes, were known to Timothy. Because Paul asks Timothy to greet them (4:19), this family obviously lived in or near Ephesus.

Onesiphorus had befriended Paul while he was in prison. **He often refreshed Paul and was not afraid of his chains,** that is, of his being a prisoner. He regularly visited the aging apostle and ministered to his needs, without fear and without shame. When this friend first came to **Rome,** perhaps on business, **he eagerly searched for** Paul until he **found** him, suggesting that the search involved considerable time, effort, and possibly danger.

In deep gratitude, Paul again prays that **the Lord [would] grant to him to find mercy from the Lord on that day,** the same day of believers' judgment for works he mentioned in verse 12 and refers to again in 4:8. Onesiphorus's devotion to Paul had begun many years earlier. He had proved his courage and faithfulness by the **services he rendered at Ephesus,** when the apostle ministered there.

Like Onesiphorus, Martin Luther, the leading instrument of God in the Reformation, possessed such godly courage in great abundance. One biographer, Roland Bainton, writes of him: "Luther had set his face to go up to Jerusalem and would not be turned aside. He would enter Worms though there were as many devils as tiles on the roofs. . . . He disregarded all human considerations and threw himself utterly upon God" (*Here I Stand: A Life of Martin Luther* [New York: Abingdon, 1950], 181).

The Elements of a Strong Spiritual Life

3

You therefore, my son, be strong in the grace that is in Christ Jesus. And the things which you have heard from me in the presence of many witnesses, these entrust to faithful men, who will be able to teach others also. Suffer hardship with me, as a good soldier of Christ Jesus. No soldier in active service entangles himself in the affairs of everyday life, so that he may please the one who enlisted him as a soldier. And also if anyone competes as an athlete, he does not win the prize unless he competes according to the rules. The hard-working farmer ought to be the first to receive his share of the crops. Consider what I say, for the Lord will give you understanding in everything. (2:1–7)

Some years ago, two teenagers were discovered in an attic room chained to their beds, where they had been confined since early childhood. They were totally disoriented and almost animalistic in behavior. They had been undernourished and unloved, and, as would be expected, were underdeveloped in every way—physically, emotionally, socially, and mentally. They were the product of child abuse at its most malevolent extreme.

Equally tragic is the condition of many children of God today who are undernourished spiritually and, consequently, are underdeveloped, confused, disoriented, and immature in the things of the Lord. There are more popular preachers today than at any time in church history, but few powerful ones. There also are more popular churches, but few powerful ones. There is much activity, but little spiritual fruit; much talk about Christianity, but little conviction; high moral proclamations, but little accountability; doctrinal creeds, but much compromise.

In the great majority of cases, weak churches are the result of weak leadership, especially weak pastoral leadership. Spiritual weakness makes both leaders and congregations subject to almost every religious fad, no matter how frivolous. Like an undernourished and anemic physical body, they have little resistance to disorders and maladies that weaken them still further. And because they have no resources but their own, the smallest difficulty is distressing. Because they have so little understanding of and confidence in the Word of God, they turn to psychological bandages and worldly solutions. They have little defense against Satan and are easy prey for false teachers. They are spiritual "children, tossed here and there by waves, and carried about by every wind of doctrine, by the trickery of men, by craftiness in deceitful scheming" (Eph. 4:14; cf. Heb. 13:9). Because they have left "the elementary teaching about the Christ," and failed to "press on to maturity" (Heb. 6:1), they may even find themselves "paying attention to deceitful spirits and doctrines of demons" (1 Tim. 4:1).

Spiritual weakness also can come from fatigue, frustration, and seemingly insurmountable obstacles in the Lord's work. After Moses died, Joshua faced the formidable task of leading Israel in the conquest of Canaan. The Lord therefore encouraged Joshua, saying, "Be strong and courageous, for you shall give this people possession of the land which I swore to their fathers to give them. Only be strong and very courageous; be careful to do according to all the law which Moses My servant commanded you; do not turn from it to the right or to the left, so that you may have success wherever you go" (Josh. 1:6–7). To wavering believers in Corinth, Paul said, "Be on the alert, stand firm in the faith, act like men, be strong" (1 Cor. 16:13). Even to the faithful church at Ephesus he felt it necessary to say, "Be strong in the Lord, and in the strength of His might" (Eph. 6:10).

Several years ago, engineers in New Jersey were building a bridge over the mouth of a river on the Atlantic coast. As they were putting down pilings, they came across the hull of an old ship that was buried in the sand. To keep the bridge on the planned route, the hull would have to be removed. After they tried every mechanical means they could think of, the ship remained in place. A young engineer suggested placing several large barges above the hull on either side, running cables underneath the hull, and attaching them tightly to the barges at low tide. When the tide rose, the hull was loosened some. At the next low tide the cables were tightened again, and at high tide the ship was loosened some more. After following that procedure for several cycles of tides, the ship eventually was freed. What humanly devised mechanical force could not accomplish, the immeasurably greater forces of nature accomplished easily.

Many Christians and churches are like that hull, embedded in spiritual immobility. They recognize the problem and try every human means to extricate themselves, but to no avail. But what His children cannot accomplish in their own strength, their heavenly Father can do by the power of His Spirit.

THE COMMAND TO BE STRONG

You therefore, my son, be strong in the grace that is in Christ Jesus. (2:1)

As mentioned in the Introduction and the previous chapters of this commentary, Timothy was facing a time of spiritual vacillation and weakness. He may have been questioning his calling or his gifts or the sufficiency of God's provision. He was mired in difficulties of some sort and could not extricate himself. Whatever the particulars, Paul realized that his son in the faith needed "to kindle afresh the gift of God which" was in him (2 Tim. 1:6). As we noted in the last chapter, he did not need more from God but needed to use, with commitment and confidence, the divine provisions he already possessed. He needed to remember and to exercise the "power and love and discipline" (v. 7) that the Holy Spirit had provided him and provides every believer. He needed to discard his being ashamed of "the testimony of the Lord" and to be willing to join Paul in "suffering for the gospel according to the power of God" (v. 8). He needed, like the apostle, to be "convinced that He is able to guard what I have entrusted to Him until that day" (v. 12), to "retain the standard of sound words which [he had] heard from [Paul], in the faith and love which are in Christ Jesus" (v. 13), to avoid faithless church members such as Phygelus and Hermogenes, and to identify with faithful believers such as Onesiphorus and those in his household (vv. 15–16).

Summing up that counsel, Paul said, "**You therefore, my son, be strong in the grace that is in Christ Jesus.**" The verb **be strong** is an imperative, making it a command. Yet it is a command tempered by Paul's deep love for Timothy, his **son.** There was tenderness in Paul's heart because there is tenderness in God's heart. Even the Lord's strongest commands are given in love. He admonishes His children firmly but lovingly, and that is the way Paul admonished his spiritual **son** Timothy. Because Timothy had "sincere faith" and was nourished in that faith by his godly mother and grandmother (1:5), because he was specially gifted by God and ordained by the laying on of Paul's hands (v. 6) and the hands of the Ephesian elders (1 Tim. 4:14), and because of the abundant resources mentioned in the remainder of chapter 1, Timothy had no reason for not being **strong.** Paul was saying to Timothy, "My son, the Lord's work in Ephesus depends on you, its divinely appointed and divinely endowed minister." The effectiveness of his ministry depended not simply in his *having* that call and those resources but in his faithfully *using* them in God's power and to God's glory.

It is an amazing paradox, but fully biblical, that, although God is sovereign and all-powerful, He nevertheless entrusts His adopted children with propagating the saving gospel of His true Son, Jesus Christ.

The verb **be strong** is also passive, however, indicating that the source of Timothy's strength was not in himself but **in the grace that is in Christ Jesus.** A somewhat better rendering would be, "by *means* of **the grace that is in Christ Jesus.** Just as we are saved solely "by grace . . . through faith; and that not of [ourselves, but by] the gift of God" (Eph. 2:8), we also are kept saved by the grace of God, who "is faithful and righteous [to continue] to forgive us our sins and [to continue] to cleanse us from all unrighteousness" (1 John 1:9). Our only effective spiritual strength is "in the Lord, and in the strength of His might" (Eph. 6:10). We build ourselves up in the "most holy faith" by "praying in the Holy Spirit" and keeping ourselves "in the love of God" (Jude 20–21).

God's continuing **grace** in the lives of believers operates in justification and sanctification, in forgiveness and in holiness, and in His grace applied to our service. The same grace that forgives us and makes us holy is the grace that empowers us. Because we belong to Christ, we are continually in the sphere of grace. But to enjoy the sphere of blessing, we must live in the sphere of obedience.

In 2 Timothy 2:2–6, Paul presents four key elements of a strong, obedient, spiritual life, using the vivid analogies of teacher (v. 2), soldier (vv. 3–4), athlete (v. 5), and farmer (v. 6).

THE TEACHER

And the things which you have heard from me in the presence of many witnesses, these entrust to faithful men, who will be able to teach others also. (2:2)

The first metaphor is that of a teacher teaching a teacher, who, in turn, teaches other teachers, who then teach still other teachers. Although Paul mentions only four generations of teachers, the idea is that of a continuing process.

The New Testament neither teaches nor supports the idea of apostolic succession. But it does clearly teach, in this passage and elsewhere, that the gospel is to be promulgated from generation to generation. Jesus, of course, was the Master Teacher. He taught the apostles, who then taught others, who taught others, who are still teaching others, and so on throughout the church age. William Barclay comments, "The teacher is a link in the living chain which stretches unbroken from this present moment back to Jesus Christ. The glory of teaching is that it links the present with the earthly life of Jesus Christ" (*The Letters to Timothy, Titus and Philemon* [Philadelphia: Westminster, 1957], 182). In every generation, God has raised up new links in this living chain of **faithful men** to pass on the good news of Jesus Christ to the people of their day.

John ends his gospel by stating that "there are also many other things which Jesus did, which if they were written in detail, I suppose that even the world itself would not contain the books which were written" (John 21:25). Luke was not an apostle but was a close associate of apostles, so that much of what we know of the Lord's earthly ministry and of the apostles' ministry in the early church we know from Luke's Spirit-guided hand. In the book of Acts, Luke begins by saying, "The first account [the gospel of Luke] I composed, Theophilus, about all that Jesus began to do and teach until the day when He was taken up" (Acts 1:1–2). Like John, he reports that what is recorded accounts only for those things "that Jesus *began* to do and teach" [emphasis added] until the Ascension. Just before He ascended, He told the awaiting disciples on the Mount of Olives, "You shall receive power when the Holy Spirit has come upon you; and you shall be My witnesses both in Jerusalem, and in all Judea and Samaria, and even to the remotest part of the earth" (Acts 1:8).

That evening, the Eleven returned to the Upper Room where they were staying and, under the Lord's guidance, chose Matthias to replace Judas (vv. 21–26). Some years later, Christ personally and directly called Paul to be the thirteenth apostle (see Acts 9:3–20), "one untimely born," whom he himself considered to be "the least of the apostles, who am not fit to be called an apostle, because I persecuted the church of God" (1 Cor. 15:8–9). But, by God's sovereign grace and choice, he was as fully an apostle as the others (see, e.g., Rom. 1:1, 11:13; 1 Cor. 9:1).

The apostles, some for only a brief time before they were martyred, proclaimed the gospel they had received from Christ to other faithful men—prophets, elders, deacons, and many others—among whom was

Timothy. It was now Timothy's turn to **entrust** the gospel, and all other divinely revealed truths, to others.

In a state invitational track meet during my college years, I represented my team as the second man in the mile relay. The first man ran a fast first leg, and I did well on the second. But soon after I passed off the baton to the third man, one of our best runners, he stopped, walked onto the infield, and sat down. Our first horrified thought was that he had pulled a hamstring or twisted an ankle. I ran across the field and asked, "What happened?" "I don't know," he replied, "I just didn't feel like running anymore." Understandably, his teammates, the coach, and everyone else from our college were sickened and disgusted. "How could you do that?" we asked. "Don't you know you're not just representing yourself, but your team and your school? Have you forgotten all the time the coach has invested in you and that your teammates have invested to get where we are? How could you, in one brief, selfish second, destroy all of that?"

On an infinitely more important level, countless leaders in the church have simply dropped out of the Lord's service, some with no better reason than the apathy of that collegiate runner.

Timothy had not reached that point of defection, but it is clear that Paul knew his young friend, his son in the faith, was being tempted in that direction. Before such a serious crisis occurred, therefore, he was saying in effect, "Don't even consider dropping out or curtailing your work to suit your own desires. This isn't your ministry but the Lord's, and you have no right to quit or to slack until He 'takes you out of the game,' as it were, either by death or by rapture. I can't let you become a broken link in God's chain of faithful witnesses. You not only have to keep going yourself but you have to help others get going and keep going as well."

The first stage in the spiritual "relay" was the truth being handed from Paul to Timothy, which the apostle describes here as Timothy's careful receiving and studying **the things which** he had **heard from** Paul over the period of several years traveling with the apostle and of ministering with him in Ephesus.

In the presence of many witnesses carries the fuller idea of "supported by the confirming testimony of other teachers"—including the teaching of other apostles. In his second letter (written about the same time as 2 Timothy), Peter attested that Paul authoritatively preached God's Word (see 2 Peter 3:14–16). Those **witnesses** certainly would have included Paul's fellow preachers and teachers, such as Barnabas and Silas (see Acts 14:1–3, 21–22; 15:35; 20:4). Other well-taught leaders in the church such as Luke, a companion of Paul on many of his trips, also would have been qualified to confirm to Timothy the divine authenticity of Paul's teaching. From the time he first met and began accompanying

Paul (Acts 16:1–3), Timothy was exposed to the public teaching and private counsel of **many** godly **witnesses** in addition to Paul.

Paratithēmi (**entrust**) is here an imperative and carries the idea of depositing something valuable for safekeeping. It is a verb form of the noun (*parathēkē*), used twice in the previous chapter, referring to the treasure Paul had entrusted to the Lord (1:12) and that Paul had entrusted to Timothy (v. 14)—namely, the treasure "of sound words which you have heard from me" (v. 13). Now it was time for the treasure with which Timothy had been entrusted to be entrusted by him to others.

Timothy's assignment was to run the second lap, as it were, of this spiritual relay, in which he was to **entrust** the **things** he had been taught by Paul—that is, pass on the in-depth teaching of God's Word—**to faithful men** under his care. That which he was to carefully guard (1:14: cf. 1 Tim. 6:20) he also was to carefully teach.

The truth Paul is talking about here is beyond the basic gospel message of salvation, which is to be preached to all who will hear. He is rather talking about the careful, systematic training of church leaders who will teach and disciple other believers in the fullness of God's Word. This particular ministry is to be selective. It is reserved for **faithful men, who will be able to teach others also.** He is directing Timothy to invest in the lives of spiritually devout men who are gifted to teach potential pastors and evangelists. Such men must already have proved their love for the Lord and their giftedness in His service. They must be prequalified by proven spiritual character and ability, as well as by fruitful labor.

Pistos (**faithful**) is used later in this chapter of the trustworthiness of God's promise that "if we died with Him, we shall also live with Him" (v. 11), and a few verses later of Christ Himself, who, even "if we are faithless, . . . remains faithful; for He cannot deny Himself" (v. 13). In other words, this special entrustment is reserved for **men** whose character reflects the faithfulness of God's own Word and of God's own Son. In this context, **faithful** not only refers to spiritual character but to spiritual giftedness. God does not call every believer to be a teacher and a teacher of teachers. Paul knew Timothy had such giftedness (see 1:6) and here instructs him to find others who were so gifted and to teach them.

Like Timothy, every preacher and teacher is to guard the purity and integrity of God's Word. Some of those also are called to accurately and fully teach other godly leaders in the church. As already mentioned, if the church is weak, it is because its leaders are weak. Conversely, if the church is to be strong, its leaders must be strong. And leaders can become strong only if they are carefully built up in the Word of God. We all received the truth from faithful men before us, and we are to preserve it so that it is passed on accurately and fully to the next generation (cf. 1 Tim. 6:20; 2 Tim. 2:14).

It is for that primary purpose that Bible schools, Christian colleges, and seminaries are founded and that books and commentaries are written—to prepare dedicated Christian men and women for effective service to the church and in the world. And within that broader purpose is the narrower one of giving special attention to raising up new generations of mature spiritual leaders who are uniquely trained and assigned to carefully guard and faithfully articulate God's truth.

Both before and under the Old Covenant, God raised up many faithful men and women to be His witnesses. He also called Israel as a nation to "be to Me a kingdom of priests and a holy nation" (Ex. 19:6). Not just the priests and prophets, but all the people, were "entrusted with the oracles of God" (Rom. 3:2). They were to be a *nation* of God's intermediaries and witnesses to the pagan, Gentile world. Centuries before Christ gave the Great Commission to His disciples to "go therefore and make disciples of all the nations" (Matt. 28:19), God had given a similar commission to His chosen people Israel. Sadly, it was a commission they had failed to heed and fulfill, and, by the time of our Lord, the leadership of Israel was apostate and satanic (cf. John 8:44).

The third lap in the relay is for spiritually mature leaders, or **faithful men,** who themselves have been carefully trained, to teach others who show promise. This is just the start of a continuous process of spiritual reproduction, of being taught and of teaching, that is to continue until our Lord returns.

On a more general level, a similar process should involve all believers, whatever their particular spiritual gifts might be. This responsibility applies especially to elders "who work hard at preaching and teaching" (1 Tim. 5:17). But parents, Sunday school teachers, and youth leaders also are responsible, to the best of their ability, to pass on God's Word to those under their care. Every Christian has such a responsibility for any brother or sister in Christ whom he has opportunity to disciple, even briefly.

In a still wider sense, every believer has a responsibility to teach God's truth to any other believer, even one who is older and more mature in the faith. Pastors can learn from other church members, parents can learn from their children, teachers can learn from their students, wives can learn from their husbands, husbands can learn from their wives, and friends can learn from friends.

THE SOLDIER

Suffer hardship with me, as a good soldier of Christ Jesus. No soldier in active service entangles himself in the affairs of every-

day life, so that he may please the one who enlisted him as a soldier. (2:3–4)

The second figure Paul uses to illustrate characteristics of a strong spiritual life is that of a soldier. In his letter to the church at Ephesus, Paul expands on this figure. After his counsel cited above, to "be strong in the Lord, and in the strength of His might" (6:10), he says, "Put on the full armor of God, that you may be able to stand firm against the schemes of the devil. For our struggle is not against flesh and blood, but against the rulers, against the powers, against the world forces of this darkness, against the spiritual forces of wickedness in the heavenly places. Therefore, take up the full armor of God, that you may be able to resist in the evil day, and having done everything, to stand firm" (vv. 11–13). He admonished believers at Corinth about the offensive side of that battle, saying, "Though we walk in the flesh, we do not war according to the flesh, for the weapons of our warfare are not of the flesh, but divinely powerful for the destruction of fortresses" (2 Cor. 10:3–4).

Paul not only calls on Timothy to serve the Lord as a soldier, **but as a good soldier of Christ Jesus.** A spiritual Christian does not simply do minimum duty for his Lord, **Christ Jesus,** but serves Him with everything he is and has.

The first mark of **a good soldier** that Paul mentions is the willingness to **suffer hardship.** By adding **with me,** he gives assurance that he would not ask anything of Timothy that he himself was not doing or willing to do. *Sunkakopatheō* (**suffer hardship with**) is a compound verb that means to suffer evil or pain along with someone else. One scholar translates the phrase, "take one's share of rough treatment." **With** does not represent a separate Greek preposition but is a part (*sun*) of the verb. **Me** is only implied in the Greek, the context indicating that Paul was speaking of himself.

It is difficult for Christians in most of the Western world to understand what serious spiritual warfare and suffering for Christ mean. The secular environment in our society is becoming more and more hostile to Christianity and to religion in general. But we are not faced with loss of job, imprisonment, and execution because of our faith. With few exceptions, being a Christian will not keep a student out of college or a worker from getting a good job. But the more faithful a Christian becomes and the more the Lord blesses his work, the more Satan will put roadblocks, hardships, and rejection in the way, the more evident the spiritual warfare will become, and the more frequent and obvious the **hardship** will become.

A **soldier in active service** does not have a 9 to 5 job, or even a long 60– or 70–hour work week. He is a **soldier** 24 hours a day, every day of the year. His body, his health, his skills, his time—all that he is—belong to the military in which he serves. Even when on leave, he is subject to recall at any time, without notice and for any reason. And whenever ordered into dangerous duty, he is expected to put his very life on the line without question or hesitation.

Consequently, he is separated from his normal environment, so that he will not **entangle himself in the affairs of everyday life. Entangle himself** translates a passive form of *emplekō*, which literally means to weave. Paul is not speaking about things that necessarily are wrong in themselves. It is not that a soldier should have no contact at all with his former friends and surroundings, but that he is not to become caught up and enmeshed in them. Those things are irrelevant to his soldiering and are always subject to being relinquished. In the same way, a good soldier of Christ Jesus refuses to allow earthly matters to interfere with the fulfillment of his duty to his Lord. Many Christians, pastors, special ministries, and doctrinally sound churches have been undermined by concerns and activities that are innocent in themselves but have been allowed to crowd out the primary purpose of serving Jesus Christ in the advancing of His kingdom against the forces of darkness.

Jesus recognized that such disconnection and call to duty required of His faithful disciple, a soldier in His active service, is not easy. As He and His disciples

> were going along the road, someone said to Him, "I will follow You wherever You go." And Jesus said to him, "The foxes have holes, and the birds of the air have nests, but the Son of Man has nowhere to lay His head." And He said to another, "Follow Me." But he said, "Permit me first to go and bury my father." But He said to him, "Allow the dead to bury their own dead; but as for you, go and proclaim everywhere the kingdom of God." And another also said, "I will follow You, Lord; but first permit me to say good-bye to those at home." But Jesus said to him, "No one, after putting his hand to the plow and looking back, is fit for the kingdom of God." (Luke 9:57–62)

In the parable of the soils, Jesus identifies false believers whose nonsaving faith is short-lived with "the one on whom seed was sown among the thorns, this is the man who hears the word, and the worry of the world, and the deceitfulness of riches choke the word, and it becomes unfruitful" (Matt. 13:22). Those are the kind of temporary professing Christians of whom Peter speaks: "If after they have escaped the defilements of the world by the knowledge of the Lord and Savior Jesus Christ, they are again entangled in them and are overcome, the last state has become worse for them than the first" (2 Peter 2:20).

"The worry of the world, and the deceitfulness of riches" of which Jesus spoke are among **the affairs of everyday life** that can keep an unbeliever from receiving Christ and can keep believers from faithfully serving Him. Just as the dutiful soldier places his life willingly on the line in service of his country, so the faithful Christian will willingly "deny himself, and take up his cross, and follow [Christ]" (Matt. 16:24). He will say with Paul, "I do not consider my life of any account as dear to myself, in order that I may finish my course, and the ministry which I received from the Lord Jesus" (Acts 20:24).

The third mark of a good soldier is a genuine desire to **please the one who enlisted him as a soldier.** In the same way, but of far greater importance, a Christian's deepest desire is to please the Lord Jesus Christ, his commander in chief, **the one who enlisted him.** It is impossible to serve two commanders in chief, just as it is impossible to serve two masters (Matt. 6:24). The faithful Christian's fondest hope is to be rewarded for loyal service and to hear his Master say, "Well done, good and faithful slave; you were faithful with a few things, I will put you in charge of many things, enter into the joy of your master" (Matt. 25:21).

The strong desire to please other people is an integral characteristic of fallen man. And because of the continued influence of the old self (Eph. 4:22), even Christians are tempted to be men-pleasers. Many Christians succumb to that temptation and become more concerned about pleasing their fellow workers, their neighbors, and their friends than about pleasing the Lord. And for the same reason, many pastors fall into the trap of wanting to please their congregations or their communities more than to please the Lord. That desire inevitably leads to moral and spiritual decline, because pleasing the world, including worldly Christians, demands compromise of God's truth, God's standards, and personal holiness. It demands forsaking Christ as our first love. From the situation of the Ephesian church some years after Paul wrote this letter to Timothy (who was pastoring in Ephesus), we know that forsaking Christ as our first love is possible even when our doctrine is sound and we toil and persevere for Him (see Rev. 2:2–4). When that happens, we must "remember therefore from where [we] have fallen, and repent" (v. 5). We must remind ourselves of Paul's sobering testimony: "If I were still trying to please men, I would not be a bond-servant of Christ" (Gal. 1:10). When Christ is our first love, we will "have as our ambition, whether at home or absent, to be pleasing to Him" (2 Cor. 5:9; 1 Thess. 2:4).

THE ATHLETE

And also if anyone competes as an athlete, he does not win the prize unless he competes according to the rules. (2:5)

The third figure Paul uses to illustrate characteristics of a strong spiritual life is that of **an athlete,** a metaphor he uses several times in his letters.

The phrase **competes as an athlete** translates the verb *athleō,* which means to contest, contend, wrestle, struggle. The idea is that of a struggle that requires great determination to win. Athletes struggle, contend, compete, and strive to win.

The difference between first and second places in an athletic event is not always a matter of talent. As in the fable of the tortoise and the hare, a less gifted athlete often surpasses another who is physically superior and more experienced, simply by having greater determination and persistence.

While watching a decathlon meet between the United States, Poland, and the U.S.S.R., I asked a friend, who was coaching the American team, to identify the best athlete among all those competitors. He pointed to a slender, lithe young man, and I asked, "Do you think he will win today?" Surprisingly, he answered, "No." When I asked why, he pointed to another athlete and said, "He's going to win, because he has the greatest determination, the strongest will to win. He is the most mentally tough competitor I have ever seen." Sure enough, he did win that day. His name was Bruce Jenner, and two years later he won the Olympic gold medal in the decathlon, which ranked him as the greatest athlete in the world.

Our spiritual competition is not, of course, against other Christians. Trying to outperform another believer is far from spiritual. Rather, our competition is against our fleshly old self, against the world, and against Satan and those who serve him. And our goal is to "press on toward the goal for the prize of the upward call of God in Christ Jesus" (Phil. 3:14).

Even the most gifted and determined **athlete,** bringing the most effort to the struggle, however, **does not win the prize unless he competes according to the rules.**

In the Greek games, which continued for centuries under Roman rule and were still being held in Paul's time, every participant had to meet three qualifications—of birth, of training, and of competition. First, he had to be a true-born Greek. Second, he had to prepare at least ten months for the games and swear to that before a statue of Zeus. Third, he had to compete within the specific rules for a given event. To fail in any of those requirements meant automatic disqualification.

Comparable rules apply to spiritual Christians. We must be truly born again; we must be faithful in study and obedience of God's Word, in self-denial, and in prayer; and we must live according to Christ's divine standards of discipleship.

The very fact that we are Christians means we have met the qualification of being born again. But the other two requirements are far from automatic and involve constant dedication and constant effort. Together they constitute spiritual discipline, which comes from the same root as "disciple" and is the foundation of spiritual maturity. The disciplined disciple has control of his affections, his emotions, his priorities, and his objectives.

It goes without saying that all serious athletes must exert special effort not just during a game or a race but for many months, even years, beforehand. Writing to believers at Corinth, who were very familiar with the Isthmian games, which were played nearby, Paul asked rhetorically, "Do you not know that those who run in a race all run, but only one receives the prize? Run in such a way that you may win. And everyone who competes in the games exercises self-control in all things. They then do it to receive a perishable wreath, but we an imperishable. Therefore I run in such a way, as not without aim; I box in such a way, as not beating the air; but I buffet my body and make it my slave, lest possibly, after I have preached to others, I myself should be disqualified" (1 Cor. 9:24–27). Paul's victory in the realm of ministry was dependent on his body, with its lusts and impulses, not being in control of him, but rather he of it.

As Paul emphasizes in that passage, the wreath (*stephanos*) for which the Greek athletes competed was perishable, but the one for which the spiritual Christian competes is imperishable. It is "the crown [*stephanos*] of righteousness, which the Lord, the righteous Judge, will award to me on that day; and not only to me, but also to all who have loved His appearing" (2 Tim. 4:8), "the unfading crown of glory" we will receive "when the Chief Shepherd appears" (1 Peter 5:4), "the crown of life, which the Lord has promised to those who love Him" (James 1:12; Rev. 2:10). One day, like the twenty-four elders, we "will fall down before Him who sits on the throne, and will worship Him who lives forever and ever, and will cast [our] crowns before the throne" (Rev. 4:10).

THE FARMER

The hard-working farmer ought to be the first to receive his share of the crops. (2:6)

The fourth and final familiar image Paul uses to illustrate characteristics of a strong spiritual life is that of a **farmer.** The farmer works to gain the crop for himself. That is how he makes his living. In New Testament times, farm laborers often were paid with a portion of the crops they helped to plant, cultivate, and harvest. The **hard-working**

farmer received not only a greater share but also **the first . . . share of the crops.** The teacher has reward in knowing he has enriched the lives of his students, the soldier has the reward of pleasing his commander in chief, the athlete has the reward of a trophy, and the farmer has the reward of the first and best share of the crops.

Hard-working is a participle form of the verb *kopiaō,* which means to toil intensely, to sweat and strain to the point of exhaustion if necessary. The industrious farmer starts his hard and demanding work early and quits late. He endures the cold, the heat, the rain, and the drought. He plows the soil whether it is hard or loose. He does not wait for his own convenience, because the seasons do not wait for him. When the time comes to plant, he must plant; when weeds appear, he must remove them; and when the crop is mature, he must harvest it. What drives the man to such hard toil is the harvest.

The teacher often finds exhilaration in the aspiring minds of his students, the soldier often has the excitement of battle, and the athlete the thrill of competing. But most of a farmer's working hours are tedious, humdrum, and unexciting. And, unlike the teacher, the soldier, and the athlete, a farmer often works alone. He has no students to stimulate him, no fellow soldiers to fight with him, no teammates or crowd to cheer him.

Many Christians' lives are like the farmer's. Although there may be occasional times of excitement and special satisfaction, the daily routine is often, in itself, unattractive and unrewarding. But whatever their day-to-day responsibilities may involve, all faithful believers are promised God's blessing and reward. We may be underpaid, treated unfairly by our boss or fellow employees, and misunderstood or unappreciated by fellow Christians. But Christ's reward to His faithful disciples is never deficient, never unfair, never late, and never omitted.

Our good works have nothing to do with keeping our salvation, no more than they had anything to do with our receiving salvation. But they have everything to do with working out our salvation (Phil. 2:12). Not only are "we . . . [God's] workmanship," Paul reminds us, but we are "created in Christ Jesus for good works, which God prepared beforehand, that we should walk in them" (Eph. 2:10). When believers stand before the Lord's judgment seat, His *bēma,* "each man's work will become evident; for the day will show it, because it is to be revealed with fire; and the fire itself will test the quality of each man's work. If any man's work which he has built upon it remains, he shall receive a reward" (1 Cor. 3:13–14).

CONCLUSION

Consider what I say, for the Lord will give you understanding in everything. (2:7)

There are certain things the spiritual Christian has to endure, such as suffering for the faith. There are certain things he has to avoid, such as becoming entangled with the affairs of the world. There are certain mandates he has to obey, namely, the commands of his Lord. There are certain things he has to do, including tasks that seem mundane and ordinary. And, just as surely, there are things he will be given to enjoy, the victory and the rewards of a dedicated, selfless, and disciplined life. Through His apostle, the Lord assures us: "Be steadfast, immovable, always abounding in the work of the Lord, knowing that your toil is not in vain in the Lord" (1 Cor. 15:58).

Consider what I say, Paul continues. The verb *noeō* (**consider**) is used only here in the New Testament. It denotes perceiving clearly with the mind, of understanding fully, of considering carefully, of pondering and mulling over. The form here is an imperative, indicating that Paul was giving a strong admonition, not mere advice.

The apostle was saying to Timothy, and still says to believers today: "Under the Lord, think over and carefully ponder what I have been saying. Look at your own life and ask yourself if you are a strong Christian, a spiritual Christian, a mature Christian. Are you devoting yourself to guarding and teaching God's Word? Do you deny yourself and count your life as nothing in order to faithfully serve the Lord? Do you keep a distance between yourself and the affairs of the world? Do you continually prepare yourself to serve your Master? Do you understand self-denial and self-sacrifice? Are you willing to pay the price that He demands?"

"If you can answer yes to those questions," we are promised, **the Lord will give you understanding in everything.** You will be led with wisdom and insight through the challenges to victory.

Motives for Sacrificial Ministry

4

Remember Jesus Christ, risen from the dead, descendant of David, according to my gospel, for which I suffer hardship even to imprisonment as a criminal; but the word of God is not imprisoned. For this reason I endure all things for the sake of those who are chosen, that they also may obtain the salvation which is in Christ Jesus and with it eternal glory. It is a trustworthy statement: For if we died with Him, we shall also live with Him; if we endure, we shall also reign with Him; if we deny Him, He also will deny us; if we are faithless, He remains faithful; for He cannot deny Himself. (2:8–13)

Jeremiah was far and away the most godly man of his day. But he is a poor advertisement for the contemporary prosperity gospel. During most of his earthly life, his godliness brought greater and greater ridicule and persecution, ending, as tradition has it, by merciless stoning. He was born into a priestly family but was called to be a prophet, the most persecuted prophet in the Old Testament. He refused to compromise God's truth, and for that faithfulness suffered what might be called a life-long martyrdom. Yet he continued yearning for the salvation of his people, praying, "Oh, that my head were waters, and my eyes a fountain of tears, that I might weep day and night for the slain of the daughter of my people!" (Jer. 9:1).

After years of opposition and torment, Jeremiah cried out in bewilderment to God: "Righteous art Thou, O Lord, that I would plead my case with Thee; indeed I would discuss matters of justice with Thee: Why has the way of the wicked prospered? Why are all those who deal in treachery at ease?" (Jer. 12:1). Patience with his ungodly countrymen was exhausted, and he now begged God to "drag them off like sheep for the slaughter and set them apart for a day of carnage!" (v. 3). He also lost patience with God, asking, "How long is the land to mourn and the vegetation of the countryside to wither? For the wickedness of those who dwell in it, animals and birds have been snatched away, because men have said, 'He [God] will not see our latter ending'" (Jer. 12:4).

God's response was not what Jeremiah, and most of us, would have expected. "If you have run with footmen and they have tired you out," the Lord asked His prophet, "then how can you compete with horses?" (v. 5). God told Jeremiah, in effect, "Your suffering for Me has just begun. You are just learning to endure." Instead of being offered sympathy, he was called to have courage and strength.

That is essentially the admonition Paul gave to Timothy, who at this time faced increased opposition from within the church as well as increased persecution from without. Timothy was not to retreat or wallow in self-pity. He was instead to "be strong in the grace that is in Christ Jesus. . . . [and to] suffer hardship . . . as a good soldier of Christ Jesus" (2 Tim. 2:1, 3).

Any careful student of the New Testament knows that a true confession of Jesus as Savior and Lord involves willing, unconditional submission to Him and to the work of His kingdom—whatever the cost might be, even if it is death.

Near the end of the Sermon on the Mount, Jesus said, "Not everyone who says to Me, 'Lord, Lord,' will enter the kingdom of heaven; but he who does the will of My Father who is in heaven" (Matt. 7:21; cf. Luke 6:46). A short while later, He told the Twelve, "He who does not take his cross and follow after Me is not worthy of Me. He who has found his life shall lose it, and he who has lost his life for My sake shall find it" (Matt. 10:38–39). Near the end of His earthly ministry, as "Christ began to show His disciples that He must go to Jerusalem, and suffer many things from the elders and chief priests and scribes, and be killed, and be raised up on the third day," He repeated the earlier truth in slightly different words: "If anyone wishes to come after Me, let him deny himself, and take up his cross, and follow Me. For whoever wishes to save his life shall lose it; but whoever loses his life for My sake shall find it" (Matt. 16:21, 24–25). In what is commonly called His second farewell discourse, Jesus said, "Remember the word that I said to you,

'A slave is not greater than his master.' If they persecuted Me, they will also persecute you" (John 15:20).

Faithful service to the Lord has always been costly. Speaking of Old Testament saints, the writer of Hebrews said that some "were tortured, not accepting their release, in order that they might obtain a better resurrection; and others experienced mockings and scourgings, yes, also chains and imprisonment. They were stoned, they were sawn in two, they were tempted, they were put to death with the sword; they went about in sheepskins, in goatskins, being destitute, afflicted, ill-treated (men of whom the world was not worthy), wandering in deserts and mountains and caves and holes in the ground" (Heb. 11:35–38). Those godly men and women could have echoed Paul's words: "I do not consider my life of any account as dear to myself, in order that I may finish my course, and the ministry which I received from the Lord" (Acts 20:24).

Throughout the history of the church, the cost of discipleship has continued to be high. Millions upon millions have severely suffered for the cause of Christ, including those who have laid down their lives. Many believers have been maligned and deserted by unbelieving spouses, a desertion that is particularly hard on wives who are left with children to support. Often there is rejection and ostracism by family, friends, or business associates who are offended by the gospel. Even in the church, "those who desire to make a good showing in the flesh" resent true godliness. They substitute humanly achievable standards, as the Judaizers did in regard to circumcision, for God's spiritual standards, in order "that they may not be persecuted for the cross of Christ" (Gal. 6:12). Believers who are self-centered and self-willed find God's standards to be onerous and often make life difficult for believers who seek, in the Spirit's power, to live up to them.

During World War II, eleven missionaries were martyred on the Island of Panay in the Philippines. One of these was Dr. Francis Rose, who had penned these poignant and challenging words in what is commonly called "The Martyr's Hymn":

> All human progress up to God
> Has stained the stairs of time with blood;
> For every gain for Christendom
> Is bought by someone's martyrdom.
>
> For us he poured the crimson cup,
> And bade us take and drink it up.
> Himself he poured to set us free.
> Help us, O Christ, to drink with Thee.

Ten thousand saints come thronging home,
From lion's den and catacomb.
The fire and sword and beasts defied;
For Christ, their King, they gladly died.
With eye of faith we see today
That cross-led column wind its way
Up life's repeated Calvary.
We rise, O Christ, to follow Thee!

Until Christ returns, the bold proclamation of the gospel will continue to stir up the animosity and opposition of the spiritually blind, Christ-rejecting world. In the farewell discourse mentioned above, Jesus told the disciples, "In the world you have tribulation, but take courage; I have overcome the world" (John 16:33). Later in the present letter, Paul would remind Timothy that "all who desire to live godly in Christ Jesus will be persecuted" (2 Tim. 3:12). Satan makes certain that persecution accompanies faithfulness to Christ.

In 2 Timothy 2:8–13, Paul assures this young pastor that, nevertheless, there is more than reason enough for him, and all Christians, to willingly suffer for Christ, to put everything in this life on the line for Him. No sacrifice—mockery, alienation, rejection, desertion, imprisonment, or even death—is too high a price to pay. The importance and the rewards of a faithful life and ministry, not to mention the honor and glory of the Lord we trust and serve, far outweigh any personal sacrifice that our trust and service may incite.

Less than ten years earlier, Paul had written the church at Rome,

Who shall separate us from the love of Christ? Shall tribulation, or distress, or persecution, or famine, or nakedness, or peril, or sword? Just as it is written, "For Thy sake we are being put to death all day long; we were considered as sheep to be slaughtered." But in all these things we overwhelmingly conquer through Him who loved us. For I am convinced that neither death, nor life, nor angels, nor principalities, nor things present, nor things to come, nor powers, nor height, nor depth, nor any other created thing, shall be able to separate us from the love of God, which is in Christ Jesus our Lord." (Rom. 8:35–39)

It was because of that confidence that the apostle also could say, "Therefore I am well content with weaknesses, with insults, with distresses, with persecutions, with difficulties, for Christ's sake; for when I am weak, then I am strong" (2 Cor. 12:10).

While writing this last inspired letter of his life, Paul knew he was near the end. "The time of my departure has come," he said. "I have fought the good fight, I have finished the course, I have kept the faith" (2 Tim. 4:6–7). Timothy understood quite well that if he ministered as courageously and faithfully as Paul he might also suffer as severely as Paul. The apostle therefore entreats Timothy to have the same unshakable confidence in Christ and the same unqualified willingness to suffer for His sake that had sustained him throughout his own productive but pain-filled years and that enabled him to "have fought the good fight" and to "have kept the faith," even when facing the most threatening enemies.

Paul may have anticipated questions that would come to Timothy's mind after the admonitions of 2:1–6. *"Why* should I be a faithful teacher of teachers?" he may have wondered. *"Why* should I suffer hardship like a soldier, compete to win like an athlete, and toil hard like a farmer?"

Whatever Timothy may have been thinking, the apostle offers four powerful motives for faithfulness. He calls him to remember the preeminence of the Lord (v. 8), the power of the Word (v. 9), the purpose of the work (v. 10), and the promise of reward (vv. 11–13).

THE PREEMINENCE OF THE LORD

Remember Jesus Christ, risen from the dead, descendant of David, according to my gospel, (2:8)

"Timothy," Paul is saying, "your service will be more aggressive, you will have greater courage, greater boldness, greater endurance of evil treatment and of suffering for the Lord if you **remember** His preeminence, who He really is—none other than God incarnate, Jesus Christ."

As with the preceding verbs "be strong" (v. 1), "entrust" (v. 2), and "consider" (v. 7), the Greek verb rendered **remember** is an imperative—as also are the following: "remind" (v. 14), "be diligent" (v. 15), "avoid" (v. 16), "abstain" (v. 19), "flee" and "pursue" (v. 22), and "refuse" (v. 23). These are gentle commands, but commands nonetheless. For a faithful and productive spiritual life, they are not options but imperatives, because they all characterize the sinless life of our supreme example, **Jesus Christ.** As John reminds us, "The one who says he abides in Him [Christ] ought himself to walk in the same manner as He walked" (1 John 2:6). Peter asks, "For what credit is there if, when you sin and are harshly treated, you endure it with patience? But if when you do what is right and suffer for it you patiently endure it, this finds favor with God. For you have been called for this purpose, since Christ also suffered for you, leaving you an example for you to follow in His steps, who committed no sin, nor was any deceit found in His mouth" (1 Peter

2:20–22). We are to fix "our eyes on Jesus, the author and perfecter of faith, who for the joy set before Him endured the cross, despising the shame, and has sat down at the right hand of the throne of God" (Heb. 12:2).

Because the Greek verb behind **remember** is in the active voice, it carries the idea of "continue to remember" or "keep on remembering." The preeminence of our Lord **Jesus Christ** should always be in the forefront of our minds. He is the supreme and ultimate teacher of teachers. He was the greatest soldier, the greatest athlete, and the greatest farmer, as it were. He fought the greatest battle and won the greatest victory. He ran the greatest race and won the greatest prize. He sowed the perfect seed and reaped the perfect harvest.

We must keep in mind that Jesus' path to glory was marked by pain before pleasure, sorrow before joy, humiliation before glorification, persecution before exaltation, death before resurrection, earthly hatred before heavenly worship. To remember those truths about our Lord's earthly life will protect us from the foolish and ungodly promises of the so-called health and wealth gospel, which vitiates His command to take up our crosses as He took up His. If Jesus' perfect and sinless obedience of His heavenly Father did not bring Him earthly prosperity and well-being, how much less can we expect to receive those things because of our imperfect service of Him? If our Lord Jesus Christ, "although He was [God's] Son, . . . learned obedience from the things which He suffered" (Heb. 5:8), how much more should we?

We are to **remember Jesus Christ** first of all because He is **risen from the dead,** more literally, "having been raised from the dead." It is that great truth on which Paul focuses in 1 Corinthians 15. "For I delivered to you as of first importance what I also received," he said, "that Christ died for our sins according to the Scriptures, and that He was buried, and that He was raised on the third day according to the Scriptures" (1 Cor. 15:3–4). That truth is of "first importance" because, "if Christ has not been raised, [our] faith is worthless; [and we] are still in [our] sins. . . . If we have hoped in Christ in this life only, we are of all men most to be pitied" (vv. 17, 19).

Our Lord Himself promised difficulty. "You will be hated by all on account of My name," He said, "but it is the one who has endured to the end who will be saved. But whenever they persecute you in this city, flee to the next; for truly I say to you, you shall not finish going through the cities of Israel, until the Son of Man comes. A disciple is not above his teacher, nor a slave above his master" (Matt. 10:22–24).

Paul is not speaking of remembering the resurrection, important as that is, but rather of remembering **Jesus Christ,** who is alive because of the resurrection, having been **risen from the dead.** We do not serve a past event or a merely historical person. Jesus did indeed live a human life and die a human death. But we worship and serve Him because He is no longer dead but alive. We **remember** and worship and serve the *living* **Jesus Christ.**

By His resurrection, Christ became "the first-born from the dead; so that He Himself might come to have first place [preeminence] in everything" (Col. 1:18). Not only that, however; for our sakes, He also became "the first-born among many brethren" (Rom. 8:29), in order that we might be raised and live with Him through all eternity, as "the general assembly and church of the first-born who are enrolled in heaven" (Heb. 12:23).

When we remember Christ as our resurrected Lord, we focus on His nature as God and His role as Savior. Through His death and resurrection, Christ broke the shackles of sin and of its wages, death, which is the greatest weapon of Satan. When we trusted in Him, He became *our* Savior and *our* Lord, breaking the power of sin, of death, and of Satan in *our own* lives. What greater motivation for service to Him could there be than to serve the One who conquered death and did it for us (John 14:19)?

We also should remember Jesus Christ in His humanity, in His identification with fallen mankind as a **descendant of David** "according to the flesh" (Rom. 1:30). His human descent from David not only speaks of His humanity as our sympathetic and merciful High Priest, who knows all our suffering and has felt all our pain (Heb. 2:14, 18), but also of His royalty and majesty. Before Jesus' conception, the angel proclaimed to Mary, "He will be great, and will be called the Son of the Most High; and the Lord God will give Him the throne of His father David; and He will reign over the house of Jacob forever; and His kingdom will have no end" (Luke 1:32–33). In his last direct words to the apostle John on Patmos, Jesus spoke of Himself as "the root and the offspring of David, the bright morning star" (Rev. 22:16).

Therefore, if Jesus Christ is our divine Savior and sovereign Lord, why should we worry about what happens to us in this life? As our perfect High Priest, He is able to "sympathize with our weaknesses," because He "has been tempted in all things as we are, yet without sin. Let us therefore draw near with confidence to the throne of grace, that we may receive mercy and may find grace to help in time of need" (Heb. 4:16).

As our sovereign Lord, Jesus Christ controls everything that we are and everything that happens to us. We must resist temptation, but we need not fear it, because our Lord "will not allow [us] to be tempted beyond what [we] are able, but with the temptation will provide the way of escape also, that [we] may be able to endure it" (1 Cor. 10:13). We have no need to worry about the depths of our troubles or our sorrows. Isaiah gives comfort to all those who belong to the Messiah, Jesus

Christ. "Like a shepherd He will tend His flock, in His arm He will gather the lambs, and carry them in His bosom" (Isa. 40:11). "Surely our griefs He Himself bore, and our sorrows He carried" (53:4), the prophet later writes.

We have no need to fear the loss of salvation, because our Lord assures us of our perfect and absolute security in Him. "My sheep hear My voice, and I know them, and they follow Me," He said; "and I give eternal life to them, and they shall never perish; and no one shall snatch them out of My hand" (John 10:27–28). "He is able to save forever those who draw near to God through Him, since He always lives to make intercession for them" (Heb. 7:25). We have no need to fear death. "Because I live," Jesus said, "you shall live also" (John 14:19). Every believer can say with Paul, "To me, to live is Christ, and to die is gain" (Phil. 1:21).

According to my gospel does not refer to Paul's personal opinion about the gospel but to the divinely revealed message of Jesus Christ entrusted to him and that he proclaimed as "an apostle of Christ Jesus by the will of God" (2 Tim. 1:1). It was the One who was the theme of the gospel he was referring to when he said, "Timothy, keep your eyes on the preeminent Jesus Christ as the Son of God as well as the Son of man, and as Savior as well as Lord and King."

THE POWER OF THE WORD

for which I suffer hardship even to imprisonment as a criminal; but the word of God is not imprisoned. (2:9)

A second great motivation for faithfulness is the power of God's Word. Paul contrasts his own **imprisonment** to the freedom of **the word of God,** which **is not imprisoned.** As suggested in this translation, the Greek noun behind **imprisonment** is from the verb that is here rendered **is . . . imprisoned.** Even though Paul was a man under the authority of Jesus Christ, he was subject to **imprisonment** by ungodly men, just as Jesus Himself had been subject to evil treatment by ungodly men during His incarnation. Although Paul was not sinless, as was his Lord, he nevertheless was like his Lord in being guiltless of the charges for which he was imprisoned. Paul was not a robber, murderer, or traitor, even by the standards of Roman law. Yet he was incarcerated as a criminal, probably in the infamous Mamertine prison in Rome, awaiting certain death.

Paul was not, however, lamenting the injustice of his imprisonment. He had already admonished Timothy not to "be ashamed of the testimony of our Lord, or of me His prisoner; but join with me in suffering for the gospel according to the power of God" (2 Tim. 1:8). Whether or not he was familiar with Peter's first letter (written several years before 2 Timothy), he certainly would have agreed with the attitude of his fellow apostle, who, as quoted above, wrote, "If when you do what is right and suffer for it you patiently endure it, this finds favor with God. For you have been called for this purpose, since Christ also suffered for you, leaving you an example for you to follow in His steps" (1 Peter 2:20–21). Paul was "well content with weaknesses, with insults, with distresses, with persecutions, with difficulties, for Christ's sake; for when I am weak," he testified, "then I am strong" (2 Cor. 12:10).

Paul's point in the present verse, therefore, is not to complain about his own lamentable condition but rather to point up, by contrast, the sovereign, unfettered **word of God.** The apostle would have agreed fully with the writer of Hebrews, who declared, "The word of God is living and active and sharper than any two-edged sword, and piercing as far as the division of soul and spirit, of both joints and marrow, and able to judge the thoughts and intentions of the heart" (Heb. 4:12). As Paul had written the Ephesian church, "The sword of the Spirit . . . is the word of God" (Eph. 6:17), and this divine "sword" cannot be taken out of the Spirit's hand—by men, by demons, or even by Satan himself.

There have always been people in the church, and never more than in our own day, who believe that the power of the gospel is restricted by social or political opposition. Consequently, they argue that risking public censure, not to mention arrest and imprisonment for boldly preaching sin, repentance, and the gospel, should be avoided. They counsel discretion and sometimes even compromise in order to make the message more acceptable and, supposedly, more effective.

Many Christians are under the illusion that God's Word has been influential in the Western world, especially in such democracies as the United States, primarily because of legal guarantees of freedom of religion, and that the fight to keep that freedom is therefore a fight to preserve the power of the gospel. In fact, some Christians who would never think of confronting society with the bold and demanding gospel and being censured for it will strongly fight for some social or political issue in ways that might get them arrested. Religious freedom is certainly commendable, and Christians who enjoy it should be grateful for and take advantage of the opportunities it affords for worship, witness, and service. But the power of God's Word has never been dependent on man's protection or subject to man's restriction. That is precisely Paul's point. **The word of God is not,** and cannot be, **imprisoned.**

At one time there were some 600 miles of catacombs under the city of Rome, nearly all them dug and used by ten generations of Christians over a period of 300 years. In the early centuries of the church, the catacombs served as meeting and burial places for perhaps as many as four million Christians. A common inscription found on walls there is "The Word of God is not bound." In his famous hymn "A Mighty Fortress Is Our God," Martin Luther declared, "The body they may kill; God's truth abideth still."

John Bunyan wrote his most famous work, *Pilgrim's Progress,* while jailed in Bedford, England, for preaching the gospel. Yet for several centuries that book was second in sales only to the Bible. Bunyan's cell window faced a high stone wall that surrounded the prison, making it impossible to see into or out of his cell. On many days, however, he would preach loudly enough for his voice to be heard on the outside of the wall, where hundreds of listeners, believers and unbelievers, eagerly awaited his proclamation of God's Word, which was unconfined by stone walls or iron bars.

Before the Communist conquest in the late 1940s and early 1950s, there were more than 700,000 Christians in China. During the subsequent "cultural revolution," at least 30 million Chinese were slaughtered, including most of the Christians. Yet, after more than forty years of brutal oppression, imprisonment, and executions, the church of Jesus Christ in that vast country has a current membership of an estimated 30 million to 100 million. Although written copies of Scripture are still scarce, the truth of God's Word endures in their hearts. Its power cannot be bound. The more it is assailed, the more it prevails.

Andrew Melville was the successor of John Knox in the Scottish Reformation. On one occasion, a certain official had him arrested and said, "There will never be quietness in this country till half a dozen of you be hanged or banished [from] the country." With perfect composure, Melville fearlessly replied, "It is the same to me whether I rot in the air or in the ground. The earth is the Lord's; my fatherland is wherever well-doing is. I have been ready to give my life, when it was not half as well worn, at the pleasure of my God. I lived out of your country ten years as well as in it. Yet God be glorified, it will not lie in your power to hang nor exile His truth!"

THE PURPOSE OF THE WORK

For this reason I endure all things for the sake of those who are chosen, that they also may obtain the salvation which is in Christ Jesus and with it eternal glory. (2:10)

A third motivation for faithfulness is the divine purpose of the Lord's work on earth before He returns.

For this reason refers to what Paul has said in the preceding verse about remembering the preeminence of Christ and the power of God's word. Those divine motivations gave the apostle the willingness to **endure all things for the sake of those who are chosen.** He is not speaking here of fellow believers, but of God's **chosen** who had yet to **obtain the salvation which is in Christ Jesus.**

That translates *hina,* which, when used with a subjunctive, as here with *tunchanō* (**to obtain**), indicates a purpose clause. A more exact rendering, therefore, would be "in order **that**" the unbelievers to whom he witnessed might **obtain the salvation which is in Christ Jesus.** Paul not only suffered because his faithfulness to Christ provoked it but also because, like the Lord, he was "not wishing for any to perish but for all to come to repentance" (2 Peter 3:9). His heart reflected God's heart, because, like Peter, he knew with certainty that "there is salvation in no one else; for there is no other name under heaven that has been given among men, by which we must be saved" (Acts 4:12).

God's Word clearly reveals that "He chose us in Him [Christ] before the foundation of the world, [and] predestined us to adoption as sons through Jesus Christ to Himself, according to the kind intention of His will" (Eph. 1:4–5), that "whom He foreknew, He also predestined to become conformed to the image of His Son" (Rom. 8:29). Disregarding other Scripture, some fatalistic interpreters use texts such as those just cited to argue that evangelism not only is unnecessary but presumptuous, claiming that God will sovereignly save those whom He has predestined, regardless of whether or not they hear and believe the gospel. But God's Word just as clearly teaches the necessity of faith for salvation as it does that salvation is by God's free and sovereign grace. Jesus said, "No one can come to Me, unless it has been granted him from the Father" (John 6:65). But He also said, "For God so loved the world, that He gave His only begotten Son, that whoever *believes* in Him should not perish, but have eternal life. . . . He who *believes* in Him is not judged; he who does not believe has been judged already, because *he has not believed* in the name of the only begotten Son of God" (John 3:16, 18, emphasis added; cf. v. 36). Paul succinctly states those companion truths in the familiar and priceless words "By grace you have been saved through faith; and that not of yourselves, it is the gift of God" (Eph. 2:8).

Scripture also is clear that, despite the Lord's sovereign calling of men to Himself, He calls those who belong to Him to extend His call to those who have not heard and heeded it. "Go therefore and make disciples of all the nations," Jesus said, "baptizing them in the name of the Father and the Son and the Holy Spirit" (Matt. 28:19). We are called to be Christ's "witnesses both in Jerusalem, and in all Judea and Samaria, and even to the remotest part of the earth" (Acts 1:8).

In his letter to the church at Rome, immediately after declaring that "whoever will call upon the name of the Lord will be saved," Paul goes on to ask rhetorically, "How then shall they call upon Him in whom they have not believed? And how shall they believe in Him whom they have not heard? And how shall they hear without a preacher?" (Rom. 10:14).

The fact that our finite minds cannot fully understand or reconcile such truths in no way affects their validity. God sovereignly calls every believer in His grace; He sovereignly demands their faith to make His gracious calling effective; and He sovereignly calls those who are saved to be His witnesses to those who are not.

John Wesley traveled by foot or horseback some 250,000 miles, preaching more than 40,000 sermons, and he wrote, translated, or edited more than 200 books. He lived simply and gave away most of whatever income he received. Yet he was continually ridiculed and pelted with stones by ungodly mobs and was ostracized by fellow clergymen in the Church of England. When maligned, he answered, "I leave my reputation where I left my soul, in the hands of God." He never lost his joy of service or his love for the Lord and for men, both saved and unsaved. One biographer commented, "To Wesley was granted the task which even an archangel might have envied."

George Whitefield, a close friend and fellow worker with John and Charles Wesley during his early ministry, spent thirty-four years preaching the gospel in the British Isles and in America. He made thirteen transatlantic voyages, which were still perilous in those days, and preached at least 18,000 sermons on the two continents. The noted poet and hymnwriter William Cowper—who wrote "Oh! For a Closer Walk with God" and "There Is a Fountain Filled with Blood"—penned the following tribute to Whitefield:

> He loved the world that hated him.
> The tear that dropped upon his Bible was sincere.
> Assailed by scandal and the tongue of strife,
> His only answer was a blameless life.

That resolute man of God heeded Peter's counsel to "keep a good conscience so that in the thing in which you are slandered, those who revile your good behavior in Christ may be put to shame. For it is better, if God should will it so, that you suffer for doing what is right rather than for doing what is wrong" (1 Peter 3:16–17).

And **with it,** Paul continues—that is, with "the salvation which is in Christ Jesus"—comes **eternal glory.** In his letter to the church at Rome, Paul presents that truth more fully: "The Spirit Himself bears witness with our spirit that we are children of God, and if children, heirs also, heirs of God and fellow heirs with Christ, if indeed we suffer with Him in order that we may also be glorified with Him" (8:16–17).

THE PROMISE OF ETERNAL BLESSING

It is a trustworthy statement: For if we died with Him, we shall also live with Him; if we endure, we shall also reign with Him; if we deny Him, He also will deny us; if we are faithless, He remains faithful; for He cannot deny Himself. (2:11–13)

A fourth motivation for faithfulness to Christ is the promise of eternal blessing.

Paul uses the phrase **It is a trustworthy statement** five times in the Pastoral Epistles (1 & 2 Timothy, Titus), but it is found nowhere else in the New Testament. He seems to have used it to introduce a truth that was axiomatic, a truism in the early church that was commonly known and believed. The long sentence beginning **For if we died with Him** and continuing through verse 13 may have been used as a creed in the early church. Its parallelism and rhythm suggest that these two verses (like 1 Timothy 3:16) may have been sung as a hymn, and it is for that reason that some Greek texts and several modern translations set it in verse form.

If we died with Him may refer to the spiritual death of which Paul speaks in Romans. "Therefore we have been buried with Him through baptism into death," he explains, "in order that as Christ was raised from the dead through the glory of the Father, so we too might walk in newness of life. For if we have become united with Him in the likeness of His death, certainly we shall be also in the likeness of His resurrection, . . . for he who has died is freed from sin. Now if we have died with Christ, we believe that we shall also live with Him" (Rom. 6:4–5, 7–8).

But the context of 2 Timothy 2:11 seems to suggest that Paul here has martyrdom in mind. In that case, if someone has sacrificed his life for Christ, that is, has **died with Him,** that martyrdom gives evidence that he had spiritual life in **Him** and will **live with Him** throughout eternity. The martyr's hope is eternal life after death.

In the same way, **if we endure** persecution and hostility without being killed, we give evidence that we truly belong to Christ and that **we shall also,** therefore, **reign with Him.** That is also the hope of believers who live in difficulty—the eternal kingdom. *Basileuō* means literally to rule as a king (*basileus*). The verb here is the compound *sumbasileuō*, which means to **reign with.** The other side of that truth is that those who do *not* **endure** give equally certain evidence that they do not belong to Christ and will *not* **reign with Him.**

Although you were formerly alienated and hostile in mind, engaged in evil deeds," Paul explained to believers at Colossae, "yet He has now reconciled you in His fleshly body through death, in order to present you before Him holy and blameless and beyond reproach—if indeed you continue in the faith firmly established and steadfast, and not moved away from the hope of the gospel that you have heard, which was proclaimed in all creation under heaven, and of which I, Paul, was made a minister" (Col. 1:21–23). Only if Christ is Lord of a life, can He present that life before His Father "holy and blameless and beyond reproach." The only life that can **endure** is an obedient life. A life that will not serve Him will never **reign with Him.**

Jesus promised the Twelve, "Truly I say to you, that you who have followed Me, in the regeneration when the Son of Man will sit on His glorious throne, you also shall sit upon twelve thrones, judging the twelve tribes of Israel" (Matt. 19:28; cf. Luke 22:29–30). Believers also have positions of authority in the millennial kingdom, as 1 Corinthians 6:2–3 indicates: "Do you not know that the saints will judge the world? And if the world is judged by you, are you not competent to constitute the smallest law courts? Do you not know that we shall judge angels? How much more, matters of this life?" (1 Cor. 6:2–3). Speaking of all Christians in the final glory, Paul declared, "For if by the transgression of the one, death reigned through the one, much more those who receive the abundance of grace and of the gift of righteousness will reign in life through the One, Jesus Christ" (Rom. 5:17).

To **endure,** or persevere, with Christ does not protect salvation, which is eternally secured when a person trusts in Him as Savior and Lord. We can no more ensure salvation by our own efforts or power than we first gained it by our own efforts or power.

The next two conditions and promises are negative and are parallel, at least in form, to the preceding positive ones.

First, Paul says, **If we deny Him,** that is, Jesus Christ, **He also will deny us.** The Greek verb rendered **deny** is in the future tense, and the clause is therefore more clearly rendered, "If we ever deny Him" or "If in the future we deny Him." It looks at some confrontation that makes the cost of confessing Christ very high and thereby tests one's true faith. A person who fails to endure and hold onto his confession of Christ will **deny Him,** because he never belonged to Christ at all. "Anyone who . . . does not abide in the teaching of Christ, does not have God; the one who abides in the teaching, he has both the Father and the Son" (2 John 9). Those who remain faithful to the truth they profess give evidence of belonging to God.

"What about Peter's denial?" we may ask. "Can a true believer deny the Lord?" (cf. Matt. 26:69–75; Mark 14:66–72; Luke 22:54–62; John 18:16, 25–27). Obviously believers like Peter can fall into temporary cowardice and fail to stand for the Lord. We all do it in various ways when we're unwilling to openly declare our love for Christ in a given situation.

Confronted by the cost of discipleship, Peter was facing just such a test as Paul had in mind. Did he thereby evidence a lack of true saving faith? His response to the denial, going out and weeping bitter tears of penitence (Matt. 26:75), and the Lord's restoration of him in Galilee (John 21:15–17) lead one to conclude that Peter was truly justified, though obviously not yet fully sanctified. And until Pentecost, Peter did not have the fulness of the Holy Spirit. After the Spirit came to live in him in New Covenant fullness, however, his courage, boldness, and willingness to face any hostility became legendary (cf. Acts 1:5, 8; 2:4, 14–36; 3:1–6, 12–26; 4:1–4, 8–13, 19, 21, 31). Peter died a martyr, just as Jesus had foretold he would—faithful in the face of execution for his Lord (John 21:18–19). Tradition holds that, by his own request, he was crucified upside down, because he felt unworthy to die in the same manner as his Lord.

So perhaps the answer to the issue of Peter's denial is that his was a momentary failure, followed by repentance. He did not as yet have the fullness of the Spirit, but during the rest of this life after Pentecost he boldly confessed Christ, even when it cost him his life.

Jesus Himself gave the sobering warning, "Whoever shall deny Me before men, I will also deny him before My Father who is in heaven" (Matt. 10:33). There is a settled, final kind of denial that does not repent and thereby evidences an unregenerate heart. After the lame man was healed near the Beautiful gate of the temple, Peter testified to the seriousness of denying Christ. "The God of Abraham, Isaac, and Jacob, the God of our fathers, has glorified His servant Jesus," he said, "the one whom you delivered up, and disowned [denied] in the presence of Pilate, when he had decided to release Him. But you disowned [denied] the Holy and Righteous One, and asked for a murderer to be granted to you, but put to death the Prince of life, the one whom God raised from the dead, a fact to which we are witnesses" (Acts 3:13–15).

The most dangerous of those who deny Christ are "false teachers . . . who will secretly introduce destructive heresies, even denying the Master who bought them" (2 Peter 2:1). They are, in fact, no less than antichrists. To those who claim to belong to God as Father without belonging to Christ as His Son, John unequivocally says, "Who is the liar but the one who denies that Jesus is the Christ? This is the antichrist, the one who denies the Father and the Son. Whoever denies the Son does not have the Father; the one who confesses the Son has the Father also" (1 John 2:22–23).

In the present text, however, Paul's warning could include those who once claimed Christ but later **deny Him** when the cost of discipleship becomes too high. Such were the "disciples [who] withdrew and were not walking with Him [Jesus] anymore" (John 6:66). It is about such false Christians that the writer of Hebrews says: "For in the case of those who have once been enlightened and have tasted of the heavenly gift and have been made partakers of the Holy Spirit, and have tasted the good word of God and the powers of the age to come, and then have fallen away, it is impossible to renew them again to repentance, since they again crucify to themselves the Son of God, and put Him to open shame" (Heb. 6:4–6).

Later in 2 Timothy, Paul describes such false Christians as "lovers of self, lovers of money, boastful, arrogant, revilers, disobedient to parents, ungrateful, unholy, unloving, irreconcilable, malicious gossips, without self-control, brutal, haters of good, treacherous, reckless, conceited, lovers of pleasure rather than lovers of God; holding to a form of godliness, although they have denied its power" (3:2–5). In his letter to Titus, he says of such people that "they profess to know God, but by their deeds they deny Him, being detestable and disobedient, and worthless for any good deed" (Titus 1:16). Continual disobedience inevitably confirms faithlessness by eventuating in denial.

The second negative condition and promise are: **If we are faithless,** Christ **remains faithful.** In this context, *apisteō* (**are faithless**) means lack of saving faith, not merely weak or unreliable faith. The unsaved ultimately deny Christ, because they never had faith in Him for salvation. But **He remains faithful,** not only to those who believe in Him but to those who do not, as here. God's divine assurance to save "whoever believes in Him [Christ]" (John 3:16) is followed almost immediately by another divine assurance that "he who does not believe has been judged already, because he has not believed in the name of the only begotten Son of God" (John 3:18). Just as Christ will never renege on His promise to save those who trust in Him, He also will never renege on His promise to condemn those who do not. To do otherwise would be to **deny Himself,** which His righteous and just nature **cannot** allow Him to do.

It was on the basis of Christ's absolute faithfulness that Paul declared earlier in this letter, "I know whom I have believed and I am convinced that He is able to guard what I have entrusted to Him until that day" (2 Tim. 1:12). It was on that basis that the writer of Hebrews admonished, "Let us hold fast the confession of our hope without wavering," and then exulted, "for He who promised is faithful" (Heb. 10:23).

The Danger of False Teaching

Remind them of these things, and solemnly charge them in the presence of God not to wrangle about words, which is useless, and leads to the ruin of the hearers. Be diligent to present yourself approved to God as a workman who does not need to be ashamed, handling accurately the word of truth. But avoid worldly and empty chatter, for it will lead to further ungodliness, and their talk will spread like gangrene. Among them are Hymenaeus and Philetus, men who have gone astray from the truth saying that the resurrection has already taken place, and thus they upset the faith of some. Nevertheless, the firm foundation of God stands, having this seal, "The Lord knows those who are His," and, "Let everyone who names the name of the Lord abstain from wickedness." (2:14–19)

Scripture clearly affirms that God is truth and that He speaks only truth and cannot lie. Jesus testified of His Father, "Thy word is truth" (John 17:17); of Himself, "I am the way, and the truth, and the life" (John 14:6); and of the Holy Spirit, He "is the Spirit of truth" (v. 17).

Scripture also affirms that Satan is a liar and the father of lies (John 8:44). His very nature is to lie and deceive. Since he fell from his exalted position in heaven, he and the angels who rebelled with him against God and became demons have been at complete, unredeemable enmity with God and separation from Him. That enmity has brought un-interrupted conflict between God and Satan. His evil angels have been in continual conflict with the holy angels of God, and on earth there has been relentless conflict between the truth of God and the lies of Satan.

God's own people have not escaped the plague of falsehood. False prophets were the bane of ancient Israel. Likewise, false teachers, preachers, and even false Christs have been the bane of the church, and will continue to be until the Lord returns. Jesus predicted that, in the last days, "false Christs and false prophets will arise and will show great signs and wonders, so as to mislead, if possible, even the elect" (Matt. 24:24).

Satan attempts to obliterate God's truth with his own falsehood. He attempts to keep the fallen world in spiritual darkness and to con-fuse and discourage God's people. It was Satan's deceit that lured Eve and then Adam to distrust God, which brought sin and death into His perfect creation and separated now-sinful mankind from the holy God. Since that time, humanity has existed in the muck and morass of sin and deceit. Through the centuries, the steady stream of falsehood has become a deeper, wider, and increasingly more destructive sea of un-godliness. False teaching about God, about Christ, about the Bible, and about spiritual reality is pandemic. The father of lies is working relent-lessly to pervert and corrupt the saving and sanctifying truth of God's written Word, the Bible, and of the living Word, His Son, Jesus Christ.

"Christian" cults abound today as never before, as does every type of false religion. Many Protestant denominations that once cham-pioned God's inerrant Word and the saving gospel of Jesus Christ have turned to human philosophy and secular wisdom. In doing so, they have abandoned the central truths of biblical Christianity—including the Trinity, the deity of Christ, His substitutionary atonement, and salva-tion by grace alone. In rejecting God's truth, they have come to condone and embrace countless evils—universalism, hedonism, psychology, self-salvation, fornication and adultery, homosexuality, abortion, and a host of other sins. The effects of ungodly teaching have been devastating and damning, not only for the members of those churches but for a count-less number of the unsaved who have been confirmed in their ungodli-ness by false religion.

Peter reminded believers of his day that "false prophets also arose among the people [of Israel], just as there will also be false teachers among you, who will secretly introduce destructive heresies, even denying the Master who bought them, bringing swift destruction upon themselves. And many will follow their sensuality, and because of them the way of the truth will be maligned" (2 Peter 2:1–2).

Paul warned the Ephesian elders, "Be on guard for yourselves and for all the flock, among which the Holy Spirit has made you overseers, to shepherd the church of God which He purchased with His own blood. I know that after my departure savage wolves will come in among you, not sparing the flock; and from among your own selves men will arise, speaking perverse things, to draw away the disciples after them" (Acts 20:28–30). It was this threat of deception that caused the Holy Spirit to inspire Paul to write, "Examine everything carefully; hold fast to that which is good; abstain from every form of evil" (1 Thess. 5:21–22).

As a young man probably past his mid-thirties, Timothy had been assigned by Paul to minister to the church in Ephesus and to correct some of the problems mentioned in the previous reference. The "savage wolves" had already begun their disruptive and destructive work, and the congregation was suffering serious spiritual and moral decline. As it always does, ungodly teaching led to ungodly living.

In his first letter to Timothy, Paul said,

> As I urged you upon my departure for Macedonia, remain on at Ephesus, in order that you may instruct certain men not to teach strange doctrines, nor to pay attention to myths and endless genealogies, which give rise to mere speculation rather than furthering the administration of God which is by faith. . . . This command I entrust to you, Timothy, my son, in accordance with the prophecies previously made concerning you, that by them you may fight the good fight, keeping faith and a good conscience, which some have rejected and suffered shipwreck in regard to their faith. (1 Tim. 1:3–4, 18–19)

He continued to inform the young pastor that "the Spirit explicitly says that in later times some will fall away from the faith, paying attention to deceitful spirits and doctrines of demons, by means of the hypocrisy of liars seared in their own conscience as with a branding iron. . . . In pointing out these things to the brethren, you will be a good servant of Christ Jesus, constantly nourished on the words of the faith and of the sound doctrine which you have been following" (4:1–2, 6; cf. 6:3–4, 20–21).

Already in the second letter, Paul has admonished Timothy, "Retain the standard of sound words which you have heard from me, in the faith and love which are in Christ Jesus. Guard, through the Holy Spirit who dwells in us, the treasure which has been entrusted to you" (2 Tim. 1:13–14). In a later passage he cautions:

Realize this, that in the last days difficult times will come. For men will be lovers of self, lovers of money, boastful, arrogant, revilers, disobedient to parents, ungrateful, unholy, unloving, irreconcilable, malicious gossips, without self-control, brutal, haters of good, treacherous, reckless, conceited, lovers of pleasure rather than lovers of God; holding to a form of godliness, although they have denied its power; and avoid such men as these. For among them are those who enter into households and captivate weak women weighed down with sins, led on by various impulses, always learning and never able to come to the knowledge of the truth. (3:1–7; cf. 4:1–3)

WARN THEM ABOUT FALSE TEACHING

Remind them of these things, and solemnly charge them in the presence of God not to wrangle about words, which is useless, (2:14a)

Paul's purpose was to motivate and encourage Timothy to keep a firm grasp on that truth himself and to pass it on to others who would do likewise (2:2). It is only with a thorough knowledge of God's truth that falsehood and deceit can be recognized, resisted, and opposed.

For that reason Paul introduces this passage about false teaching with **Remind them of these things.** As mentioned in the previous commentary chapter, **remind** translates an imperative, as do many other verbs in 2 Timothy 2, e.g., "be strong" (v. 1), "entrust" (v. 2), and "consider" (v. 7), "be diligent" (v. 15), "avoid" (v. 16), and "abstain" (v. 19). Because of the present tense in the Greek, **remind** carries the further idea of persistence.

Them refers to the whole congregation at Ephesus as well as to the "faithful men" mentioned in 2:2. **Things** refers to that about which he has just been speaking in this chapter, namely, the *positive* responsibility to pass on God's truth to others, who will, in turn, pass it on to still others; to work diligently in the Lord's work like a soldier, athlete, and farmer; to remember that Jesus is alive, risen from the dead; and to remind them of Christ's preeminence, the power of God's Word, and the purpose of His work. The call is to continually preach the truth, sound doctrine, so that it cannot be forgotten (cf. Titus 2:1, 15).

Peter was committed to this very duty, as he expresses in his second letter:

Therefore, I shall always be ready to remind you of these things, even though you already know them, and have been established in the truth which is present with you. And I consider it right, as long as I am in this earthly dwelling, to stir you up by way of reminder, knowing that the laying aside of my earthly dwelling is imminent, as also our Lord Jesus Christ has made clear to me. And I will also be diligent that at any time after my departure you may be able to call these things to mind. (2 Peter 1:12–15)

Beginning with verse 14, the apostle focuses on Timothy's *negative* responsibility to oppose and correct false teaching in the church. Timothy was to **solemnly charge them in the presence of God not to wrangle about words, which is useless.**

Diamarturomai (**solemnly charge**) is a strong verb, here used as an imperative participle, which carries the idea of stern warning. The seriousness of the admonition is made clear first of all because it intensifies still further Paul's forceful command at the beginning of this verse to remember and, second, because the warning is to be given **in the presence of God.** God is always present, of course, and He is never unaware of what His children are doing. But because of the profound danger of false teaching, Paul wanted to make sure that Timothy and those he admonished were consciously and continually aware of **the presence of God.** Being specially aware of God's presence adds a measure of healthy fear of the Lord and therefore of increased determination to serve Him faithfully.

Paul used the phrase "in the presence of God" twice in his first letter to Timothy (5:21; 6:13). He uses it again in this letter, saying, "I solemnly charge you in the presence of God," and then strengthens the charge by adding, "and of Christ Jesus, who is to judge the living and the dead, and by His appearing and His kingdom" (2 Tim. 4:1).

Sometimes in Scripture the phrase "the presence of God" is used to comfort believers. Nearing death, Isaac implored Esau, "Bring me some game and prepare a savory dish for me, that I may eat, and bless you in the presence of the Lord before my death" (Gen. 27:7). In his grand psalm of victory, David rejoiced, "O God, when Thou didst go forth before Thy people, when Thou didst march through the wilderness, the earth quaked; the heavens also dropped rain at the presence of God; Sinai itself quaked at the presence of God, the God of Israel" (Ps. 68:7–8). Reassuring Zacharias about the birth of John the Baptist, the angel said, "I am Gabriel, who stands in the presence of God; and I have been sent to speak to you, and to bring you this good news" (Luke 1:19). To a crowd of Jews outside the Temple shortly after Pentecost, Peter implored, "Repent therefore and return, that your sins may be wiped away, in order that times of refreshing may come from the presence of the Lord" (Acts 3:19). The writer of Hebrews assures us of Christ's appearing in heaven on our behalf "in the presence of God" (Heb. 9:24).

But in most cases, "the presence of the Lord" has to do with God's severity, often in judgment. Near the beginning of the psalm quoted above, David exclaims, "As smoke is driven away, so drive them away; as wax melts before the fire, so let the wicked perish before God" (Ps. 68:2; cf. 97:5; 114:7). When Christ returns in judgment, unbelievers "will pay the penalty of eternal destruction, away from the presence of the Lord and from the glory of His power" (2 Thess. 1:9).

In view of the presence of the eternal God, Paul solemnly charges the church at Ephesus **not to wrangle about words, which is useless.** As becomes clear in the following verses, Paul was not speaking about immature wrangling over secondary matters, disruptive as that can be. *Logomacheō* (**wrangle about words**) carries the idea of waging a war of words, in this instance with false teachers, who are later described as "always learning and never able to come to the knowledge of the truth" (2 Tim. 3:7). Such deceivers use human wisdom and reason to undermine God's Word, and believers are not to debate with them, especially within the church.

Even from a human perspective, it is obvious that no debate can be carried on effectively when the two sides argue from completely opposite and contradictory presuppositions. Unbelievers put no stock in the divine authority of God's Word, and believers should put no stock in the presumed authority of men's words. No matter how biblically sound their arguments may be in themselves, Christians who debate with unbelievers inadvertently allow Scripture to be considered on the same level as human wisdom.

To discuss interpretations of Scripture and doctrine with other believers who recognize the Bible as God's inerrant and authoritative Word is important when it is done in a spirit of humility and civility and is an honest attempt to grasp the truth. In the early days of the church, the Jerusalem Council was called to settle a dispute about the circumcision of believers (see Acts 15). Throughout church history, equally godly believers have differed on certain points of doctrine, as they still do today. But to argue doctrine with someone who disdains Scripture is both futile and foolish.

In his fictional but spiritually insightful *The Screwtape Letters,* C. S. Lewis has an older demon give a junior demon named Wormwood the following advice about tempting a certain human being who has been assigned to him: "Your man has been accustomed, ever since he was a boy, to have a dozen incompatible philosophies dancing about together inside his head. He doesn't think of doctrines as primarily 'true' or 'false,' but as 'academic' or 'practical.'. . . Jargon, not argument, is your best ally in keeping him from the Church" ([New York: Macmillan, 1961], 8).

Satan does indeed know that most people, including many who are intelligent and well-educated, are more apt to be persuaded by popular jargon than by biblical argument or actual proof—despite what they may claim to the contrary. In the last several centuries, the most unbiblical, humanistic, and destructive philosophies have come through channels of higher education, including many colleges, universities, and seminaries that claim to be Christian, and once were. Human intelligence has never been a match for the wiles of Satan. The sinful pride of man is nowhere more clearly seen than in exalting his own intellect over Scripture and in considering such utter foolishness to be scholarship. Many undiscerning students line up to learn from these pseudo-scholars and have the strength of any remaining convictions turned into weakness.

The barrage of ungodly ideas and verbiage that today is assaulting society in general, and even the evangelical church, is frightening. More frightening than the false ideas themselves, however, is the indifference to them, and often acceptance of them, by those who name the name of Christ and claim to be born again. Abortion, theistic evolution, homosexuality, no-fault divorce, feminism, and many other unbiblical concepts and attitudes have invaded the church at an alarming rate and to an alarming degree. One of the most popular and seductive false teachings is the promotion of high self-esteem as a Christian virtue, when, in reality, it is the very foundation of sin. Such destructive notions are inevitable when Christians listen to the world above the Word, and are more persuaded by men's wisdom than by God's. Far too few leaders in the church today can say honestly with Paul that their "exhortation does not come from error or impurity or by way of deceit" (1 Thess. 2:3).

As Christians become less and less familiar with Scripture and sound doctrine on a firsthand, regular basis, they become easy prey for jargon that sounds Christian but strongly mitigates against God's truth. Such unbiblical and arbitrary ideas as being "slain in the Spirit" and "binding Satan" frequently replace or are valued above the clear teaching of and submission to Scripture.

Whatever the specific doctrinal errors were that threatened the church at Ephesus, they obviously were serious. In his first letter to Timothy, Paul warned that "the Spirit explicitly says that in later times some will fall away from the faith, paying attention to deceitful spirits and doctrines of demons" (1 Tim. 4:1). Doubtless some of those demonic doctrines already were corrupting the church there.

In any case, Paul gives six specific reasons for avoiding and opposing *all* false teaching: it ruins the hearers (2:14b), it brings shame on the teacher (v. 15), it leads to ungodliness (v. 16), it spreads rapidly (v. 17a), it upsets the faith of some (vv. 17b–18), and it characterizes those who do not belong to the Lord (v. 19).

FALSE TEACHING RUINS THE HEARERS

and leads to the ruin of the hearers. (2:14b)

The first and most obvious harm of false teaching is the damage it does to those who hear it. It puts an obstacle in the way of unbelievers, who may be turned away from the true way of salvation. It also does harm to believers, by causing confusion, doubt, discouragement, and disobedience.

As one might guess, *katastrophē* (**ruin**) is the word from which we get *catastrophe*. False teaching has a catastrophic effect. The Greek word has the basic idea of being overturned or overthrown, and in this context it carries the more explicit connotation of being spiritually ruined. Paul is talking about teaching that intentionally subverts the truth by replacing it with falsehood. Consequently, instead of building up the hearers, it tears them down; instead of bringing enrichment, it brings disaster.

The only other use of that Greek word in the New Testament is found in Peter's second epistle, where its extreme seriousness is even clearer. "[God] condemned the cities of Sodom and Gomorrah to destruction [*katastrophē*] by reducing them to ashes, having made them an example to those who would live ungodly thereafter" (2 Peter 2:6). In that epistle Peter confronts false teaching which, by that time, was perverting God's truth and ruining its hearers throughout the world. Those "untaught and unstable" men distorted Paul's teaching, just as they did "the rest of the Scriptures, to their own destruction" (2 Peter 3:15–16). Even more dangerous, however, were the "false teachers among [them in the church], who [would] secretly introduce destructive heresies, even denying the Master who bought them" (2 Peter 2:1).

FALSE TEACHING BRINGS SHAME ON THE TEACHERS

Be diligent to present yourself approved to God as a workman who does not need to be ashamed, handling accurately the word of truth. (2:15)

Paul's second warning about false teaching is by means of contrast. Contrary to such perverters of God's truth as those mentioned by Peter, Timothy was to **be diligent to present [himself] approved to God**.

Spoudazō (to **be diligent**) carries the idea of having zealous persistence to accomplish a particular objective. The **diligent** believer

—in this context, the **diligent** teacher—gives maximum effort to impart God's truth as completely, as clearly, and as unambiguously as possible. He gives unreserved commitment to excellence in examining, interpreting, explaining, and applying God's Word. It is for that reason that "elders who rule well be considered worthy of double honor, especially those who work hard at preaching and teaching" (1 Tim. 5:17).

The purpose of that diligence is not to please others, and certainly not to please oneself, but to **present yourself approved to God.** *Paristēmi* (**to present yourself**) literally means to stand alongside of. The idea in this passage is that of standing alongside of or before God, of presenting oneself for inspection, as it were, in order to be approved by Him. *Dokimos* (**approved**) refers to favorably passing careful scrutiny and thereby being counted worthy.

The supreme purpose of the diligent and selfless teacher is to please God. "For am I now seeking the favor of men, or of God?" Paul asked Galatian believers. "Or am I striving to please men? If I were still trying to please men, I would not be a bond-servant of Christ" (Gal. 1:10). Every Christian teacher and preacher should be able to say, "Just as we have been approved by God to be entrusted with the gospel, so we speak, not as pleasing men but God, who examines our hearts" (1 Thess. 2:4). His greatest desire is to hear his Master say, "Well done, good and faithful servant" (Matt. 25:21). Such a teacher or preacher is **a workman who does not need to be ashamed.**

The clear implication, especially in light of the following three verses, is that false teachers, on the other hand, have great reason to **be ashamed.** One dictionary defines **shame** as "a painful emotion caused by consciousness of guilt, shortcoming, or impropriety." Another states that it is "the painful feeling arising from the consciousness of having done something dishonorable." Therefore, unlike a teacher who stands **as a workman who does not need to be ashamed,** a teacher who propagates falsehood, especially in the name of God and under the guise of Christianity, *ought* to be ashamed (cf. 1 John 2:28).

It is obvious, though, that those who have the most reason to be ashamed are the most shameless. They are among those Paul speaks of in his letter to the Philippian church: "For many walk, of whom I often told you, and now tell you even weeping, that they are enemies of the cross of Christ, whose end is destruction, whose god is their appetite, and *whose glory is in their shame,* who set their minds on earthly things" (Phil. 3:18–19, emphasis added). Those who persist in perverting the gospel are no less than "enemies of Christ." The most damning indictment of them is from the pen of Jude, who calls them "hidden reefs in your love feasts when they feast with you without fear, caring for themselves; clouds without water, carried along by winds; autumn trees without fruit, doubly dead, uprooted; wild waves of the sea, casting up their own shame like foam; wandering stars, for whom the black darkness has been reserved forever" (Jude 12–13).

It is clear from both the Old and New Testaments, as well as from church history and our own time, that many of the worst false teachers claim to be servants of God. The majority of scribes, Pharisees, and other Jewish leaders of Jesus' day considered themselves to be the godliest of the godly, as well as the only reliable interpreters of Scripture. Yet Jesus said of them, "You are of your father the devil, and you want to do the desires of your father. He was a murderer from the beginning, and does not stand in the truth, because there is no truth in him. Whenever he speaks a lie, he speaks from his own nature; for he is a liar, and the father of lies" (John 8:44).

Even apart from those extremes, *anyone* who ignores, misrepresents, misinterprets, or detracts from God's truth by adding to it or taking away from it (Rev. 22:18–19) has reason to be ashamed as well as fearful. Whether consciously or not, those who corrupt and denigrate God's truth are the spiritual children of Satan. They are purveyors of his abominable lies and are under God's sovereign and certain judgment.

The mark of a faithful teacher or preacher is his **handling accurately the word of truth. Handling accurately** translates a participle of *orthotomeō*, which means literally to cut straight. It was used of a craftsman cutting a straight line, of a farmer plowing a straight furrow, of a mason setting a straight line of bricks, or of workmen building a straight road. Metaphorically, it was used of carefully performing any task. Because Paul was a tentmaker by trade (Acts 18:3), he may have had in mind the careful, straight cutting and sewing of the many pieces of leather or cloth necessary to make a tent.

Sometimes in the New Testament, the phrase **word of truth,** or message of truth, refers specifically to the gospel. Paul reminded believers in Ephesus, "In Him, you also, after listening to the message of truth, the gospel of your salvation—having also believed, you were sealed in Him with the Holy Spirit of promise" (Eph. 1:13; Col. 1:5). James speaks of the Father's exercising His will in bringing "us forth by the word of truth, so that we might be, as it were, the first fruits among His creatures" (James 1:18). Many other references to God's **truth** refer to the full revelation of His Word in Scripture. Jesus doubtless had this broad meaning in mind when He prayed to His Father on our behalf, "Sanctify them in the truth; Thy word is truth" (John 17:17). In any case, Paul's point here is the same. Every aspect of God's **truth** is to be handled **accurately,** as a sacred trust by those who teach it and by those who hear it.

The careful exegete and expositor of God's word of truth must be meticulous in the way he interprets and pieces together the many individual truths found in Scripture. The first and most important principle is that of basing doctrine and standards of living on Scripture alone (*sola scriptura*), a key watchword of the Protestant Reformation.

Because the Bible is God's inerrant, authoritative, sufficient, and sole source of His divine **word of truth,** every other truth rests on that **truth.** It is not that the inerrancy of Scripture is a more important truth than, say, the deity of Christ or the Trinity. But it is only from the **truth** of Scripture that we can know all other truths. God's **word of truth** in Scripture is the source and measure not only of all spiritual and moral truth but of all truth of *any sort* on which it speaks.

In explaining, and evidently trying to justify, the conception of his first child out of wedlock, a prominent evangelical leader maintained that true marriage with his wife began at that time, rather than at the time of their wedding. That claim, of course, utterly contradicts what Scripture teaches about the unconditional sinfulness of fornication. When the man's wife was asked how she felt about that "indiscretion" being made public, she added to her husband's twisting of Scripture by responding, "Well, now I understand the meaning of John 8:23, 'the truth shall make you free.'" The most cursory look at that passage reveals that Jesus was not speaking about the feeling of relief that often comes with having a sin justified. He was speaking about the truth of His divinity and messiahship. He was speaking "to those Jews who had believed Him," explaining that their knowing and being made free by that truth was conditioned on their abiding in His Word, which would mark them as "truly [His] disciples" (v. 31).

Equally blasphemous was a young woman who posed nude for a pornographic magazine and said the experience had drawn her closer to God. She even claimed the scriptural promise "Draw near to God and He will draw near to you" (James 4:8). The arrogant folly of her statement is made clear in the next half of that verse, which commands: "Cleanse your hands, you sinners; and purify your hearts, you double-minded."

It is one thing to genuinely repent of a sin and to have the assurance of God's forgiveness. It is a different thing entirely to twist God's Word in an effort to justify the sin. It is one thing for an unbeliever, who makes no claim of godliness, to be unashamed of a sin. It is quite another thing, and immeasurably worse, for a person who claims salvation to be unashamed of a sin, especially when God's Word is used to defend it.

FALSE TEACHING LEADS TO UNGODLINESS

But avoid worldly and empty chatter, for it will lead to further ungodliness, (2:16)

A third danger of false teaching is its leading to ungodliness. **But** indicates the contrast of "handling accurately the word of truth" with the warning to **avoid worldly and empty chatter.** Such talk should not be "handled" at all.

Paul gave similar advice to Titus: "Shun foolish controversies and genealogies and strife and disputes about the Law; for they are unprofitable and worthless" (Titus 3:9). The apostle had given Timothy such advice earlier, adding the warning to also avoid "the opposing arguments of what is falsely called 'knowledge'" (1 Tim. 6:20). That sort of talk is time-wasting and confusing at best and spiritually harmful at worst, which obviously is what Paul has in mind here. Words of **worldly** human opinion are no more than evil **chatter.**

Paul is not talking of idle chitchat or gossip, which can do considerable damage in a church. He is speaking of destructive heresy that perverts divine truth and **will lead to further ungodliness.** The chatter itself is evil enough, but when it infects the hearers, the evil is compounded.

This danger is not restricted to unbelievers or even immature believers. Paul is speaking directly to Timothy, who, despite his timidity and temporary discouragement, was nevertheless a gifted spiritual leader in whom the apostle had much confidence. He had been appointed leader as the official representative of Paul in the church at Ephesus. No one is exempt from the corruptive influence of falsehood. Just as a doctor cannot help being exposed to a dangerous disease he is treating, a godly preacher or teacher cannot help being exposed to dangerous ideas. But just as a doctor keeps exposure to the minimum and concentrates on destroying the disease, so the godly preacher or teacher must keep exposure to falsehood at a minimum, while opposing and seeking to exterminate it with the truth.

When false teachers are unopposed or unexposed, "many will follow their sensuality, and because of them the way of the truth will be maligned" (2 Peter 2:2). The spiritual plight of many denominations and Christian institutions that once were solidly biblical is abundant proof of the pernicious and pervasive destructiveness of false doctrine. The legacy of false doctrine is the **further ungodliness** of false living. Error cannot restrain the flesh, cannot halt the devil, and cannot protect from the world. False teaching provides no defense against iniquity and no strength for doing what is right and God-honoring.

FALSE TEACHING SPREADS RAPIDLY

and their talk will spread like gangrene. (2:17a)

The Danger of False Teaching   2:17b–18

Not only that, but false doctrine propagated by the **talk** of false teachers **will spread** its infection **like gangrene. Gangrene** transliterates *gangraina,* the Greek word from which it is derived. In the ancient world, the term was used of cancer as well as gangrene, both of which diseases **spread** rapidly and are deadly. Even in modern warfare, **gangrene** is one of the worst dangers in battlefield injuries. If not treated promptly and carefully, it can quickly lead to amputation or death. False religion and satanic lies spread faster than the truth, because the sinful human heart is more receptive to them.

Religious deceptions are so infectious, malicious, and insidious that they are to be handled only with protective mask and gloves, as it were. Using another figure, Jude says that those who are in grave spiritual danger should be snatched "out of the fire" (Jude 23) like a hot ember. It was in a similar figurative way that the high priest Joshua, who had become corrupted like the rest of the priesthood, was divinely retrieved and spared, like "a brand plucked from the fire" (Zech. 3:2).

"The whole world lies in the power of the evil one," John says in his first letter (1 John 5:19). Earlier in that epistle he says we are not to "love the world, nor the things in the world," because "if anyone loves the world, the love of the Father is not in him. For all that is in the world, the lust of the flesh and the lust of the eyes and the boastful pride of life, is not from the Father, but is from the world" (2:15–16). James likewise warns, "Do you not know that friendship with the world is hostility toward God? Therefore whoever wishes to be a friend of the world makes himself an enemy of God" (James 4:4). The world is the partner with demons in developing and spreading the epidemic of deadly spiritual gangrene.

It is because false teachers are of the world and serve the prince of this world that they are so dangerous. And rapidly growing technology has helped worldliness and every other form of ungodliness to also grow more rapidly, exposing more people to more evil teaching than those who lived even a few generations ago could have imagined. Consequently, Christians today have more reason than ever to "test the spirits to see whether they are from God; because many false prophets have gone out into the world" (1 John 4:1). "They are from the world; therefore they speak as from the world, and the world listens to them" (v. 5). Christians therefore have no excuse even for listening to them, much less buying into their ungodly beliefs and ways.

FALSE TEACHING UPSETS THE FAITH OF SOME

Among them are Hymenaeus and Philetus, men who have gone astray from the truth saying that the resurrection has already taken place, and thus they upset the faith of some. (2:17b–18)

Paul identifies one of the false teachers as **Hymenaeus,** who, because he was denounced in the previous letter, obviously had been a threat to the Ephesian church for some time. Although Paul had put him out of the church when he himself was still in Ephesus, having "delivered [him] over to Satan," **Hymenaeus** obviously persisted in his efforts to mislead believers there, **and Philetus** had replaced Alexander as his co-conspirator (see 1 Tim. 1:20).

Those men were apostates, like those of whom the writer of Hebrews wrote: "In the case of those who have once been enlightened and have tasted of the heavenly gift and have been made partakers of the Holy Spirit, and have tasted the good word of God and the powers of the age to come, and then have fallen away, it is impossible to renew them again to repentance, since they again crucify to themselves the Son of God, and put Him to open shame" (Heb. 6:4–6). They have "trampled under foot the Son of God, and [have] regarded as unclean the blood of the covenant by which [they were] sanctified, and [have] insulted the Spirit of grace" (Heb. 10:29). As Jesus said of Judas (Matt. 26:24), it would have been better if those men had not been born.

The particular heresy of **Hymenaeus and Philetus** was their claiming **that the resurrection [had] already taken place** (cf. 1 Cor. 15:12). Paul does not explain what resurrection they had in mind. Neither Jesus' resurrection (which had occurred) nor the physical resurrection of believers (which had not yet occurred) makes sense in this context. It seems probable, therefore, that these men propounded some form of spiritual resurrection as the only resurrection. Perhaps they taught that the only resurrection was the spiritual union with Christ in His death and resurrection (cf. Rom. 6:1–11). Such a view would have been based on pagan Greek philosophy, perhaps incipient gnosticism, whose adherents believed that the body and all other material things are intrinsically evil. Some of the Greeks of Athens who sneered "when they heard [Paul speak] of the resurrection of the dead" (Acts 17:32) were doubtless into such philosophical dualism and were horrified at the idea of the body's being restored in the afterlife. **Hymenaeus and Philetus** possibly held the belief of many pagans that the only immortality is in life carried on through one's progeny. By denying bodily resurrection, they were destroying the very foundation of the Christian faith—denying both the reality and the implications of Christ's resurrection.

In his first letter to the church at Corinth, Paul makes clear the monumental importance of both Christ's and the believer's resurrection and of a right understanding of those truths. "If there is no resurrection of the dead," Paul says, "not even Christ has been raised; and if Christ has not been raised, then our preaching is vain, your faith also is vain. Moreover we are even found to be false witnesses of God, because we witnessed against God that He raised Christ, whom He did not raise, if in fact the dead are not raised, . . . and if Christ has not been raised, your faith is worthless; you are still in your sins" (1 Cor. 15:13–15, 17).

To deny or distort the truth about the **resurrection** is to deny and distort the heart of the gospel. It is therefore a tragic and damnable thing to teach falsehood about that doctrine. Not only does it blaspheme God and denigrate His Word but inevitably it will **upset the faith of some.**

Anatrepō (to **upset**) carries the idea of overturning or overthrowing, indicating that the **faith** held by **some** of those who listened to false teachers was not saving faith, which cannot be overthrown or destroyed. Those hearers apparently had heard the gospel and been attracted to Christianity as a possible answer to their religious quest. But because they had not placed their **faith** in Christ as Savior and Lord and were exposed to deception, they fell prey to corrupt teaching and remained lost.

Again, that sad truth reveals one of the greatest perils of a false gospel: It keeps **some** souls—over the centuries, countless millions of them—out of the kingdom.

FALSE TEACHING CHARACTERIZES
THOSE WHO DO NOT BELONG TO THE LORD

Nevertheless, the firm foundation of God stands, having this seal, "The Lord knows those who are His," and, "Let everyone who names the name of the Lord abstain from wickedness." (2:19)

The last danger of false teaching mentioned here is that it fits those who are unsaved and ungodly.

Paul again makes his point by contrast. **Nevertheless,** he continues, **the firm foundation of God stands.** Unlike those who trust in a satanic scheme of religion, those who are truly saved, who are God's spiritual children and genuine disciples of Jesus Christ, are part of **the firm foundation of God.**

In this context, **the firm foundation of God** seems most likely to refer to the church. In the previous letter to Timothy, Paul speaks of "the household of God, which is the church of the living God, the *pillar and support* of the truth" (1 Tim. 3:15, emphasis added). The **foundation** of Christ's church **stands** on the truth, "and the gates of Hades shall not overpower it" (Matt. 16:18).

On that promise, we have God's seal. A *sphragis* (**seal**) was a sign of ownership, and **God** has placed His divine **seal** of ownership on the church. In the end times, those "who do not have the seal of God on their foreheads" will be tormented by the locusts (Rev. 9:4). It is also doubtless that God's seal on their foreheads will protect believers from taking the mark of the beast (see Rev. 13:16).

God's **seal** of ownership is on the church in two ways. First, every member of the body of Christ, the church, has God's divine assurance of election, in that **"the Lord knows those who are His."** The source of this quotation is not certain, but is possibly from the book of Numbers. When some Israelites were about to rebel against the Lord and His appointed leaders Moses and Aaron, Moses declared to Korah and the other rebels, "The Lord will show who is His, and who is holy, and will bring him near to Himself; even the one whom He will choose, He will bring near to Himself" (Num. 16:5).

"My sheep hear My voice, and I know them, and they follow Me," Jesus assures us; "and I give eternal life to them, and they shall never perish; and no one shall snatch them out of My hand" (John 10:27–28). Like Satan, false teachers can cause great confusion and apprehension among God's people, but they cannot corrupt or destroy His people, because "God has chosen [us] from the beginning for salvation" (2 Thess. 2:13a).

The New Testament is replete with such guarantees. "All that the Father gives Me shall come to Me," Jesus promises, "and the one who comes to Me I will certainly not cast out. For I have come down from heaven, not to do My own will, but the will of Him who sent Me. And this is the will of Him who sent Me, that of all that He has given Me I lose nothing, but raise it up on the last day. For this is the will of My Father, that everyone who beholds the Son and believes in Him, may have eternal life; and I Myself will raise him up on the last day" (John 6:37–40). God chose us for salvation in Christ "before the foundation of the world" (Eph. 1:4), and those "whom He [God] foreknew, He also predestined to become conformed to the image of His Son, that He might be the first-born among many brethren; and whom He predestined, these He also called; and whom He called, these He also justified; and whom He justified, these He also glorified" (Rom. 8:29–30).

The second way in which God has placed His **seal** on the church is through personal sanctification, personal holiness. Paul therefore says, **"Let everyone who names the name of the Lord abstain from wickedness."** This quotation may be adapted from the same passage in the book of Numbers, in which Moses later warned the godly: "Depart now from the tents of these wicked men, and touch nothing that belongs to them, lest you be swept away in all their sin" (Num. 16:26). Those who did not separate themselves from the wicked rebels were destroyed with them when "the earth opened its mouth and swallowed them up" (v. 32).

This second aspect of sanctification is both an exhortation and an affirmation. The exhortation is: "Do you not know that your body is a temple of the Holy Spirit who is in you, whom you have from God, and that you are not your own? For you have been bought with a price: therefore glorify God in your body" (1 Cor. 6:19–20). Peter likewise admonishes, "Like the Holy One who called you, be holy yourselves also in all your behavior" (1 Peter 1:15).

But our sanctification is also divinely affirmed. In the verse in 2 Thessalonians cited above, in which Paul assures believers that God has chosen them for salvation, he adds, "through sanctification by the Spirit and faith in the truth" (2:13b). Despite our many failures and our frequent unfaithfulness, God will graciously complete our sanctification. "For I am confident of this very thing," Paul testified, "that He who began a good work in you will perfect it until the day of Christ Jesus" (Phil. 1:6).

An Honorable Vessel

6

Now in a large house there are not only gold and silver vessels, but also vessels of wood and of earthenware, and some to honor and some to dishonor. Therefore, if a man cleanses himself from these things, he will be a vessel for honor, sanctified, useful to the Master, prepared for every good work. Now flee from youthful lusts, and pursue righteousness, faith, love and peace, with those who call on the Lord from a pure heart. But refuse foolish and ignorant speculations, knowing that they produce quarrels. And the Lord's bond-servant must not be quarrelsome, but be kind to all, able to teach, patient when wronged, with gentleness correcting those who are in opposition, if perhaps God may grant them repentance leading to the knowledge of the truth, and they may come to their senses and escape from the snare of the devil, having been held captive by him to do his will. (2:20–26)

A chorus by Audrey Mieir beautifully expresses the spirit of dedication of which Paul speaks in this passage.

> To be used of God
> To sing, to speak, to pray.

To be used of God
To show someone the way.
I long so much to feel
The touch of His consuming fire,
To be used of God is my desire.

Every believer should have that compelling desire to be used of God in whatever way He chooses. The flow of 2 Timothy 2 moves from the call to "be strong in the grace that is in Christ Jesus" (2:1) to being "a workman who does not need to be ashamed" (v. 15) in order to be "useful to the Master, prepared for every good work" (v. 21).

THE ILLUSTRATION

Now in a large house there are not only gold and silver vessels, but also vessels of wood and of earthenware, and some to honor and some to dishonor. (2:20)

As in several other letters, Paul uses the figure of a vessel to describe Christians. For example, in defending God's sovereign right to save and to condemn according to His own divine and perfect will, the apostle asks rhetorically, "Does not the potter have a right over the clay, to make from the same lump one vessel for honorable use, and another for common use?" (Rom. 9:21). Pointing up our utter dependence on God's enabling grace and power in order to minister, he reminded Corinthian believers that "we have this treasure in earthen vessels, that the surpassing greatness of the power may be of God and not from ourselves" (2 Cor. 4:7).

Using the illustration of **a large house** whose owners were affluent and which would have many occupants, many rooms, and many furnishings, he says **there are not only gold and silver vessels, but also vessels of wood and of earthenware, and some to honor and some to dishonor.**

As mentioned in the previous commentary chapter, the context strongly suggests that "the firm foundation of God" (v. 19) refers to the church, the earthly custodian of God's truth (v. 18). God's ownership of, or "seal" on, the church is in two parts. From the divine perspective, it is His sovereign election of "those who are His," and from the human perspective it is the righteousness of the faithful believer, the one "who names the name of the Lord" and abstains "from wickedness."

The **large house** would therefore represent the entire church of God, the body of Christ, composed of all true believers, the **vessels** in which represent individual believers—the honorable **gold and silver vessels** and the dishonorable **vessels of wood and of earthenware.**

Skeuos (**vessel**) was used of a wide variety of domestic implements, utensils, and furnishings, including furniture and tools. Because of the materials mentioned here of which these items were made, it seems likely that Paul had in mind serving **vessels** and perhaps utensils. But whatever the articles might be, his point is the same. Articles made of **gold** or **silver** are more valuable and presentable than those of **wood** or **earthenware.** The former would be prominently displayed as decorations or used for serving important guests as a gesture of **honor.** The inferior articles, on the other hand, were strictly utilitarian. They were common, plain, replaceable, unattractive, and often dirty and vile, because some were used for the garbage and human waste of the house. They were used for those duties that were never seen and were kept out of sight as much as possible. To display them before guests would be an act of unspeakable **dishonor.**

(It should be noted that in this context the wood and clay vessels are despised from the Lord's perspective, whereas in 2 Corinthians 4:7 Paul is glad to be an "earthen vessel," because he is there using the analogy to express his personal self-evaluation and humility.)

Honor and **dishonor** do not refer to true and false Christians, respectively. Jesus makes clear in the parable of the wheat and tares (Matt. 13:24–30) and in His teaching about the sheep and goats judgment of the nations (Matt. 25:31–46) that the visible church on earth will contain both unbelievers and believers until He returns and orders the final separation. But Paul is not speaking about that distinction.

Nor is he speaking here of the God-given differences among believers. In his letter to Rome, he says that "God has allotted to each a measure of faith. For just as we have many members in one body and all the members do not have the same function, so we, who are many, are one body in Christ, and individually members one of another. And since we have gifts that differ according to the grace given to us, let each exercise them accordingly" (Rom. 12:3–6). He emphasizes the same truth in his first letter to the Corinthians, saying, "If the whole body were an eye, where would the hearing be? If the whole were hearing, where would the sense of smell be? But now God has placed the members, each one of them, in the body, just as He desired" (1 Cor. 12:17–18).

The honorable **vessels** represent believers who are faithful and useful to the Lord. They are the good soldiers, the competitive athletes, the hard-working farmers mentioned in verses 3–6. By contrast, the dishonorable **vessels** are the cowardly soldiers, the lazy athletes, and the slothful farmers, defiled people fit only for the most menial, undistinguished purposes. **Honor** and **dishonor** therefore refer to the ways in which genuine believers are found useful to the Lord in fulfilling the work to which He has called them. In this sense, all believers *should be*, but are not always, **vessels** of **honor.**

Some Ephesian leaders, including Timothy, were becoming discouraged and apathetic. Part of the problem was their apparent intimidation by false teachers such as Hymenaeus, Alexander, and Philetus, whom Paul specifically denounces (1 Tim. 1:20; 2 Tim. 2:17). Because Paul repeats many of his strong admonitions to Timothy and the other leaders in Ephesus, the serious problems he sought to correct must have been ongoing or recurring.

And because this letter is addressed to Timothy, the foremost overseer, or elder, and apostolic legate in the church at Ephesus, Paul's admonitions in 2:20–26 seem directed first of all to leaders in that church. That interpretation is supported by the reference to "the Lord's bond-servant" (v. 24), which, in this context, probably is used as an official term referring to overseers. In addition, the characteristics mentioned in verses 24–25 correspond to several qualifications for that office listed in 1 Timothy 3:2–3 and Titus 1:5–9.

In verses 21–26, Paul sets forth nine characteristics that mark the faithful, godly believer who is the vessel of honor. He will have a cleansed life (v. 21a), a sanctified soul (v. 21b), be useful to God (v. 21c), be prepared for service (v. 21d), have a pure heart (v. 22), and have a discerning mind (v. 23), a gentle manner (v. 24), a humble spirit (v. 25a), and a compassionate attitude (vv. 25b–26).

A CLEANSED LIFE

Therefore, if a man cleanses himself from these things, he will be a vessel for honor, (2:21a)

Cleanses is from *ekkathairō,* an intensified form of *kathairō* (from which we get "catharsis"), which means to clean out thoroughly, to completely purge. **These things** refer to the vessels of dishonor mentioned in the previous verse, **from** which **a man** who is faithful **cleanses himself.** As noted, vessels of dishonor are defiled people in the church, and Paul's exhortation is therefore for godly believers to separate themselves from the fellowship of impure believers, who are not clean, not obedient, not submissive to the Lord, and not eager to serve.

Sin is contagious, and association with openly sinful and shameless people is morally and spiritually dangerous. "He who walks with wise men will be wise, but the companion of fools will suffer harm" (Prov. 13:20). The Lord's exhortation to Jewish exiles in pagan Babylon applies to every believer who seeks to faithfully serve Him. "Depart, depart, go out from there," Isaiah proclaimed. "Touch nothing unclean; go out of the midst of her [Babylon], purify yourselves" (Isa. 52:11).

An immoral and/or doctrinally corrupt believer, especially a leader who is influential, is more dangerous than a pagan or atheist, because weak or careless brothers and sisters may assume—or rationalize—that certain practices and ideas are permissible simply because they are practiced and taught by some church leaders.

Paul explained to believers in Corinth,

I wrote you in my [previous] letter not to associate with immoral people; I did not at all mean with the immoral people of this world, or with the covetous and swindlers, or with idolaters; for then you would have to go out of the world. But actually, I wrote to you not to associate with any so-called brother if he should be an immoral person, or covetous, or an idolater, or a reviler, or a drunkard, or a swindler—not even to eat with such a one. For what have I to do with judging outsiders? Do you not judge those who are within the church? But those who are outside, God judges. Remove the wicked man from among yourselves. (1 Cor. 5:9–13)

You do not expect unbelievers to think, talk, and behave like Christians, and your guard tends to be up against their influence. But, like "worldly and empty chatter" that leads "to further ungodliness" and spreads "like gangrene" (2 Tim. 2:16–17), willing association with ungodly believers, vessels of dishonor, inevitably will cause some of their sin to infect you, whether you realize it or not. "Do not be deceived," Paul therefore warns; "Bad company corrupts good morals" (1 Cor. 15:33). Fellowship with defiled church members develops tolerance for their defilement.

Faithful service of the Lord requires separation from those who can contaminate you. Warning Jeremiah about associating with ungodly Israelites, God said, "If you extract the precious from the worthless, you will become My spokesman. They for their part may turn to you, but as for you, you must not turn to them" (Jer. 15:19). In other words, the influence should be but one way. If those unfaithful Israelites were led to repentance by Jeremiah's preaching and example, the Lord would be pleased. But the prophet was never to allow their corruption to infect him.

The writer of Hebrews gives this sobering warning: "See to it that no one comes short of the grace of God; that no root of bitterness springing up causes trouble, and by it many be defiled" (Heb. 12:15). Unchecked bitterness, even in a believer who otherwise is upright, is not a trivial and purely personal sin. It is highly destructive and can seriously demoralize and weaken an entire congregation.

Refusing to associate with sinning believers is also for their own benefit. If they are not disciplined and are readily accepted into church fellowship, they will become more comfortable in their sin. Being ostracized from the church, on the other hand, may help them become ashamed and repentant. "If anyone does not obey our instruction in this letter," Paul instructed the Thessalonian church, "take special note of that man and do not associate with him, so that he may be put to shame" (2 Thess. 3:14).

No Christian should associate with professing Christians who are morally and spiritually defiled. We should not want to be around those whose language and lifestyle do not honor Christ. We should not want to associate with those who have a critical tongue, who tolerate evil in their lives and in the lives of other believers, or whose commitment to the Lord is shallow and artificial. **A vessel for honor** cannot remain honorable and usable if it is continually contaminated by vessels of dishonor. It cannot remain pure apart from pure fellowship.

A Sanctified Soul

sanctified, (2:21b)

A second characteristic of a vessel for honor is a **sanctified** soul. **Sanctified** is from *hagiazō,* which has the basic meaning of being set apart. A Christian is **sanctified,** set apart, in two ways. Negatively, he is set apart *from* sin. Positively, he is set apart *for* God and for His righteousness. Just as the vessels in the tabernacle and temple were set apart from all mundane uses and dedicated solely to God and His service, so are those believers who are vessels of honor in the church. Their supreme purpose as Christians, the purpose from which all duties derive, is to serve God. For that they keep themselves pure. It would be inconceivable that a vessel could alternate between being used for vile waste and for food for guests. An honorable vessel is kept pure.

Sanctified translates a perfect passive participle, indicating a condition that already exists. When we trusted in Jesus Christ as Lord and Savior, He immediately "became to us wisdom from God, and righteousness and sanctification, and redemption" (1 Cor. 1:30). Every believer has been chosen by God "from the beginning for salvation through sanctification by the Spirit and faith in the truth" (2 Thess. 2:13; cf. 1 Peter 1:2). Salvation itself is a sanctification, setting us apart to God. But it also is the beginning of a lifelong process. It is both a reality and a progressive experience.

Christians not only are **sanctified** by having a right relationship to God but also are being **sanctified** as they grow in fulfilling God's purpose of righteous living. That is the meaning of the term used here. "For this is the will of God, your sanctification," Paul declares; "that is, that you abstain from sexual immorality. . . . For God has not called us for the purpose of impurity, but in sanctification" (1 Thess. 4:3, 7). The **sanctified** life is a life of purity, holiness, and godliness. It is **a vessel for honor,** worthy for the Lord to use.

On the negative side, the believer is being **sanctified,** or set apart, *from* unrighteousness. Our new, redeemed life in Christ is to be in stark contrast to our former, unsaved life. "For just as you presented your members as slaves to impurity and to lawlessness, resulting in further lawlessness, so now present your members as slaves to righteousness, resulting in sanctification" (Rom. 6:19; cf. v. 22). Honorable vessels are separated from sin, from the world, from the flesh, from Satan, and from the self-will of the old self.

USEFUL TO GOD

useful to the Master, (2:21c)

A vessel for honor is **useful to the Master.** Using the same Greek word (*euchrēstos*), Paul later in this letter speaks of Mark as "useful to me for service" (4:11). The apostle wanted Timothy to be **useful to** Jesus Christ, **the Master,** just as Mark was useful to him in his apostolic work.

The deepest desire of Paul's own heart was to be **useful to the Master.** He testified, "Do you not know that those who run in a race all run, but only one receives the prize? Run in such a way that you may win. And everyone who competes in the games exercises self-control in all things. They then do it to receive a perishable wreath, but we an imperishable" (1 Cor. 9:24–25). On the other hand, it was the apostle's greatest fear that he would lose his usefulness to **the Master** because of sin. "Therefore I run in such a way, as not without aim," he continued; "I box in such a way, as not beating the air; but I buffet my body and make it my slave, lest possibly, after I have preached to others, I myself should be disqualified" (vv. 26–27).

Master translates *despotēs,* from which we get "despot." Christians are not simply rightly related to God; they wholly *belong* to God. He is our sovereign Master, our loving and benevolent Lord, who actually owns us. "Do you not know that your body is a temple of the Holy Spirit who is in you, whom you have from God, and that you are not your own?" Paul asks rhetorically. "You have been bought with a price" (1 Cor. 6:19–20).

PREPARED FOR GOOD WORK

prepared for every good work. (2:21d)

A vessel of honor to the Lord is **prepared for every good work.** *Hetoimazō* (**prepared**) carries the idea of willingness and eagerness as well as of readiness. Like "sanctified," **prepared** translates from a perfect passive, indicating a condition that already exists. When we were saved, the Lord placed us in a state of divine preparedness, in which we received His own Holy Spirit to indwell us and empower us. We also have His divine Word in Scripture to teach us His truth and His will. But unlike a metal, earthenware, or wooden vessel, a human vessel has a will. Our full preparedness for the Lord's service therefore demands more than simply *having* His Spirit within us and *possessing* the particular talents and gifts He has provided and *knowing* the truth He has revealed. It also demands our genuine and unreserved willingness to *submit* to His Spirit, to *use* those talents and gifts, and to *obey* His revealed truth in His service and in His power. In the words of the hymn quoted on pages 85–86, the truly **prepared** Christian can honestly say, "To be used of God is my desire."

A PURE HEART

Now flee from youthful lusts, and pursue righteousness, faith, love and peace, with those who call on the Lord from a pure heart. (2:22)

This verse presents five characteristics of **a pure heart,** which itself is a fifth characteristic of an honorable vessel for the Lord. This verse is almost identical to the apostle's admonition in his previous letter to Timothy: "Flee from these things, you man of God; and pursue righteousness, godliness, faith, love, perseverance and gentleness" (1 Tim. 6:11).

The first attribute of **a pure heart** is negative, expressed here in the command to **flee youthful lusts. Flee** is from *phuegō,* from which "fugitive" is derived. The Greek verb is here a present imperative of command, indicating that fleeing is not optional but is to be persistent. That meaning is reflected in the term "fugitive," which refers to a person who is continually on the run in order to escape capture. The faithful Christian is continually on the run, as it were, from the sinful passions that started when we were young.

Timothy was some thirty years younger than Paul when this letter was written. He therefore was relatively **youthful** and was still tempted by many sinful **lusts** that are characteristic of young people. These lusts involve much more than sinful sexual desire. They also include pride, craving for wealth and power, inordinate ambition, jealousy, envy, an argumentative and self-assertive spirit, and many other sinful **lusts.**

Timothy was timid and apparently sometimes embarrassed by his close association with the apostle Paul and the uncompromising gospel he proclaimed. He probably was fearful of persecution and may not have boldly confronted all those who compromised and misinterpreted God's revealed truth. He seems to have been especially intimidated by older men in the church who resented his leadership (1 Tim. 4:12). Losing the battle to **youthful lusts** would not help him resolve the problem of leadership or effectively correct wrong doctrine and immoral practices but would aggravate the conflict. For his own sake and the sake of the church, he was to **flee** such temptations and inclinations.

The next four attributes of **a pure heart** are positive and comprehensive: **righteousness, faith, love and peace.** To **pursue** those virtues is the other side of fleeing **youthful lusts.** As with **flee,** the Greek verb translated **pursue** is an imperative. Paul is not making a suggestion.

A believer who does not run *from* sin and *toward* **righteousness** will be overtaken by sin. "When [an] unclean spirit goes out of a man," Jesus said, "it passes through waterless places seeking rest, and not finding any, it says, 'I will return to my house from which I came.' And when it comes, it finds it swept and put in order. Then it goes and takes along seven other spirits more evil than itself, and they go in and live there; and the last state of that man becomes worse than the first" (Luke 11:24–26). The only way not to "be overcome by evil" is to "overcome evil with good" (Rom. 12:21). Understanding that truth, the psalmist wrote, "How can a young man keep his way pure? By keeping it according to Thy word" (Ps. 119:9). In whatever age the faithful live, the only infallible and effective guide to **righteousness** is God's divine Word. Living a pure life does not involve following an esoteric system of ritual, having a mystical experience, achieving a special level of human wisdom, or making a decision to do so. But by faithfully pursuing and obeying the truth of Scripture, even the most unsophisticated child of God is able to successfully **pursue** the Lord's **righteousness.**

The godly believer also will **pursue . . . faith.** In this context, *pistis* (faith) is better rendered "faithfulness," as it is of God in Romans 3:3 and of the fruit of the Spirit in Galatians 5:22. The supreme purpose of a believer with **a pure heart** is to please and glorify God by pursuing integrity, loyalty, and trustworthiness. It was for lack of such "weightier provisions of the law—"justice and mercy and faithfulness"—that Jesus excoriated the hypocritical scribes and Pharisees (Matt. 23:23). The truly faithful Christian will be loyal to God, to God's Word, to God's work, and to God's people.

He also will **pursue . . . love,** the first and foremost fruit of the Spirit (Gal. 5:22). Of the several words in Greek that are translated **love,** *agapē* is the noblest, because it is the word of choice, not of feelings or sentiment, as fine as those sometimes may be. It is the love of the mind and the will, not of emotion or affection even of the highest sort. It is the love of conscious determination, not impulse. It is the love that focuses on the welfare of the one loved, not on self-gratification or self-fulfillment. *Agapē* **love** is not based on the attractiveness or worthiness of those who are loved, but on their needs, even when they are most unattractive and unworthy. It is selfless and self-giving.

Agapē **love** is used countless times of God Himself. It is that **love** which God the Father has for His own Son, Jesus Christ (John 17:26) and for those who belong to the Son by faith (John 14:21). It is the love which our gracious Lord has for even fallen, sinful mankind (John 3:16; Rom. 5:8). *Agapē* **love** is so characteristic of God that John twice tells us that He *is* love (1 John 4:8, 16).

The godly believer also will **pursue . . . peace.** *Eirēnē* (**peace**) is the word from which we get "serene" and "serenity." In this context it does not refer to absence of warfare but to harmonious relationships, between men and God and between men and other men, especially between Christians. "If possible, so far as it depends on you," Paul commands, "be at peace with all men" (Rom. 12:18).

Although the church at Ephesus was one of the most mature and faithful congregations mentioned in the New Testament, at the time Paul wrote his letters to Timothy it was experiencing serious internal conflict. Paul's prediction to the elders of the church as they met on the beach near Miletus was already being fulfilled. "I know that after my departure savage wolves will come in among you," he warned, "not sparing the flock; and from among your own selves men will arise, speaking perverse things, to draw away the disciples after them" (Acts 20:29–30). Confronting all of that and maintaining peace requires a delicate balance.

Those who call on the Lord is a description of genuine Christians, referring specifically to their calling **on the Lord** for salvation— for His grace, His mercy, His forgiveness. To **call on the Lord** is the equivalent of placing saving faith in Him. "For there is no distinction between Jew and Greek; for the same Lord is Lord of all, abounding in riches for all who call upon Him," Paul assures believers in Rome. Quoting Joel 2:32, he then adds, "For 'Whoever will call upon the name of the Lord will be saved'" (Rom. 10:12–13). The apostle opens his first letter to the church at Corinth with these words: "Paul, called as an apostle of Jesus Christ by the will of God, and Sosthenes our brother, to the church of God which is at Corinth, to those who have been sanctified in Christ Jesus, saints by calling, with *all who in every place call upon the name of our Lord Jesus Christ*, their Lord and ours" (1 Cor. 1:1–2, emphasis added).

But not everyone who calls on the Lord for salvation continues to faithfully serve and obey Him. From **a pure heart** therefore further identifies the godly believers who qualify as honorable vessels. The term **pure** comes from the same root word as "cleanses" in verse 21 and takes us back to where Paul's thought began—to the truth that a clean vessel is a useful one. They continue to **call on the Lord** for guidance, strength, and wisdom in living for Him. The Christian with **a pure heart** diligently pursues the righteousness, faith, love, and peace mentioned in the first half of this verse. He is the "vessel for honor, sanctified, useful to the Master, prepared for every good work" mentioned in the previous verse.

A Discerning Mind

But refuse foolish and ignorant speculations, knowing that they produce quarrels. (2:23)

A vessel of honor to God must develop a discerning mind. An unguarded mind, even of a believer, is subject to deceit, misunderstanding, and confusion, which inevitably produce false doctrine and sinful living. The undiscerning mind is "tossed here and there by waves, and carried about by every wind of doctrine, by the trickery of men, by craftiness in deceitful scheming" (Eph. 4:14).

That danger is what prompted Paul to establish the basic safeguard of discernment with the command to "examine everything carefully; hold fast to that which is good; abstain from every form of evil" (1 Thess. 5:21–22).

Paul also emphasized the importance of discernment in his first letter to Timothy:

> As I urged you upon my departure for Macedonia, remain on at Ephesus, in order that you may instruct certain men not to teach strange doctrines, nor to pay attention to myths and endless genealogies, which give rise to mere speculation rather than furthering the administration of God which is by faith. But the goal of our instruction is love from a pure heart and a good conscience and a sincere faith. For some men, straying from these things, have turned aside to fruitless discussion. (1 Tim. 1:3–6; cf. 4:7)

Later in that epistle he gravely warns, "If anyone advocates a different doctrine, and does not agree with sound words, those of our Lord Jesus Christ, and with the doctrine conforming to godliness, he is conceited and understands nothing; but he has a morbid interest in controversial questions and disputes about words, out of which arise envy, strife, abusive language, evil suspicions, and constant friction between men of depraved mind and deprived of the truth, who suppose that godliness is a means of gain" (1 Tim. 6:3–5). As he ends the letter, he implores, "O Timothy, guard what has been entrusted to you, avoiding worldly and empty chatter and the opposing arguments of what is falsely called 'knowledge'—which some have professed and thus gone astray from the faith" (6:20–21).

As we saw in the second chapter of the second letter, Paul admonishes the younger pastor to warn those under his care "not to wrangle about words, which is useless, and leads to the ruin of the hearers" and to "avoid worldly and empty chatter, for it will lead to further ungodliness, and their talk will spread like gangrene" (2 Tim. 2:14–17).

The truth and purity of ideas that go into the mind are of the utmost importance. An automobile needs filters to trap harmful objects in the gasoline, oil, and air. If not filtered out, even small particles of dust or grime can cause an engine to lose power, stop running, and suffer permanent damage. In the same way, an accumulation of even seemingly insignificant moral and spiritual pollution can corrupt a Christian's mind and heart, making him less and less effective and usable in the Lord's work. The things we allow to enter our minds affect our thinking, our beliefs, our values, our motives, and our priorities. And the more willingly we allow them to enter, the more powerfully they affect us. The writer of Proverbs wisely observed that "a fool does not delight in understanding, but only in revealing his own mind," and that "a fool's lips bring strife, and his mouth calls for blows" (Prov. 18:2, 6).

Of the ten billion or so cells in the human brain, by far the majority are used for memory. And although the ease of forgetting makes it hard to believe, scientists have determined that everything the brain registers it retains. The passing of time and lack of use make information harder and often impossible to retrieve, but all the information received is still there, no matter how far it recedes from consciousness. The memory cells are interconnected by equally microscopic fibers, which enable stored facts, ideas, visual images, feelings, and experiences to be associated with each other to produce thought patterns, which store still more permanent information in the brain.

Paul may not have been aware of those facts of physiology, but he well understood the power of ideas on a Christian's mind and knew that the only protection against false and evil notions is God's truth and righteousness. He therefore advised, "Finally, brethren, whatever is true, whatever is honorable, whatever is right, whatever is pure, whatever is lovely, whatever is of good repute, if there is any excellence and if anything worthy of praise, let your mind dwell on these things" (Phil. 4:8). Our mind is to be a treasure house, not a garbage dump.

From the early days of the church and continuing almost unabated to our own day, many believers have carelessly forsaken personal study of Scripture and have fallen prey to every sort of false idea and practice. Not bothering to check what they read and hear against God's own Word—as did the God-fearing, noble-minded Jews in Berea (Acts 17:11)— they are corrupted by **foolish and ignorant speculations,** which make them stumble and fall, often without knowing it.

Mōros (**foolish**) has the root meaning of being mentally dull, silly, or stupid, and is the word from which we get "moron." *Apaideutos* (**ignorant**) means unlearned and untrained and often carried the additional idea of undisciplined. *Zētēsis* (**speculations**) refers to that which is controversial and seriously disputed, having no certain basis in truth.

Paul is not, of course, advising believers to avoid all controversy and discussion of the faith. We are to "sanctify Christ as Lord in [our] hearts, always being ready to make a defense to everyone who asks [us] to give an account for the hope that is in [us]," and we are to do so "with gentleness and reverence" (1 Peter 3:15). Paul spent much time presenting and defending the gospel as he went from city to city. "According to Paul's custom," Luke reports, "he went to them [Jews in the synagogue at Thessalonica], and for three Sabbaths reasoned with them from the Scriptures" (Acts 17:2). "He was reasoning in the synagogue [at Corinth] every Sabbath and trying to persuade Jews and Greeks" (Acts 18:4). He began his ministry at Ephesus in the same way (18:19). In defending the gospel and himself as he stood before the Roman governor Felix in Caesarea, "he was discussing righteousness, self-control and the judgment to come" (Acts 24:25). In the above passages, "reasoned," "reasoning," and "discussing" all translate *dialegomai,* from which we get the English "dialogue."

In this Timothy passage, Paul makes clear that he is not speaking about responsible discussion of Scripture and theology, either with the unsaved or among believers. He rather forbids **speculations,** fruitless and unproductive debates **that . . . produce quarrels.** Such **speculations** not only are worthless but are ungodly. They question Scripture, distort the truth, create doubt, weaken faith, undermine confidence in the Lord, often lead to compromise of convictions, and produce quarrels. Earlier in this chapter, the apostle commanded Timothy to "solemnly charge [believers] in the presence of God not to wrangle about words, which is useless, and leads to the ruin of the hearers" (v. 14).

Paul gives almost identical counsel to Titus, warning him to "shun foolish controversies and genealogies and strife and disputes about the Law; for they are unprofitable and worthless" (Titus 3:9). Any church member who persists in such "unprofitable and worthless" behavior is to be severely disciplined. "Reject a factious man after a first and second warning," the apostle continues, "knowing that such a man is perverted and is sinning, being self-condemned" (vv. 10–11).

A GENTLE MANNER

And the Lord's bond-servant must not be quarrelsome, but be kind to all, able to teach, patient when wronged, (2:24)

Doulos (**bond-servant**) is a description Paul frequently used of himself. In several epistles he refers to his being a bond-servant of the Lord—ranking himself with all other believers—before declaring his divine call as an apostle (see Rom. 1:1; Phil. 1:1; Titus 1:1). Here he uses the description **the Lord's bond-servant** to refer to Timothy and to other preachers of divine truth.

Every **bond-servant** of **the Lord's** is to take care **not [to] be quarrelsome, but be kind to all, able to teach, patient when wronged.** Similarly, in his first letter he points out that pastors "must be above reproach, the husband of one wife, temperate, prudent, respectable, hospitable, able to teach, not addicted to wine or pugnacious, but gentle, uncontentious, free from the love of money" (1 Tim. 3:2–3). The apostle gives an expanded list of qualifications in his letter to Titus: "The overseer must be above reproach as God's steward, not self-willed, not quick-tempered, not addicted to wine, not pugnacious, not fond of sordid gain, but hospitable, loving what is good, sensible, just, devout, self-controlled, holding fast the faithful word which is in accordance with the teaching, that he may be able both to exhort in sound doctrine and to refute those who contradict" (Titus 1:7–9).

Leaders in the church, are **not [to] be quarrelsome, but . . . kind to all.** Those qualities characterized Jesus in His incarnation. He said of Himself, "Take My yoke upon you, and learn from Me, for I am gentle and humble in heart" (Matt. 11:29). In recording Jesus' triumphal entry into Jerusalem, Matthew quotes Zechariah: "Say to the daughter of Zion, 'Behold your King is coming to you, gentle, and mounted on a donkey, even on a colt, the foal of a beast of burden'" (Matt. 21:5). In his second letter to them, Paul reminded Corinthian believers of "the meekness and gentleness of Christ" and of his own meekness as an apostle, "I who am meek when face to face with you" (2 Cor. 10:1).

As much as we are to speak boldly for the Lord without compromise, we are to do so with the attitude of meekness, gentleness, and humility. We are never to be harsh, abusive, overbearing, unkind, thoughtless, or pugnacious. There is to be a softness in the authority of a Christian leader, just as there was in Paul's and in the Lord's when He was on earth. "We proved to be gentle among you," Paul reminded believers in Thessalonica, "as a nursing mother tenderly cares for her own children" (1 Thess. 2:7).

The responsible and godly preacher must also be **able to teach.** That phrase translates the single Greek adjective *didaktikos,* which carries the idea of being highly skilled in teaching. The only other time it is used in the New Testament is in Paul's first letter to Timothy, where it is also applied to elders (1 Tim. 3:2). The term does not refer so much to *possessing* vast knowledge or understanding as to having notable ability to *communicate effectively* whatever knowledge and understanding one may have—in this case, knowledge and understanding of God's Word.

The godly leader who is an honorable vessel must be **patient when wronged,** which is perhaps the hardest qualification mentioned here. If the old self is not firmly resisted, we are likely to become more offended **when** we ourselves are **wronged** than when our Lord and His truth are attacked. When we are faithfully witnessing and living for the Lord, it is not easy to graciously accept unjust criticism. But again Jesus is our example. "Christ also suffered for you, leaving you an example for you to follow in His steps," Peter reminds us. He "committed no sin, nor was any deceit found in His mouth; and while being reviled, He did not revile in return; while suffering, He uttered no threats, but kept entrusting Himself to Him who judges righteously" (1 Peter 2:21–23). In addition to being our example, Jesus is also our resource for being **patient.** Patience is a fruit of Christ's own Holy Spirit (cf. Gal. 5:22), who will provide the strength we need for bearing His fruit.

The effective **bond-servant** of the Lord is not concerned about justifying or vindicating himself but about serving the Lord without bitterness, vengeance, or anger, and with graciousness, kindness, and patience.

A HUMBLE SPIRIT

with gentleness (2:25a)

Prautēs (**gentleness**) can also be rendered "meekness." In the ancient Greek world the word was used of colts that were broken for riding. In such training, care must be taken to bring the animal's will into submission to the rider without breaking its energetic and lively spirit. Contrary to the connotation that "meekness" often carries today, *prautēs* has no relation to weakness but denotes power that is under willing control.

Again Jesus is the supreme example. In the two passages already cited referring to His manner, the adjective *praus* describes Him as gentle, or meek (Matt. 11:29; 21:5). Although He was God incarnate, and at any moment could have destroyed His enemies with a word or had at His "disposal more than twelve legions of angels" (Matt. 26:53), He chose rather to submit to every indignity, because that was His Father's will for Him in His incarnation.

In the same way, though to a much more limited degree, the faithful bond-servant of Jesus Christ who has great strength of conviction, and who may have leadership authority in the church, willingly expresses and defends his convictions and exercises his authority in a spirit of gentleness. The truly meek person is submissive as a matter of choice, because he *wants* to obey his Master and to be like Him.

In my book *Kingdom Living Here and Now,* I commented,

> Jesus never defended Himself, but when they desecrated His Father's Temple, He made a whip and beat them. Meekness says, "I'll never defend myself, but I'll die defending God." Twice Jesus cleansed the Temple. He blasted the hypocrites. He condemned false leaders of Israel. He fearlessly uttered divine judgment upon people. And yet the Bible says He was meek. [For the Christian, therefore], meekness is power used only in the defense of God ([Chicago: Moody, 1980], 79).

The *prautēs* kind of **gentleness** reflects a spirit of humility that does not focus on self but on the Lord and on others in His name. It has nothing to do with impotence or shyness or weakness or cowardice. It is power supplied by, and willingly put under the control of, the Holy Spirit, in faithful submission to the Word and will of God. When one is truly meek, he talks not of himself but of his Lord.

A COMPASSIONATE ATTITUDE

correcting those who are in opposition, if perhaps God may grant them repentance leading to the knowledge of the truth, and they may come to their senses and escape from the snare of the devil, having been held captive by him to do his will. (2:25b–26)

Finally, an honorable vessel and bond-servant of the Lord will have a compassionate attitude. Paul here focuses on the expression of compassion and meekness when **correcting those who are in opposition.**

Correcting is from *paideuō,* which means to instruct, educate, or give guidance. Because the objects of this instruction are those who teach false doctrine and live ungodly lives, this particular instruction is in the form of correction.

Much of the self-righteousness of the scribes and Pharisees was based on their carefully following human tradition that had no basis in Scripture and often was in contradiction of it. They "invalidated the word of God for the sake of [their] tradition," Jesus said (Matt. 15:6). But the godly Christian has no reason for being self-righteous even when he is humbly obeying Scripture, because he knows that his obedience is the product of the Holy Spirit rather than his own goodness. Consequently, when confronting believers who are teaching falsehood and living sinfully, one must never do so with an attitude of personal superiority. Christians are to have compassion for them in their sin just as the Lord has compassion.

Paul is not speaking of personal differences of opinion but of the **opposition** of disobedient believers. The **opposition** may pertain to "foolish and ignorant speculations" (v. 23) or to the more serious matters of doctrine or morals they lead to. Every minister encounters situations in the church that demand correction and sometimes rebuke. "For the grace of God has appeared, bringing salvation to all men," Paul reminded Titus, "instructing us [that is, *every* believer] to deny ungodliness and worldly desires and to live sensibly, righteously and godly in the present age, looking for the blessed hope and the appearing of the glory of our great God and Savior, Christ Jesus" (Titus 2:11–13). The faithful bond-servant of Christ is to be God's instrument for correcting fellow believers, whatever their position in the church, who persist in "ungodliness and worldly desire" and to admonish them to live "righteously and godly in the present age."

The motivation of such correction should be the sincere desire that **perhaps God may grant them repentance.** That is always the motivation of a humble and compassionate heart. Paul told the immature, worldly believers in Corinth, "I now rejoice, not that you were made sorrowful, but that you were made sorrowful to the point of repentance; for you were made sorrowful according to the will of God, in order that you might not suffer loss in anything through us" (2 Cor. 7:9). Even when those who are corrected are resentful of us and unrepentant, as some in Corinth were in regard to Paul, there is never a place in godly correction for personal animosity or judgmental self-righteousness.

The hope that **God may grant them repentance** is not a last resort. The idea is not that we must try to persuade **them** to repent by their own efforts and in their own power and that, if they fail, we then *hope* that **perhaps God** will **grant them** the **repentance** they were unable to achieve for themselves. *Metanoia* (**repentance**) does not mean simply being sorry for what we have done. It signifies a genuine change of mind, change of heart, and change of direction. It is for that reason that *all* genuine **repentance** must be the product of God's sovereign grace, just as is *every* aspect of salvation—"in order that in the ages to come He might show the surpassing riches of His grace in kindness toward us in Christ Jesus" (Eph. 2:7). No person, no matter how sincere and determined, can truly repent and change his own sinful thoughts and ideas and correct his own sinful life. Only God can work that miracle in the heart. In the same way, we are able to love only "because [Christ] first loved us" (1 John 4:19), "because the love of God has been poured out within our hearts through the Holy Spirit who was given to us" (Rom. 5:5). God works repentance in the willing heart of one who truly desires holiness.

Repentance leads disobedient believers out of their sin and falsehood into **the knowledge of the truth.** *Epignōsis* represents more than mere factual information. It is deep, thorough spiritual *knowledge* of God's truth, which, as with repentance, only He can supply.

It is only through God's gracious provision of repentance and knowledge of His truth that anyone, including sinning believers, **may come to their** spiritual **senses.** *Ananēphō* (**come to their senses**) literally means to return to soberness, indicating that falsehood and sin produce what might be called a type of spiritual inebriation, a stupor resulting in loss of judgment and proper control of one's faculties. The destructive effect of false teaching and sin numbs the conscience, confuses the mind, erodes conviction, and paralyzes the will.

God's provision of genuine repentance and knowledge of His truth enable a believer to **escape from the snare of the devil,** after **having been held captive by him to do his will.** As Paul apprised Timothy in the previous letter, even an overseer can "fall into reproach and the snare of the devil" (1 Tim. 3:7). It is a fearful thing that, because of sin and unfaithfulness, **the devil** can actually **snare** and hold a believer **captive . . . to do his will.** The vessel of dishonor becomes a pawn of Satan to work his evil **will** within the very body of Christ. Such is the terrible and tragic power of sin.

But our gracious "God is faithful," Paul assures us. He "will not allow you to be tempted beyond what you are able, but with the temptation will provide the way of escape also, that you may be able to endure it" (1 Cor. 10:13). Not only does the Lord know "how to rescue the godly from temptation" (2 Peter 2:9), but He even promises His unfaithful, dishonorable vessels that "if we confess our sins, He is faithful and righteous to forgive us our sins and to cleanse us from all unrighteousness" (1 John 1:9).

Danger in the Church

7

But realize this, that in the last days difficult times will come. For men will be lovers of self, lovers of money, boastful, arrogant, revilers, disobedient to parents, ungrateful, unholy, unloving, irreconcilable, malicious gossips, without self-control, brutal, haters of good, treacherous, reckless, conceited, lovers of pleasure rather than lovers of God; holding to a form of godliness, although they have denied its power; and avoid such men as these. For among them are those who enter into households and captivate weak women weighed down with sins, led on by various impulses, always learning and never able to come to the knowledge of the truth. And just as Jannes and Jambres opposed Moses, so these men also oppose the truth, men of depraved mind, rejected as regards the faith. But they will not make further progress; for their folly will be obvious to all, as also that of those two came to be. (3:1–9)

The full counsel of God has been displeasing, unacceptable, and even repugnant to self-centered, self-serving, and worldly mankind throughout the ages. But even in the professing church today there is greater confusion, apostasy, moral decay, and tolerance for things that are clearly unscriptural than ever before. Sermons on current issues, selectively using Bible passages that are "relevant" and "positive," are attracting many hearers, including genuine but misled and worldly believers. "The time will come," Paul writes later in this epistle, "when [many in the church] will not endure sound doctrine; but wanting to have their ears tickled, they will accumulate for themselves teachers in accordance to their own desires" (2 Tim. 4:3).

DIFFICULT TIMES

But realize this, that in the last days difficult times will come. (3:1)

In the intervening 2,000 years, the apostle's divinely revealed prediction of **difficult times** has come true as heresies have become progressively more characteristic of nominal Christianity. In this passage he gives the most serious possible command to avoid, expose, and oppose spiritual impostors in the church.

Throughout church history the full counsel of God has been unpalatable to many who have claimed the name of Christ. In his book *Damned Through the Church* (Minneapolis: Bethany, 1970), John Warwick Montgomery discusses the **difficult times** as he offers a list of what he calls "the damnable epochs of church history." He identifies and discusses seven specific movements or theological orientations— from the sacramentalism of the Middle Ages (also called the Dark Ages) to the subjectivism that is so rampant in our own day—that are clearly unbiblical, ungodly, and destructive of the body of Christ. As the title of the book implies, these false gospels are damning to their adherents.

In each of those **difficult times,** men's ideas were substituted for God's truth and therefore for God Himself. Under sacramentalism, the church replaced God; under rationalism, reason was god; under orthodoxism, god was sterile, impersonal orthodoxy; under politicism, god was the state; under ecumenism, god was uncritical fellowship and cooperation among nominal Christians; under experientialism, god became personal experience; and under subjectivism, which still reigns in much of Christendom, self has become god.

It would be appropriate to add to Montgomery's list the current emphases on mysticism, which seeks to determine truth about God by intuition and feeling, and on pragmatism, which attempts to determine what is true by what produces desired effects. These movements do not come and go but come to stay, so that as the years go on, the church accumulates them, and the battles continue.

Besides our present text, the only other prediction Paul made to Timothy is found in the first letter, in which he gives a similar warning: "The Spirit explicitly says that in later times some will fall away from the faith, paying attention to deceitful spirits and doctrines of demons, by means of the hypocrisy of liars seared in their own conscience as with a branding iron" (1 Tim. 4:1–2).

That problem was not new to God's people. Jeremiah wrote, "The Lord said to me, 'The prophets are prophesying falsehood in My name. I have neither sent them nor commanded them nor spoken to them; they are prophesying to you a false vision, divination, futility and the deception of their own minds'" (Jer. 14:14). Later he relates that "among the prophets of Jerusalem I [the Lord] have seen a horrible thing: The committing of adultery and walking in falsehood; and they strengthen the hands of evildoers, so that no one has turned back from his wickedness. All of them have become to Me like Sodom, and her inhabitants like Gomorrah" (Jer. 23:14). The prophet then warned, "Thus says the Lord of hosts, 'Do not listen to the words of the prophets who are prophesying to you. They are leading you into futility; they speak a vision of their own imagination, not from the mouth of the Lord'" (v. 16).

The most serious and lamentable aspect of such rejection of God and His Word is that the danger comes from *within* the church. As noted several times, near the end of his third missionary journey Paul sent for the Ephesian elders to meet with him at Miletus. Pouring out his heart to them, he warned, "I know that after my departure savage wolves will come in *among you*, not sparing the flock; and from *among your own selves* men will arise, speaking perverse things, to draw away the disciples after them" (Acts 20:29–30, emphasis added).

Although our Lord assures us, "I will build My church; and the gates of Hades shall not overpower it" (Matt. 16:18), He did not promise that His people would be free from spiritual danger and harm. Much to the contrary. Near the beginning of His ministry, in the Sermon on the Mount, He warned, "Beware of the false prophets, who come to you in sheep's clothing, but inwardly are ravenous wolves" (Matt. 7:15). In the guise of spiritual shepherds and prophets, who were noted for wearing wool garments, they devour and destroy the very ones they profess to lead and protect. Zechariah spoke of such men as those who "put on a hairy robe in order to deceive" (Zech. 13:4). Earlier in His revelation to that prophet, the Lord declared, "For behold, I am going to raise up a shepherd in the land who will not care for the perishing, seek the scattered, heal the broken, or sustain the one standing, but will devour the flesh of the fat sheep and tear off their hoofs. Woe to the worthless shepherd who leaves the flock! A sword will be on his arm and on his right eye! His arm will be totally withered, and his right eye will be blind" (11:16–17).

Near the end of His ministry, Jesus expanded the warning cited above from Matthew 7. "Many false prophets will arise, and will mislead many," He said. "And because lawlessness is increased, most people's love will grow cold. . . . For false Christs and false prophets will arise and will show great signs and wonders, so as to mislead, if possible, even the elect" (Matt. 24:11–12, 24).

Similar warnings are given in the epistles. Peter warned that "false prophets also arose among the people, just as there will also be false teachers among you, who will secretly introduce destructive heresies, even denying the Master who bought them, bringing swift destruction upon themselves. And many will follow their sensuality, and because of them the way of the truth will be maligned" (2 Peter 2:1–2). John warned, "Children, it is the last hour; and just as you heard that antichrist is coming, even now many antichrists have arisen; from this we know that it is the last hour. They went out from us, but they were not really of us; for if they had been of us, they would have remained with us; but they went out, in order that it might be shown that they all are not of us" (1 John 2:18–19). Jude warned that "certain persons have crept in unnoticed, those who were long beforehand marked out for this condemnation, ungodly persons who turn the grace of our God into licentiousness and deny our only Master and Lord, Jesus Christ" (Jude 4).

Those warnings were about the contemporary as well as the future condition of the church. The dangers that plagued the New Testament church would continue and become worse throughout the church age, as "evil men and impostors will proceed from bad to worse, deceiving and being deceived" (2 Tim. 3:13).

The twin dangers are the closely related evils of ungodly teaching and ungodly living, of false doctrine and sinful lifestyle. As Jesus pointed out in the quotation above from Matthew 24:11, as "false prophets will arise, . . . lawlessness is increased," and as Jeremiah predicted, "the committing of adultery and walking in falsehood" are companion evils (Jer. 23:14). Those enemies of God and of God's people originated at the Fall and will continue to thrive until the Lord returns and takes back the world for Himself. In the meanwhile, the alliance of false teaching and ungodly living will continue to afflict the church.

The conjunction **but** indicates a change of direction, from the admonition to be a godly "vessel for honor," one characterized by kindness, patience, and gentleness (2:21–25), to the admonition to be a responsible and fearless guardian of God's people, protecting them from false doctrine and immoral living.

Realize this translates a Greek present tense, which, as often noted before, carries the ideas of constancy and continuity. As long as Timothy was given breath and energy to serve the Lord and the Lord's people, he was to heed Paul's warning.

In Scripture, the phrase **last days** can have several meanings. In his prophecies about "the latter days," Daniel referred to the entire sweep of history from the time of King Nebuchadnezzar of ancient Babylon to the time when "the God of heaven will set up a kingdom which will never be destroyed" (see Dan. 2:28–45). In Isaiah's prophecy, the phrase refers to the time just prior to and including Christ's second coming, when "the mountain of the house of the Lord will be established as the chief of the mountains, and will be raised above the hills; and all the nations will stream to it" (Isa. 2:2; cf. Micah 4:1).

The writer of Hebrews declared that "God, after He spoke long ago to the fathers in the prophets in many portions and in many ways, in *these last days* has spoken to us in His Son, whom He appointed heir of all things, through whom also He made the world" (Heb. 1:1–2, emphasis added; cf. James 5:3). It seems clear that these **last days,** which began with the earthly ministry of Jesus Christ, are the ones about which Paul is speaking here. Explaining the miraculous descent of the Holy Spirit at Pentecost, Peter made clear that "this is what was spoken of through the prophet Joel: 'And it shall be in *the last days,*' God says, 'That I will pour forth of My Spirit upon all mankind'" (Acts 2:16–17; cf. Joel 2:28, emphasis added). The Messiah, Jesus Christ, initiated these last days, the continuation of which was attested by the descent of His Holy Spirit at Pentecost and the birth of the church.

In John's first epistle, he warned his readers in the early church that "it is the last hour," which, in this context, is the equivalent of **the last days.** "And just as you heard that antichrist is coming," he continued, "even now many antichrists have arisen; from this we know that it is the last hour" (1 John 2:18). We are still living in the messianic time between Christ's first and second comings, all of which may properly be called **the last days.**

In those **days,** Paul says, **difficult times will come.** *Chelepos* (**difficult**) carries the ideas of perilous or grievous, as some English versions translate the word. In Matthew 8:28, referring to the Gadarene demoniacs, it is translated "violent" (NASB). The famous Greek writer Plutarch used the term to describe an ugly, infected, and dangerous wound.

Times does not translate *chronos,* which, as one would guess, indicates chronological time, but rather *kairos,* which refers to periods of time, to seasons, epochs, or eras. The plural **times** may indicate the epochs of varying degrees of danger and difficulty the church would experience throughout its history. As Paul makes clear a few verses later, these perilous **times** will become more and more frequent and intense, whereas the intervening periods of relative tranquillity will become less frequent and peaceful, as the return of Christ nears.

LOVERS OF SELF

For men will be lovers of self, lovers of money, boastful, arrogant, revilers, disobedient to parents, ungrateful, unholy, unloving, irreconcilable, malicious gossips, without self-control, brutal, haters of good, treacherous, reckless, conceited, lovers of pleasure rather than lovers of God; (3:2-4)

Paul's description of these seasons of danger is specific. In this context, **men** does not refer to mankind in general or to the unsaved world but to members, especially leaders, in Christ's church, **men** who not only claim the name of Christ but claim to be His ministers, His prophets, pastors, teachers, and evangelists. These **men** are apostate leaders in apostate churches. As Paul will shortly point out, they hold "a form of godliness, [but] have denied its power" (v. 5) and they pose an immeasurable threat to the spiritual health, safety, and power of the entire body of Christ. In these three verses, Paul lists eighteen characteristics of ungodly, apostate **men,** and doubtless women, who have corrupted and will continue to corrupt the church of Christ until He returns.

The first characteristic is that these **men will be lovers of self.** The pride of self-love is the pervasive deadly sin that grips the human soul and is the foundation sin of all the others. It might be called the sewer out of which the rest of these ugly sins are discharged.

Lovers of self translates the single Greek word *philautos,* a compound of the verb *phileō* (to have great affection for) and the pronoun *autos* (self). *Phileō* is not a wrong kind of loving, and the verb is frequently used positively in the New Testament. In John 16:27, it is used both of the Father's love for believers and of the believer's love for the Son. It is used of Jesus' love for John (John 20:2) and is used once even of the Father's love for the Son (John 5:20). In the present passage, it is not the *kind* of love that is evil but the wrongly elevated *object* of that love, namely **self.** Whenever love for **self** is raised, love for God and the things of God is lowered. For that reason, misdirected love always engenders vice. It was first from Lucifer's and then from Adam's and Eve's love of themselves over the Lord—and from the similar self-love of their descendants—that every other sin has issued.

It is for that reason that the most frightening development within the contemporary church is the wide acceptance and enthusiastic proclamation of self-love, not only as being allowable but as being the basic virtue. Turning God's truth completely on its head, the source of all evil is touted as the source of all good. And on the other hand, the lack of self-love and its many derivatives—such as self-esteem, self-worth, self-fulfillment, and positive self-image—have been imported almost unchanged into the church from antibiblical secular psychology.

It is widely claimed that a person cannot love God and other people rightly unless and until he loves himself rightly, completely reversing what both the Old and New Testaments teach. As already noted above, Jesus said, "'You shall love the Lord your God with all your heart, and with all your soul, and with all your mind.' This is the great and foremost commandment. The second is like it, 'You shall love your neighbor as yourself'" (Matt. 22:37–39). Instead of taking the words "as yourself" as an assumption of self-love that is natural to sinful man, many interpreters not only take these words as a command but as the *first and greatest command!*

Throughout church history, many Christians, both true and nominal, have been guilty of perverted self-love. Self-love always has been associated with worldliness, but heretofore it was never taught as a doctrinal tenet in the church, even in its most corrupt periods. It was universally acknowledged to be the sin it is. Even most neoorthodox theologians have recognized self-love, or pride, as the root sin of all others. But psychologists Carl Rogers, Erich Fromm, and many others strongly denounced that God-centered view and boldly claimed that *lack* of self-love and self-esteem is the root problem of man. That false and damnable twist has permeated the church to an alarming degree.

In *The City of God,* Augustine wrote, "Two cities have been founded by two loves, the earthly by the love of self, even to the contempt of God. The heavenly by the love of God, even to the contempt of self. The former, in a word, glorifies itself, the latter the Lord." In his great theological work *The Institutes of the Christian Religion* the Swiss Reformer John Calvin said, "For so blindly do we all rush in the direction of self-love that everyone thinks he has good reason for exalting himself. There is no other remedy than to pluck up by the roots that most noxious pest, self-love."

The concept of self-love as a positive characteristic did not find its way into the church until the late twentieth century, and, lamentably, it has spread quickly to broad portions of evangelicalism. Contrary to the unambiguous teaching of Scripture and contrary to its clearly destructive consequences, the heresy of self-love continues to find acceptance among those who claim Christ.

The roots of the modern infatuation with self-love can be traced to the humanism of the nineteenth century, especially in the development of evolutionism. If man is seen as the product of impersonal chance, God is ruled out, making the elevation of self perfectly acceptable. Because there is no basis for right and wrong, the individual's natural bent to self-centeredness is reinforced, and he finds consummate justification for being his own god who does his own will. Each man is captain of his own ship and master of his own fate and cannot allow his self-will to be hindered or he does harm to his well-being.

The philosophy and theology of existentialism have also contributed to selfism. Although some existentialists genuinely believe there is a God and even that Jesus Christ is His Son and the Savior of the world, they reject the authority of Scripture except in a mystical way and claim that God is too far removed from man to be clearly understood, much less be personally known. Man is thrust back on himself to make of God and of life what he can. Consequently, and regardless of any protests to the contrary, man becomes in effect his own interpreter of God. Because no outside absolutes are recognized, personal beliefs and personal actions must be based solely on what seems best at the moment. Rather than unconditional submission to God, there is unconditional submission to self.

Fortunately some psychologists and psychiatrists are contesting the premise that man's basic problem is low self-esteem. In a book written under the auspices of the Christian College Coalition, called *Psychology Through the Eyes of Faith,* David Meyers and Malcolm Jeeves give abundant evidence against that myth. In a chapter titled "A New Look at Pride," they write,

> Time and again, experimenters have found that people readily accept credit when told they have succeeded (attributing the success to their ability and effort), yet they attribute failure to external factors such as bad luck or the problem's inherent "impossibility." These self-serving attributions have been observed not only in laboratory situations, but also with athletes (after victory or defeat), students (after high or low exam grades), drivers (after accidents), and married people (among whom conflict often derives from perceiving oneself as contributing more and benefiting less than is fair). Self-concepts researcher Anthony Greenwald summarizes, "People experience life through a self-centered filter." . . .
>
> In virtually any area that is both subjective and socially desirable, most people see themselves as better than average. Most business people see themselves as more ethical than the average business person. Most community residents see themselves as less prejudiced than their neighbors. Most people see themselves as more intelligent and as healthier than most other people. ([New York: Harper, 1987], 130)

Later in the book the authors maintain that "the most common error in people's self-images is not unrealistically low self-esteem but rather self-serving pride; not an inferiority complex but a superiority complex." Even self-depreciation, putting yourself down, is but a thinly disguised attempt to get others to build you up.

The eighteenth-century preacher Samuel Johnson said, "He that overvalues himself will undervalue others. And he that undervalues others will oppose them." Self-love alienates men from God and from each other. Self-love is the supreme enemy of godliness and of genuine friendship and fellowship.

What a contrast self-seeking love is to the self-giving love that God requires. "Do nothing from selfishness or empty conceit," Paul adjures, "but with humility of mind let each of you regard one another as more important than himself; do not merely look out for your own personal interests, but also for the interests of others" (Phil. 2:3–4). Just as the second great commandment assumes self-love, so Paul's admonition assumes that people naturally "look out for [their] own interests." As always, the Lord Himself is our perfect example. "Have this attitude in yourselves which was also in Christ Jesus," the apostle continues, "who, although He existed in the form of God, did not regard equality with God a thing to be grasped, but emptied Himself, taking the form of a bond-servant, and being made in the likeness of men. And being found in appearance as a man, He humbled Himself by becoming obedient to the point of death, even death on a cross" (vv. 5–8). If the heavenly Lord had that attitude in His incarnation, how much more ought we to humble ourselves, empty ourselves, and become unselfishly submissive to God to the point of death.

A concomitant of being lovers of self is being **lovers of money,** a term which represents materialism, the craving for earthly possessions of whatever sort. It is being covetous, as the Greek word is here rendered in the King James Version.

Paul is not speaking of the rightful earning and use of **money** to feed, clothe, and otherwise provide necessities for ourselves and our families. "If anyone will not work," the apostle said in another letter, "neither let him eat" (2 Thess. 3:10). But as he explains in the first letter to Timothy, "If we have food and covering, with these we shall be content" (1 Tim. 6:8). Those who are *not* content with those essentials and want "to get rich fall into temptation and a snare and many foolish and harmful desires which plunge men into ruin and destruction. For the love of money is a root of all sorts of evil, and some by longing for it have wandered away from the faith, and pierced themselves with many a pang" (vv. 9–10). Because Ephesus was a wealthy city, it is likely that Paul had in mind specific members of the church there who had "wandered away from the faith" because of their love of money.

Because false teaching always leads to wrong living, it is not surprising that many false teachers, such as those who promote the so-called health and wealth gospel, "suppose that godliness is a means of gain" (1 Tim. 6:5). It is the inordinate desire for **money** and for the things money represents that has made this perverted gospel so popular in the church today. It follows logically that a Christian who thinks first of himself has no problem in expecting God to provide not only necessities but luxuries, to believe that because he is a child of the King he should live like a prince. "Godliness *actually is* a means of great gain," Paul goes on to say, but only "when accompanied by contentment" (v. 6, emphasis added).

Such false teachers "must be silenced," Paul declares, "because they are upsetting whole families, teaching things they should not teach, for the sake of sordid gain" (Titus 1:11). They are consumed with self, which inevitably leads to greed, "and in their greed they will exploit you with false words" (2 Peter 2:3). It is a cycle of sin. Greed leads to false teaching, and false teaching leads to further greed. The false gospels of self-love and prosperity go hand in hand; they promote each other and feed on each other.

Being **boastful** is the outward manifestation of self-love. **Boastful** translates *alazōn,* a noun meaning "braggart," which Plato defined as a person who claims greatness that he does not possess. **Boastful** persons brag about their accomplishments, overstating the truth to the degree that it has no basis in reality. They are know-it-alls who try to deceive people into thinking they are brilliant. They love to see their names in print and their faces on television. They exaggerate their abilities, their accomplishments, their talents, their reputations, and their value to society and to the church. They are always the heroes of their own stories.

Like self-love and love of money, being **boastful** is closely related to false teaching. Boasters want "to be teachers of the Law, even though they do not understand either what they are saying or the matters about which they make confident assertions" (1 Tim. 1:7). The boastful person "is conceited and understands nothing; but he has a morbid interest in controversial questions and disputes about words," and out of those sins arise such companion sins as "envy, strife, abusive language, evil suspicions" (6:4).

A person who is boastful is invariably **arrogant.** Those who are characterized by these twin evils are perpetually self-exalting and determined to have their own way. *Huperēphanos* (**arrogant**) has the literal meaning of placing above, hence the idea of superiority.

The **arrogant** are best illustrated in the New Testament by the Jewish religious leaders mentioned by Jesus "who trusted in themselves that they were righteous, and viewed others with contempt" (Luke 18:9). He proceeded to tell them the well-known parable of the Pharisee and the tax-gatherer, or publican, who went to pray in the temple:

> The Pharisee stood and was praying thus to himself, "God, I thank Thee that I am not like other people: swindlers, unjust, adulterers, or

even like this tax-gatherer. I fast twice a week; I pay tithes of all that I get." But the tax-gatherer, standing some distance away, was even unwilling to lift up his eyes to heaven, but was beating his breast, saying, "God, be merciful to me, the sinner!" I tell you, this man went down to his house justified rather than the other; for everyone who exalts himself shall be humbled, but he who humbles himself shall be exalted. (vv. 11–14)

Quoting from Proverbs 3:34, both James and Peter declare that "God is opposed to the proud, but gives grace to the humble" (James 4:6; 1 Peter 5:5; cf. Ps. 138:6).

William Barclay gives a helpful comparison of boastful and arrogant:

> The braggart is a swaggering creature, who shouts his claims to the four winds of heaven, and tries to boast and bluster his way into power and eminence. No one can possibly mistake him or fail to see him. But the sin of the man who is *arrogant,* in this sense, is in his heart. He might even seem to be humble; he might even seem to be quiet and inoffensive; but in his secret heart there is this contempt for everyone else. He nourishes an all-consuming, all-pervading pride. In his heart there is a little altar where he bows down before himself, and in his eyes there is something which looks at all men with a silent contempt. (*The Letters to Timothy, Titus and Philemon* [Philadelphia: Westminster, 1957], 214)

The boastful and the **arrogant** are much more alike than different. It is a rare instance when a person who is one is not also the other. Even in the modern church it becomes harder and harder to find those who are meek and humble and equally difficult to avoid those who are proud and conceited.

Revilers translates *blasphēmos,* from which we get "blasphemous," and carries the basic idea of being abusive and slanderous. It is inevitable that a person who is contemptuous of others will eventually revile them. When you elevate yourself, you automatically lower and denigrate others. Inner disdain will eventually find expression in outward slander, because the tongue always follows the heart. "For from within, out of the heart of men," Jesus made clear, "proceed the evil thoughts, fornications, thefts, murders, adulteries, deeds of coveting and wickedness, as well as deceit, sensuality, envy, slander, pride and foolishness" (Mark 7:21–22).

Disobedient to parents is the next evil in Paul's list and is self-explanatory. The disobedience of children to parents in our day has become endemic, and the cause is not hard to find. Not only are children born with a bent to self-will and disobedience, but the disappearance of mothers into the work force and the spiritual failure of fathers is exacerbated by the prevailing philosophy of self-love that is promoted in modern society, including many classrooms and churches, making being **disobedient to parents** all but compulsory. Children who will rebel against their parents will have no qualms about rebelling against anyone else. It should be no surprise that a generation whose natural, sinful self-love has been reinforced and justified by society is now undermining the family, the church, and the permissive society that has misguided it.

Like the previous sin, **ungrateful** is self-explanatory. The person who elevates self above all others will feel he deserves everything good he receives and therefore feels no need of gratitude for it. Although he may not put it into words, the **ungrateful** person despises the very idea of grace, which denotes goodness received that is undeserved. This is a particularly noxious sin to God, whose wrath is revealed against sinners for being unthankful (cf. Rom. 1:18, 21).

Unholy translates *anosias,* which carries the idea not so much of irreligion as of gross indecency. It was used of a person who refused to bury a dead body or who committed incest. The unholy person is driven by self-love to gratify his lusts and passions of whatever sort, as fully as possible with no thought to propriety, decency, or personal reputation.

Unloving translates *astorgos,* a negative adjective form of the verb *storgē,* which commonly was used of family, social, and patriotic love. The noted theologian Benjamin Warfield described it as "that quiet and abiding feeling within us, which, resting on an object as near to us, recognizes that we are closely bound up with it and takes satisfaction in its recognition." It is not natural for people to love God or the things and people of God, but it *is* natural for them to love their own families. To be *astorgos* is therefore to be "without natural affection" (KJV). Just as the self-loving person is without common decency, he also is without common affection. He cares nothing for the welfare of those who should be dearest to him. His only interest in them is for what he believes they can do for him. To be **unloving** is to be heartless.

Unloving behavior is reported daily in newspapers and broadcasts. Husbands and wives abusing one another, parents and children abusing one another—often to the point of murder—are so common that they make headlines only if they are particularly brutal or sensational. Tragically, the evangelical church has its share of the **unloving** and heartless.

The **irreconcilable** are those who refuse to change, no matter how desperate even their own situation becomes, much less the situations of those they should care about. They are determined to have their own way regardless of the consequences, even to the point of knowingly destroying their own lives and the lives of their families. They do not forgive and do not want to be forgiven. They are implacable, beyond reasoning, and inevitably self-destructive. As far as they are concerned, there is no compromise, no reconciliation, no court of appeal. Their self-love is so extreme and their egoism so massive that absolutely nothing matters except doing as they please.

Gossip is often thought of as being relatively harmless, but at best it is unkind, harmful, and ungodly. **Malicious** gossip is a sin of an even more evil and destructive sort. Whereas the irreconcilable person tends to disregard and neglect others, **malicious gossips** make a point of harming others. Whether to promote their own interests, to express jealousy or hatred, or simply to vent their anger, they take perverse pleasure in damaging reputations and destroying lives.

Malicious gossips translates *diabolos,* which, even to the person unacquainted with Greek, suggests the severity of this evil, with our English derivative "diabolical." *Diabolos* means "accuser" and is used thirty-four times in the New Testament as a title for Satan. Engulfed and blinded by self-love, **malicious gossips** do the very work of Satan.

Akratēs ("without self-control") denotes incontinence, in this context that of a moral and spiritual kind. When Jesus excoriated the hypocritical scribes and Pharisees, He told them they cleaned "the outside of the cup and of the dish, but inside they are full of robbery and self-indulgence [*akratēs*]" (Matt. 23:25).

Without self-control describes the person who has jettisoned inhibitions and shame, who does not care about what people think or about what happens to them because of what he does. Like a driverless car, he careens haphazardly and crashes into whatever gets in his way. The lover of self eventually loses control of his own life and becomes a slave to his passions and ambitions.

Brutal refers to savagery, like that of wild beasts, whose nature it is to attack enemies and tear them in pieces. Self-love that is not checked makes a person insensitive, malicious, and eventually brutal.

Next in their downward spiral, self-lovers become **haters of good,** hating what should be loved and loving what should be hated. They sink to what amounts to an animal level; but unlike animals, they know what is good yet choose to despise and oppose it. "Woe to those who call evil good, and good evil," the Lord warned the wicked; "who substitute darkness for light and light for darkness; who substitute bitter for sweet, and sweet for bitter" (Isa. 5:20). **Haters of good** remain under God's judgment.

Lovers of self eventually become **treacherous,** turning against even their own families and friends. Treachery comes naturally to a person who loves money, who is boastful and arrogant, ungrateful and unholy, unloving and irreconcilable, a malicious slanderer who has lost self-control, and who is brutal and hates what is good.

Jesus warned the Twelve that "brother will deliver up brother to death, and a father his child; and children will rise up against parents, and cause them to be put to death. And you will be hated by all on account of My name" (Matt. 10:21–22; cf. 24:9–10). Whenever the church has suffered persecution, true believers have been betrayed into the hands of the oppressors, often by members of their own families who value safety and prosperity above devotion and fidelity. Feigned love and friendship become means of treachery. That is also the time when genuine loyalty proves itself, often at a high price.

The **reckless** person is careless, negligent, and rash. This characteristic is not as serious as most of the others and often is manifested unconsciously. The self-centered person is so preoccupied with his own interests that he simply does not notice people and things around him that are not related to those egotistic concerns.

It goes without saying that the self-lover is **conceited,** having a much higher view of himself than is justified. *Tuphoō* (**conceited**) has the root meaning of being enveloped in smoke, or beclouded, so that what is outside one's circumscribed world of self cannot be seen.

Paul advised Timothy in his first letter that an elder, or overseer, should "not [be] a new convert, lest he become conceited and fall into the condemnation incurred by the devil" (1 Tim. 3:6). Later in the same letter the apostle states that conceit is a sure mark of a false teacher, again certifying the inescapable connection between wrong doctrine and wrong living. A false teacher who "advocates a different doctrine, and does not agree with sound words, those of our Lord Jesus Christ, and with the doctrine conforming to godliness, . . . is conceited and understands nothing; but he has a morbid interest in controversial questions and disputes about words, out of which arise envy, strife, abusive language, evil suspicions" (1 Tim. 6:3–4).

The final sinful characteristic of dangerous false teachers given in this extensive but not exhaustive list is their being **lovers of pleasure rather than lovers of God. Lovers of pleasure** translates the single Greek word *philēdonos,* a compound of *philos* (loving) and *hēdonē* (**pleasure**), from which we get "hedonist" and "hedonism." Along with all his other sins, the false teacher is a self-loving, pleasure-mad hedonist.

It should be noted that **pleasure,** especially in this context, is not limited to the desire for comfort, fine food, sexual satisfaction, and other indulgences normally associated with hedonism. As already mentioned, a self-centered person also derives perverse pleasure from such things as malicious gossip, brutality, and treachery. His satisfaction comes, in part, from the pain and misery he sadistically inflicts on others, including parents and supposed friends.

This depraved **pleasure** is not loved *more than* God, but **rather than . . . God.** In other words, the true God has no place at all in the thinking and living of a false teacher or of anyone who is self-centered. Jesus told Nicodemus, "And this is the judgment, that the light is come into the world, and men loved the darkness *rather than* the light; for their deeds were evil" (John 3:19, emphasis added).

Those who love **pleasure rather than . . . God** cannot possibly obey either the first or the second great commandments. They cannot truly love God or their neighbors, and have no genuine desire to do so. Jesus made clear that a person can have only one god, and for the self-lover, self is god. Satan has never had a shortage of false gods with which to tempt man, and by far the most useful to his cause is the god of self. Lucifer fell from his exalted and magnificent state in heaven because he became his own god, and since that time he has endeavored to entice fallen mankind into the same form of idolatry.

CHARLATANS OF RELIGION

holding to a form of godliness, although they have denied its power; and avoid such men as these. (3:5)

Leaders in the church who foster false systems of belief and corrupt standards of living not only are lovers of self but also are charlatans of religion.

Form comes from *morphsis,* which refers to outward shape and appearance, such as that of a silhouette, which is an undetailed outline or shadow of something. Like the unbelieving scribes and Pharisees, lovers of self are concerned only about the outward **form,** about "the outside of the cup and of the dish," while "inside they are full of robbery and self-indulgence" (Matt. 23:25). They are religious fakes, phony religionists who masquerade as Christian leaders. They claim to be servants of God and teachers of His Word, but they are really servants of Satan and purveyors of his lies. Again like the scribes and Pharisees who opposed Jesus, they "are of [their] father the devil, and [they] want to do the desires of [their] father. He was a murderer from the beginning, and does not stand in the truth, because there is no truth in him. Whenever he speaks a lie, he speaks from his own nature; for he is a liar, and the father of lies" (John 8:44).

That false teachers hold **to a form of godliness,** that is, an outline of Christianity without substance, makes them all the more dangerous, because immature members in the church will accept their paganized

Christianity as the true faith. Like most of the other vile traits Paul has just mentioned, this one was not new among God's people but was regularly recurrent in ancient Israel. Ezekiel warned against such impostors, who "do the lustful desires expressed by their mouth, and [whose] heart goes after their gain" (Ezek. 33:31). Paul warned Titus that such men "profess to know God, but by their deeds they deny Him, being detestable and disobedient, and worthless for any good deed" (Titus 1:16).

Satan is deceptive and subtle. He never tells the truth about anything, although he frequently tries to use a partial truth or a truth out of context to his advantage, as when he quoted Scripture to Jesus during the wilderness temptations (Matt. 4:6). And Satan's most dangerous attacks against God's people come from within the church by means of false preachers and teachers who pretend to speak for God.

The deception of such false leaders is seen in their denying the true, gracious, life-giving **power** of the true gospel. Although it is presented in many persuasive ways, theirs is an empty, worthless, damning message that keeps its adherents out of the kingdom. Ungodly leaders have no love for God and no love for His Word or for His people, only love for themselves.

True believers are given a standing order to **avoid such men as these** and reject the false doctrines they teach and the false standards they live by. And because the verb *apotreō* (avoid) is here in the middle voice, the idea is to *make yourself* turn away. Regardless of how convincing a false idea may appear or how sincere a false teacher may seem to be, we are to take ourselves by the scruff of the neck, as it were, and make ourselves **avoid such men as these.** We should **avoid** and keep on avoiding **such men,** whenever, wherever, and however they may confront us. Whether their heresy is sacramentalism, rationalism, ecumenism, subjectivism, experientialism, mysticism, pragmatism, or any of countless others, both they and their ungodly ideas are to be rejected. As with counterfeit money, it is not necessary to understand every false detail of a teaching but only necessary to recognize that it does not match the real thing, namely, God's Word. Whether a counterfeit is a well-done fraud or a shoddy fake, it is equally worthless.

There are three guidelines for judging whether a teacher or preacher is from God. The first thing to measure is his creed, the specific beliefs and ideas he propounds. Is Scripture, the whole of Scripture, the basis for everything he believes and does, or does he use certain Bible passages selectively to bolster unbiblical ideas? If his creed does not measure up to Scripture, or if he belittles the importance of doctrine, nothing else about him matters, because he obviously does not speak for God and has not been sent by Him.

The second guideline to examine is personal character and its reflection in his lifestyle. Even if a person's professed doctrine is orthodox, ungodly living betrays a godless heart. Godly belief always produces godly living.

A third measure of a godly leader is his converts, his most ardent followers. If his devotees are weak, confused, or unconcerned about doctrine, and if their living does not reflect biblical standards, the leader himself almost certainly is not godly, because godly leaders will not claim or be satisfied with ungodly converts. Christ-honoring, Scripture-loving teachers and preachers will produce Christ-honoring, Scripture-loving converts. Religious charlatans, on the other hand, will produce converts in their own image.

CAPTORS OF THE WEAK

For among them are those who enter into households and captivate weak women weighed down with sins, led on by various impulses, always learning and never able to come to the knowledge of the truth. (3:6–7)

A third identifying mark of false teachers is their capturing of the weak. This particular characteristic does not apply to all false teachers but is found **among them.** *Endunō* (**enter**) carries the idea of stealth and therefore of creeping in undetected. Like all ungodly leaders who come from within the church, these men go under false colors. Jude wrote of "certain persons [who had] crept in unnoticed, those who were long beforehand marked out for this condemnation, ungodly persons who turn the grace of our God into licentiousness and deny our only Master and Lord, Jesus Christ" (Jude 4).

A favorite target of these particular false teachers is **weak women [who] are weighed down with sins, [and are] led on by various impulses.** Because they are deep into **sins** and ungodly **impulses** that have **weighed [them] down** emotionally and spiritually, the weak women Paul describes here are especially vulnerable to being religiously seduced by false teachers. They are weak in truth and weak in virtue, and they feel the heavy weight of their sin and the guilt it brings. And just as wrong doctrine leads to wrong living, so can their wrong living easily lead to embracing wrong doctrine. Just as Eve was the first target, as the weaker sex (1 Peter 3:7), so Satan continues to target women as his initial captives. Cults not only are often spawned by women, but women are the most numerous and devout adherents.

Often moving from one false teacher or group to another, such women are **always learning and never able to come to the knowledge of the truth.** If they have been reared in the church, they are especially susceptible to ideas that purport to be Christian. But their ignorance of Scripture and their sinful living make them utterly undiscerning and defenseless against unbiblical and ungodly precepts. They are continually learning about everything except **the knowledge of the truth**. Because legalism deals only in outward performance, it is very attractive. Many such women, and men as well, are glad to find a way that promises to make them right with God simply by adhering to certain outward forms and conforming to certain behavioral standards.

Epignōsis (**knowledge**) refers to deep understanding, comprehension, and discernment, not merely awareness of factual truths. It is the **knowledge of the truth** that God wants all of His children to have and for which our Lord interceded on our behalf: "Sanctify them in the truth; Thy word is truth" (John 17:17). In fact, God "desires *all men* to be saved and to come to the knowledge of the truth" (1 Tim. 2:4, emphasis added; cf. 2 Tim. 2:25; 2 Peter 3:9). Reflecting that divine love, Paul sought the salvation even of those who were "in opposition" to the gospel, hoping that, "perhaps God [would] grant them repentance leading to the knowledge of the truth" (2 Tim. 2:25).

OPPOSERS OF THE TRUTH

And just as Jannes and Jambres opposed Moses, so these men also oppose the truth, men of depraved mind, rejected as regards the faith. But they will not make further progress; for their folly will be obvious to all, as also that of those two came to be. (3:8–9)

Although **Jannes and Jambres** are not mentioned in Exodus or anywhere else in the Old Testament, they may have been among the magicians in the pharaoh's court who duplicated many of the miracles the Lord performed through Moses. Because **Jannes** perhaps means "he who seduces" and **Jambres** "he who makes rebellion," those may have been symbolic names given to these men at a later time. Jewish tradition holds that they pretended to convert to Judaism in order to subvert Moses' divine assignment to liberate Israel from Egypt, that they led in making and worshiping the golden calf while Moses was on Mt. Sinai receiving the Law from God, and that they were slaughtered by the Levites along with the other idolaters (see Ex. 32). That possibility is consistent with Paul's warning about false leaders who corrupt the church from within. **Just as** those two men **opposed Moses** in his teaching and leading ancient Israel, so **these men** in Ephesus **also oppose[d] the truth** of the gospel.

If **Jannes and Jambres** were indeed among the Egyptian magicians, Paul may be warning that, similarly, **these men** in the early church also might perform magical feats. They may have been like the "false Christs and false prophets [who] will arise" in the last days, "and will show great signs and wonders, so as to mislead, if possible, even the elect" (Matt. 24:24; cf. 2 Thess. 2:9).

Those false teachers were **men of depraved mind.** The Greek word behind **depraved mind** is a perfect passive participle, indicating an established, continuous, and unalterable condition. It was of such reprobates that Paul declared, "And just as they did not see fit to acknowledge God any longer, God gave them over to a depraved mind, to do those things which are not proper, . . . and, although they know the ordinance of God, that those who practice such things are worthy of death, they not only do the same, but also give hearty approval to those who practice them" (Rom. 1:28, 32).

Because they had rejected the faith, they were themselves **rejected** by God **as regards the faith.** *Adokimos* (rejected) was used of metals that did not pass the test of purity and were discarded. The word also was used of counterfeits of various sorts. The fact that the men were rejected as regards the faith makes clear that Paul was speaking of individuals within the church who claimed to be Christians but were not.

The apostle admonished members of the church in Corinth, "Test yourselves to see if you are in the faith; examine yourselves! Or do you not recognize this about yourselves, that Jesus Christ is in you—unless indeed you fail the test [*adokimos*]?" (2 Cor. 13:5; cf. vv. 6–7). Paul used the word in his previous letter to that church, expressing fear that "possibly, after I have preached to others, I myself should be disqualified [*adokimos*]" (1 Cor. 9:27). He was not, of course, speaking of being disqualified from salvation, as were the men who were **rejected as regards the faith,** but of being disqualified as a usable instrument, a vessel of honor, of the Lord in ministry.

Paul assured Timothy that, despite the great turmoil and damage they cause the church, such men **will not make further progress.** In other words, they can seriously harm the church and can prevent many unsaved from becoming saved; but they cannot rob His redeemed people of salvation. Jesus Himself assures us that "the gates of Hades shall not overpower" His church (Matt. 16:18), and that "all that the Father gives Me shall come to Me, and the one who comes to Me I will certainly not cast out" (John 6:37). Until the Lord returns, "false Christs and false prophets will arise, and will show signs and wonders, in order, if possible, to lead the elect astray" (Mark 13:22). But they **will not make further progress** in their evil schemes.

Many times throughout history, the church has been so fiercely persecuted that believers have feared not only for their own lives but for the very existence of the church. But God has a boundary that proscribes the work of Satan, not only in the church but in the world. He is on a divine tether that he can neither break nor lengthen.

Sooner or later the **folly** of false teachers and preachers becomes obvious to all of God's people, **as also** did the folly of **those two,** Jannes and Jambres, in ancient Israel. While these "evil men and impostors will proceed from bad to worse, deceiving and being deceived" (v. 13), their plunge into the depth of sin and error, which deceives them and other ungodly men, ceases to deceive the people of God, who see the error clearly.

This passage holds several lessons, explicit or implicit, for believers today. First, we must realize that the church is in spiritual warfare, a warfare that will intensify as Christ's second coming draws nearer. Second, we must be doctrinally discerning, testing every message that claims to be Christian against God's Word, as did the God-fearing Jews of Berea, who "received the word with great eagerness," but carefully examined "the Scriptures daily, to see whether these things" that Paul and Silas preached "were so" (Acts 17:11).

Third, we must be pure and holy, vessels of honor for the Lord to use. Christ's own righteousness is our protection against false teachers, false doctrine, and ungodly living. Fourth, we must be patient, a difficult task for many Christians today who want instant answers to their questions and immediate resolution of their problems. We know the ultimate outcome is certain, that victory already belongs to Christ and His church, but the actual time of victory may be further away than we would like to think. In the meanwhile, our responsibility is to remain faithful (see 1 Cor. 4:2).

The church today faces times of unparalleled difficulty and danger. As extraordinary opportunities for spreading the gospel increase with rapidity after the breakup of much of the former Communist world, attacks on that church are also increasing with great speed. Heresy, apostasy, self-will, and their accompanying moral decadence are engulfing the evangelical church. Like cancer cells that rebel against the body, these evils are in rebellion against God by corrupting and weakening the church, the body of Christ. Also like cancer cells, the evils multiply rapidly and choke out and destroy normal cells. Much like white cells in the blood, which will not attack cancerous cells because they are identified with the body, many naive and careless church leaders take no action against corruption in the church simply because the corruption hides behind the guise of orthodoxy. Simply put, much of the church is in rebellion against the Lord.

In the days ahead, the escalation of violence against the kingdom of God by the kingdom of darkness will intensify. As in any warfare, there will be times of relative calm, but God's Word assures us of ever-increasing wickedness, which will culminate in the appearance of Antichrist, the ultimate deceiver and enemy of God except for Satan himself. Like the wolves that would come into the flock at Ephesus from within and try to destroy it (Acts 20:29–30), Antichrist, along with other false christs, false apostles, and false prophets, will come from within Christendom.

Before the Antichrist appears, Paul informs us, the great apostasy will come first, which, by definition, is a falling away, or defection, from God and His truth. At the peak of his power, Antichrist, "the man of lawlessness, . . . the son of destruction, who opposes and exalts himself above every so-called god or object of worship, [will take] his seat in the temple of God, displaying himself as being God, . . . the one whose coming is in accord with the activity of Satan, with all power and signs and false wonders" (2 Thess. 2:2–5, 9). We know that his defeat is certain, because "the Lord will slay [him] with the breath of His mouth and bring [him] to an end by the appearance of His coming" (v. 8). But before that final defeat is accomplished—before and during the great apostasy and before the Lord takes His own to Himself at the Rapture— the church will continue to experience expanded assaults from the adversary.

Even now, the attacks against God Himself and against His truth and His righteousness come from so many sides and in so many forms that it is hard for His people to know which front to defend. Discerning Christians are hard put to know which falsehood to refute or moral compromise to oppose. No believer, no matter how gifted and willing, is able to fight on all fronts. But we are not called to win God's battles single-handedly and are presumptuous and foolish to try. He does, however, expect us to yield to Him all that we are and have and to be willing to be used wherever and in whatever way He leads.

Standing
Against Apostasy

8

But you followed my teaching, conduct, purpose, faith, patience, love, perseverance, persecutions, and sufferings, such as happened to me at Antioch, at Iconium and at Lystra; what persecutions I endured, and out of them all the Lord delivered me! And indeed, all who desire to live godly in Christ Jesus will be persecuted. But evil men and impostors will proceed from bad to worse, deceiving and being deceived. You, however, continue in the things you have learned and become convinced of, knowing from whom you have learned them; (3:10–14)

As mentioned in the Introduction, Paul had three overriding priorities in his life: to know Christ, to defend Christ's truth (Scripture), and to minister in Christ's name. A major part of both of his letters to Timothy focuses on the second priority, defending God's revealed truth.

There is much relational preaching today that attempts to make people feel better about themselves and about how God might feel about them, but there is little forceful defense of the full truth. As in most periods of church history, strong and effective defenders of the faith are at a premium. Not many pastors and teachers cry out for doctrinal and moral purity, for right belief and right living.

The New Testament church faced the same deficiency. "Beloved, while I was making every effort to write you about our common salvation," Jude admonished, "I felt the necessity to write to you appealing that you contend earnestly for the faith which was once for all delivered to the saints. For certain persons have crept in unnoticed, those who were long beforehand marked out for this condemnation, ungodly persons who turn the grace of our God into licentiousness and deny our only Master and Lord, Jesus Christ" (Jude 3–4).

Paul here continues to focus on Timothy's service as a strong and loyal defender of the faith, pointing up two necessary qualifications for such a defender: having a strong example as his spiritual mentor (vv. 10–13) and having strong convictions built into a spiritual foundation (v. 14). A third qualification, strong adherence to scriptural authority and sufficiency, will be discussed in the following commentary chapter. Because Timothy already had observed these qualifications, their mention here is by way of reminder and summary. Timothy should have no excuse for not being strong and triumphant in battling apostasy, because he had been privileged to observe the noblest soldier in battle—Paul.

A Strong Example As Spiritual Mentor

But you followed my teaching, conduct, purpose, faith, patience, love, perseverance, persecutions, and sufferings, such as happened to me at Antioch, at Iconium and at Lystra; what persecutions I endured, and out of them all the Lord delivered me! And indeed, all who desire to live godly in Christ Jesus will be persecuted. But evil men and impostors will proceed from bad to worse, deceiving and being deceived. (3:10–13)

The conjunction **but** marks a contrast and a change of emphasis. The faithful character and ministry of Paul are contrasted with the ungodly character and ministry of the false preachers and teachers (the "men," v. 2) mentioned in verses 1–9. The apostle tells his son in the faith that, unlike those heretics, "**you followed my** life and ministry." Paul reminds him of the character of that ministry to lead up to the command in verse 14 to "continue in the things you have learned and become convinced of." That is the key command in this section. Timothy had the best training by spending several decades with Paul. He knew firsthand what it took to combat error and to preserve the truth. This was no time to fail under the pressure of difficulty.

Except for the Twelve and the other disciples who were taught by Jesus Himself during His incarnation, no Christian has had a greater example and mentor than Timothy had in Paul.

Often more than we realize, we are influenced by those we have lived with, worked with, and served with. Sometimes the influence is for good, sometimes for bad. Sometimes it is conscious and direct and sometimes unconscious and indirect. For that reason it is of inestimable importance that, insofar as we are able to determine it for ourselves, we should take great care in choosing those we associate with, especially if they are in positions to influence us spiritually.

In contrast to the false teachers (vv. 1–9), Timothy had observed closely the power of the truth. *Parakoloutheō* (**followed**) literally means to accompany and was used metaphorically of conforming to something as a matter of conviction. In ancient Greece, philosophers used the word to describe the close relationship between a teacher and his disciple, or student. It meant "to study with at close quarters" or "to take as an example to follow." William Barclay says of this term,

> It means to follow a person *physically*, to stick by him through thick and thin, to be by his side in fair weather and in foul. It means to follow a person *mentally*, to attend diligently to his teaching, and fully to understand the meaning and the significance of what he says. It means to follow a person *spiritually*, not only to understand what he says, but also to carry out his ideas, and to be the kind of person that he wishes us to be. (*The Letters to Timothy, Titus and Philemon* [Philadelphia: Westminster, 1957], 224)

That comprehensive meaning certainly represents what Paul had in mind. He meant for Timothy to pattern his beliefs, his thinking, and his lifestyle after him. Although in more detail, he was telling his disciple, beloved friend, and spiritual son what he had told believers in Corinth some ten years earlier: "I exhort you therefore, be imitators of me" (1 Cor. 4:16). "For this reason," he continued, "I have sent to you Timothy, who is my beloved and faithful child in the Lord, and he will remind you of my ways which are in Christ, just as I teach everywhere in every church" (v. 17). Even at that earlier date, he had great confidence in Timothy. Just as he had trusted him to minister faithfully in Corinth he now trusted him to minister faithfully in Ephesus.

Like all of us, Timothy had temptations to weakness and vacillation, and he may have been in such a struggle when Paul wrote him this second letter. Still, the apostle was certain that, with proper encouragement and reliance on the Lord, Timothy would regain his former commitment and zeal.

In the Greek text, the definite article precedes each of the descriptive nouns in verses 10 and 11, grammatically connecting each to the possessive pronoun **my** and thereby giving it repeated emphasis.

The idea is, **But you followed my teaching, [my] conduct, [my] purpose,** and so on.

Every church, Christian college, Bible school, seminary, and other Christian organization should be led by and, in turn, reproduce leaders who not only are orthodox in doctrine and moral in lifestyle but also are courageous and committed defenders of the faith. They should be willing to follow the Lord and lead His church in dangerous times and circumstances and at any cost steadfastly hold up the banner of God's divine revelation in Scripture.

The nine leadership qualities, or characteristics, mentioned in 3:10–13 can be divided into three categories: ministry duties (**teaching, conduct, purpose,** v. 10a), personal virtues (**faith, patience, love, perseverance,** v. 10b), and difficult experiences, summarized by **persecutions and sufferings** (vv. 11–13).

MINISTRY DUTIES

my teaching, conduct, purpose (3:10a)

Didaskalia (**teaching**) is a general term referring to instruction, or "doctrine," as it is sometimes rendered. The reference here is to the specific, divinely inspired, apostolic **teaching** that Timothy had heard expounded so often and so carefully by Paul (**my**), his beloved mentor. A few verses later he reminds Timothy that "all Scripture is inspired by God and profitable for teaching [*didaskalia*], for reproof, for correction, for training in righteousness" (v. 16). This **teaching** included all "the things which [Timothy had] heard from [Paul] in the presence of many witnesses," truths he, in turn, was to "entrust to faithful men, who [would] be able to teach others also" (2:2).

Because he was "an apostle of Christ Jesus by the will of God" (1:1), Paul's **teaching** was apostolic teaching and therefore divine teaching. The time would soon come when Timothy's hearers would "not endure sound doctrine; but wanting to have their ears tickled, they [would] accumulate for themselves teachers in accordance to their own desires" (4:3). For that reason Paul had just commanded, "I solemnly charge you in the presence of God and of Christ Jesus, who is to judge the living and the dead, and by His appearing and His kingdom: preach the word; be ready in season and out of season; reprove, rebuke, exhort, with great patience and instruction" (vv. 1–2).

Timothy had observed and was to continue following Paul's **conduct,** his lifestyle, his pattern of daily living. Like Paul's, Timothy's living had been consistent with his teaching. He had lived what he preached.

That combination is imperative for any effective ministry. God is able to bring good out of any preaching and teaching of His authentic Word. Even though some preachers and teachers "proclaim Christ out of selfish ambition, rather than from pure motives," Paul nevertheless rejoiced that "whether in pretense or in truth," Christ was proclaimed (Phil. 1:17–18). Yet the work of Christ is subject to ridicule and is seriously hindered when an ungodly life contradicts a godly message. Only the Lord knows how much damage to His kingdom and to His name is caused by the moral failure of those He entrusts with proclaiming and demonstrating the gospel.

A third ministry duty Timothy had observed in Paul was that of having a godly **purpose.** A leader's **purpose** relates to his personal motive for service, the driving passion of his heart. Paul was under compulsion, confessing, "Woe is me if I do not preach the gospel" (1 Cor. 9:16). Yet his was an inner compulsion, a voluntary yielding of all that he had to the Lord, to the Lord's worship, the Lord's service, and the Lord's people. He was not forced by God to minister but willingly and gladly served everywhere just as he had at Ephesus. He reminded the elders of that church, "You yourselves know, from the first day that I set foot in Asia, how I was with you the whole time, serving the Lord with all humility and with tears and with trials, . . . how I did not shrink from declaring to you anything that was profitable, and teaching you publicly and from house to house, solemnly testifying to both Jews and Greeks of repentance toward God and faith in our Lord Jesus Christ" (Acts 20:18–21). Wherever Paul ministered, he could say what he said to them: "I testify to you this day, that I am innocent of the blood of all men. For I did not shrink from declaring to you the whole purpose of God" (vv. 26–27). He continually discharged his responsibility to proclaim, without compromise or deflection, the gospel of Jesus Christ and the full counsel of God's Word.

That driving inner force creates a life of integrity and faithfulness, a life in which professed truth is lived truth. Such things as creature comforts, self-love, self-fulfillment, self-promotion, and self-preservation had been of no consequence to Paul, nor should they be to Timothy. The single great motive of their lives was the unreserved passion to fulfill the **purpose** of their divine calling to the glory of God.

PERSONAL VIRTUES

faith, patience, love, perseverance, (3:10b)

Paul also wanted Timothy to continue in **faith.** As noted in the discussion of 2:22, *pistis* (**faith**) is here better rendered "faithfulness," as it is in referring to God in Romans 3:3 and to the fruit of the Spirit in Galatians 5:22 (cf. 1 Tim. 2:15; 4:12). The apostle is not referring to saving faith but to the faithfulness and trustworthiness of those who are already saved. The idea is that of faithfully living the truth that is professed.

A second personal virtue of Paul known to Timothy was **patience,** which translates *makrothumia,* rather than *hupomonē,* the more common term for "patience" in the New Testament. *Makrothumia* carries the additional ideas of steadfastness and long-suffering. Paul is speaking of the resolute and persistent spirit of the servant of Christ who never gives up and never gives in, regardless of the cost. Such patience is more than an attitude; it is a determined way of life and is a certain mark of the Christian who lives in uncompromising devotion to his Lord and to the work of the kingdom.

Because God Himself is loving, no devoted servant of His can be without love. This is the volitional, purposeful, unselfish **love** (*agapē*) that is superior even to faith and hope (1 Cor. 13:13) and is the first fruit of the Spirit (Gal. 5:22). We are to "walk in love, just as Christ also loved [us], and gave Himself up for us, an offering and a sacrifice to God as a fragrant aroma" (Eph. 5:2). We are to "love one another, for love is from God; and everyone who loves is born of God and knows God" (1 John 4:7). **Love,** in fact, is so crucial to the Christian life that "the one who does not love does not know God, for God is love" (v. 8); and, on the other hand, "the one who abides in love abides in God, and God abides in him" (v. 16). Jesus' final petition to the Father on our behalf was "that the love wherewith Thou didst love Me may be in them, and I in them" (John 17:26).

As noted above, *hupomonē* is commonly translated "patience," but in this context the idea is more that of **perseverance,** not so much with difficult people (as earlier in this verse, "patience," *makrothumia*) as with difficult circumstances.

Hupomonē carries the idea of remaining under, and it sometimes is translated "endurance." In 2 Corinthians 6:4, Paul reminds his readers of his own "endurance [*hupomonē*], in afflictions, in hardships, in distresses." The writer of Hebrews reminds every believer of the "need of endurance [*hupomonē*], so that when [we] have done the will of God, [we] may receive what was promised" (Heb. 10:36), referring to "great reward" from the Lord (v. 35).

DIFFICULT EXPERIENCES

persecutions, and sufferings, such as happened to me at Antioch, at Iconium and at Lystra; what persecutions I endured,

and out of them all the Lord delivered me! And indeed, all who desire to live godly in Christ Jesus will be persecuted. But evil men and impostors will proceed from bad to worse, deceiving and being deceived. (3:11–13)

Like Paul, Timothy should be made stronger and his preaching made more effective because of his **persecutions and sufferings** for the sake of Christ.

Diōgmos (**persecutions**) is from the verb *diōkō,* which has the literal meaning of putting to flight. Because of their refusal to compromise or cease proclaiming the gospel, both Paul and Timothy often had been put to flight as fugitives from the **persecutions** of both Jews and pagans.

Before his conversion, Paul himself had been the greatest persecutor of Christians. Known then as Saul and "still breathing threats and murder against the disciples of the Lord, [he] went to the high priest, and asked for letters from him to the synagogues at Damascus, so that if he found any belonging to the Way, both men and women, he might bring them bound to Jerusalem" (Acts 9:1–2). He later confessed before a Jewish multitude in Jerusalem, "I persecuted this Way to the death, binding and putting both men and women into prisons" (Acts 22:4).

But the persecutor became the persecuted. Soon after his conversion, while he was preaching the gospel in Damascus and probably after his three years in Arabia (Gal. 1:17), "the Jews plotted together to do away with him" (Acts 9:23). From that day on, persecution was an almost constant companion. In Pisidian Antioch, where many Jews believed the gospel, others there "were filled with jealousy, and began contradicting the things spoken by Paul, and were blaspheming" (Acts 13:45). Many years before he wrote the second letter to Timothy, Paul could say of his own sufferings, as compared to certain Christian leaders who boasted "according to the flesh, . . ."

Are they servants of Christ? (I speak as if insane) I more so; in far more labors, in far more imprisonments, beaten times without number, often in danger of death. Five times I received from the Jews thirty-nine lashes. Three times I was beaten with rods, once I was stoned, three times I was shipwrecked, a night and a day I have spent in the deep. I have been on frequent journeys, in dangers from rivers, dangers from robbers, dangers from my countrymen, dangers from the Gentiles, dangers in the city, dangers in the wilderness, dangers on the sea, dangers among false brethren; I have been in labor and hardship, through many sleepless nights, in hunger and thirst, often without food, in cold and exposure. (2 Cor. 11:23–27)

Besides suffering "from such external things," he also suffered because of "the daily pressure upon [him] of concern for all the churches" (v. 28).

Timothy often shared **sufferings** with Paul. He was with the apostle "when the Jews of Thessalonica found out that the word of God had been proclaimed by Paul in Berea also, [and] came there likewise, agitating and stirring up the crowds" against him (Acts 17:13; cf. vv. 14–15). He was with Paul in Corinth, when unbelieving Jews "resisted and blasphemed" the gospel (18:6).

Timothy was with Paul during many, if not all, of the **sufferings** that **happened to [him] at Antioch, at Iconium and at Lystra.** Those three cities were in Timothy's home province of Galatia, the first place during Paul's missionary journeys where Luke mentions hostility against him (see Acts 13:45, 50). **Lystra** was Timothy's hometown, where he doubtless saw Paul heal the man who had been born crippled and where he witnessed the apostle's being stoned and left for dead (Acts 14:8–10, 19). During his first encounter with Paul and for the next several decades, Timothy had the unparalleled privilege of living beside and working with this man of great courage, resolution, and character.

When this letter was written, Timothy himself was facing opposition and ridicule, the normal preludes of **sufferings.** As far as we know, he did not suffer to the same degree as his mentor, but with the apostle he could say to those to whom he ministered, "If we are afflicted, it is for your comfort and salvation; or if we are comforted, it is for your comfort, which is effective in the patient enduring of the same sufferings which we also suffer" (2 Cor. 1:6). He also could say with Paul, "I consider that the sufferings of this present time are not worthy to be compared with the glory that is to be revealed to us" (Rom. 8:18) and, "I am well content with weaknesses, with insults, with distresses, with persecutions, with difficulties, for Christ's sake; for when I am weak, then I am strong" (2 Cor. 12:10).

While in Athens, Paul sent Timothy, his "brother and God's fellow worker in the gospel of Christ," back to Thessalonica, "to strengthen and encourage" believers there, in order that "no man may be disturbed by these afflictions; for you yourselves know that we have been destined for this. For indeed when we were with you, we kept telling you in advance that we were going to suffer affliction; and so it came to pass, as you know" (1 Thess. 3:2–4).

Yet, "with all those **persecutions I endured,** Paul continued, I can say that **out of them all the Lord delivered me!**" He could proclaim with David, "Many are the afflictions of the righteous; but the Lord delivers him out of them all" (Ps. 34:19). He could say with Shadrach, Meshach, and Abednego, "Our God whom we serve is able to deliver us from the furnace of blazing fire; and He will deliver us" (Dan. 3:17).

Timothy knew God had delivered Paul, and that knowledge should have reinforced his own courage to stand against the apostate teachers and persecutors.

Paul and Timothy were not exceptions, because **all who desire to live godly in Christ Jesus will be persecuted.** That also was Jesus' promise. "If the world hates you," He said,

> you know that it has hated Me before it hated you. If you were of the world, the world would love its own; but because you are not of the world, but I chose you out of the world, therefore the world hates you. Remember the word that I said to you, "A slave is not greater than his master." If they persecuted Me, they will also persecute you; if they kept My word, they will keep yours also. But all these things they will do to you for My name's sake, because they do not know the One who sent Me. (John 15:18–21)

Self-centered Christians who serve the Lord halfheartedly seldom have to pay a price for their faith. They are of little threat to Satan's work because they are of little benefit to Christ's.

It is those **who desire to live godly in Christ Jesus [who] will be persecuted.** The faithful believer should expect persecution and suffering for Christ's sake. Not every godly believer will be maligned, imprisoned, tortured, or martyred for his faith. Even Paul did not face unrelieved mistreatment. But all faithful believers should expect opposition from the world and realize that, when opposition becomes severe enough, they will suffer for their faith, just as did Paul and Timothy.

Persecution of the godly will continue until the Lord returns, because **evil men and impostors will proceed from bad to worse, deceiving and being deceived.** These are the very **evil men and impostors** Paul has vividly described in the first nine verses of this chapter.

Ponēros (**evil**) refers to malignant character or activity. In the parable of the sower, Jesus used the word to describe Satan, "the evil one [who] comes and snatches away" the good seed of the Word that is sown in the heart of a hearer (Matt. 13:19). **Impostors** translates *goēs*, which literally refers to one who wails or howls. Because sorcerers, wizards, and magicians commonly used wails in their incantations, the term was sometimes used to describe such people, and hence was used of any deceivers or **impostors.** If the Jannes and Jambres of verse 8 were among the magicians of Pharaoh's court, **impostors** obviously could here carry the meaning of sorcerer. But Paul's warning to Timothy applies to impostors of any sort who pervert God's Word.

Such enemies of Christ **will proceed from bad to worse.** Paul does not specifically state whether the regression is internal or external, and it seems likely he was referring to both. As men themselves **proceed from bad to worse,** so does their influence on others.

Paul has already given assurance that there are limits to how effective these enemies of the faith can be. They "will not make further progress" (v. 9a), because their stupidity eventually becomes apparent to those who know the truth. "Their folly," like that of Jannes and Jambres (v. 8), "will be obvious to all" (v. 9b). While they are **deceiving** others, and **being deceived** by their own wicked foolishness, the people of God will eventually expose them for what they are.

STRONG CONVICTIONS BUILT
INTO A SPIRITUAL FOUNDATION

You, however, continue in the things you have learned and become convinced of, knowing from whom you have learned them; (3:14)

A second characteristic of effective defenders of the faith is that of strong convictions being built into a solid spiritual foundation. More often than not, such leaders have been reared in a family where God's Word was loved and exalted, in practice as well as in principle.

That was Timothy's heritage. Near the beginning of this letter, Paul reminded him "of the sincere faith within you, which first dwelt in your grandmother Lois, and your mother Eunice, and I am sure that it is in you as well" and admonished him "to kindle afresh the gift of God which is in you" (1:5–6). He now repeats that admonition, saying, in effect, "Unlike the evil men and impostors about which I just gave warning, **you, however,** are fundamentally different. Whereas they are unbelievers and are characterized by self-love and its many related sins (vv. 1–9), you belong to the Lord and have emulated the godly virtues I have through God's grace (vv. 10–11)."

Like many other verbs in this epistle (see, e.g., "abstain," 2:19; "flee," "pursue," v. 22; "refuse," v. 23), **continue** translates a present active imperative, which has the force of a command. **Have learned** is from *mantanō,* which is related to *mathētēs* ("disciple") and carries the connotation of intentional learning by inquiry and observation. Timothy had not **learned** from Scripture and from Paul incidentally but by intent. He had pursued and **become convinced** of the truths of Scripture—fixed, nonnegotiable truths that are not subject to compromise or dilution. It was those strong convictions, held with equally strong tenacity, that made Timothy a worthy prospect to follow in the footsteps of Paul.

Knowing and remembering the godly people **from whom** he had **learned** those truths was, in itself, a source of great strength and encouragement. **Whom** translates a plural pronoun, indicating Timothy's obligation to several teachers and examples. To successfully learn spiritual convictions from others and to hold them as your own, it is necessary not only to hear them clearly taught but to see them consistently lived.

The Work
of the Word

9

and that from childhood you have known the sacred writings
which are able to give you the wisdom that leads to salvation
through faith which is in Christ Jesus. All Scripture is inspired
by God and profitable for teaching, for reproof, for correction,
for training in righteousness; that the man of God may be adequate, equipped for every good work. (3:15–17)

No other passage in the New Testament speaks so concisely of
the nature and work of God's Word in salvation and sanctification. In
this text, the spiritually transforming power of divine revelation is de-
lineated.

SCRIPTURE PROVIDES
INSTRUCTION FOR SALVATION

and that from childhood you have known the sacred writings
which are able to give you the wisdom that leads to salvation
through faith which is in Christ Jesus. (3:15)

Scripture is the source of saving truth (cf. Ps. 19:7; Mark 4:14–20; John 5:24, 39; James 1:18). The truth of the Word, when mixed with faith in Jesus Christ, empowered by the Holy Spirit, leads to spiritual life. In his letter to the church in Rome, Paul asks rhetorically, "How shall they [unbelievers] hear without a preacher?" (Rom. 10:14), and later explains that "faith comes from hearing, and hearing by the word of Christ" (v. 17). The Word presented by human witness is God's plan for reaching people with the gospel.

The women who heard Paul preach the Word of God at a Jewish place of prayer outside Philippi illustrate that pattern. Luke reports that "a certain woman named Lydia, from the city of Thyatira, a seller of purple fabrics, a worshiper of God, was listening; and the Lord opened her heart to respond to the things spoken by Paul" (Acts 16:14). God has chosen believers to be His spokesmen to bring His saving truth to others.

Timothy had the privilege of hearing the Word in the most marvelous manner through his family—because **from childhood**, or more literally "from infancy," he had been taught and had **known the sacred writings.** It was at the knees of his "grandmother Lois, and [his] mother Eunice" (1:5) that he was led to saving faith, and it was in their lives that he first saw genuine godliness.

Among Greek-speaking Jews, of which there were many in the time of the early church, the Jewish Scriptures (our Old Testament) were often referred to as *hieros grammata* (**the sacred writings**). It was on those **sacred writings** that the faith of Lois and Eunice was built and on which the faith and devotion of Timothy was built as well. As they became exposed to New Testament truth, the reality of the Old Testament anticipation turned to realization.

Timothy may not have had the constitutional strength of Paul and was more easily intimidated and discouraged. But he did not lack a foundation for strength of faith or character. Paul admonished him to hold on and to stand firm, but he never had to correct Timothy for faulty doctrine or sinful living. Both as a child under his mother and grandmother and as a young man under Paul, he had been taught well and had learned well. He was qualified to take the revelation he had heard from Paul "in the presence of many witnesses" and to "entrust [it] to faithful men, who [would] be able to teach others also" (2:2).

The faith of Timothy's grandmother Lois and his mother, Eunice, (1:5) were built on the Jewish Scriptures, the Old Testament, and it was on those **sacred writings** (*hieros grammata*) that those women helped build the faith and devotion of Timothy.

This text shows that the Old Testament clearly gives **the wisdom that leads to salvation.** From Genesis through Malachi, that **wisdom** reveals the holiness, majesty, and lovingkindness of God and His gracious offer of forgiveness and redemption from sin for those who trust in Him and not themselves and seek His grace and mercy.

The moral law was intended to set a righteous standard which no one could keep, thus confirming every person as a sinner under God's judgment. Since no one could be made righteous by the law, it rendered everyone doomed by guilt. Men were therefore in desperate need of grace and forgiveness, which God was eager to give to those who repented and asked. The sacrifices did not save Jews but showed that they recognized the fact that sin demands death. Every sacrifice made under the Old Covenant depicted the ultimate, perfect, and complete sacrifice of the coming Savior, Jesus Christ,

> who does not need daily, like those high priests, to offer up sacrifices, first for His own sins, and then for the sins of the people, because this He did once for all when He offered up Himself. . . . But when Christ appeared as a high priest of the good things to come, He entered through the greater and more perfect tabernacle, not made with hands, that is to say, not of this creation; and not through the blood of goats and calves, but through His own blood, He entered the holy place once for all, having obtained eternal redemption. (Heb. 7:27; 9:11–12)

Even before it occurred, the death of Jesus Christ provided the satisfaction of divine justice by which God could forgive the penitent. Even before the death of Jesus, salvation was available by grace through faith alone—based on the perfect sacrifice that was yet to be made on the cross.

In the time of Nehemiah a spiritual awakening began in Israel when the people turned to God's Word for wisdom and spiritual renewal. Faced with a new awareness of their sin and of the Lord's holiness, they confessed their sin and sought His forgiveness. By God's mercy, they began to worship with divinely cleansed hearts and in genuine reverence and praise.

> All the people gathered as one man at the square which was in front of the Water Gate, and they asked Ezra the scribe to bring *the book of the law of Moses* which the Lord had given to Israel. Then Ezra the priest brought *the law* before the assembly of men, women, and all who could listen with understanding, on the first day of the seventh month. And he read from it before the square which was in front of the Water Gate from early morning until midday, in the presence of men and women, those who could understand; and all the people were attentive to *the book of the law*. . . .
> And the descendants of Israel separated themselves from all foreigners, and stood and confessed their sins and the iniquities of

their fathers. While they stood in their place, they read from *the book of the law of the Lord their God* for a fourth of the day; and for another fourth they confessed and worshiped the Lord their God. . . .

Now the rest of the people, the priests, the Levites, the gate-keepers, the singers, the temple servants, and all those who had separated themselves from the peoples of the lands to the law of God, their wives, their sons and their daughters, all those who had knowledge and understanding, are joining with their kinsmen, their nobles, and are taking on themselves a curse and an oath to walk in *God's law,* which was given through Moses, God's servant, and to keep and to observe all the commandments of God our Lord, and His ordinances and His statutes. (Neh. 8:1–3; 9:2–3; 10:28–29, emphasis added)

In the parable of the sower, given before the New Testament was written, Jesus explained that "the seed is the word of God" and that the several types of soil represent the different ways in which people respond to God's Word (Luke 8:4–15). The power of the Word has always brought salvation, but its effectiveness in doing so depends on the condition of each heart. The only ones who hear it and understand the wisdom of the Word are "the ones who have heard the word in an honest and good heart, and hold it fast, and bear fruit with perseverance" (v. 15). For them, it **leads to salvation.**

The heart and soul of effective evangelism, therefore, is the faithful preaching, teaching, and witnessing of the truth as it is revealed in Scripture. That is the only "seed" the Lord will bless and bring to fruition. When "a certain lawyer," that is, a scribe, "stood up and put [Jesus] to the test, saying, 'Teacher, what shall I do to inherit eternal life?'" the Lord replied, "What is written in the Law? How does it read to you?" (Luke 10:25–26). In other words, the source of truth regarding eternal life is Scripture and *only* Scripture. The truth of Scripture invariably brings a genuine, Spirit-prompted seeker **to salvation.** This **salvation** is not by works but **through faith** placed **in Christ Jesus** (cf. Rom. 3:19–28; 10:9–10; Eph. 2:8–9).

The Lord Himself declared that fact unequivocally, saying to unbelieving Jews in Jerusalem, "The Father who sent Me, He has borne witness of Me. You have neither heard His voice at any time, nor seen His form. And you do not have His word abiding in you, for you do not believe Him whom He sent. You search the Scriptures, because you think that in them you have eternal life; and it is these that bear witness of Me" (John 5:37–39). In other words, any Jew—or Gentile, for that matter—who had faith in God the Father would also have faith in the Son. In the same way, anyone who truly believed the Old Testament Scriptures would have faith in the Son, because they "bear witness" to Him. "For if you believed Moses," that is, the five books of the Law,

Jesus went on to say, "you would believe Me; for he wrote of Me" (v. 46). "The Law has become our tutor to lead us to Christ," Paul explains, "that we may be justified by faith" (Gal. 3:24).

Peter also used the figure of a seed to represent Scripture, both of the Old and New Testaments. After reminding believers that they had "been born again not of seed which is perishable but imperishable, that is, through the living and abiding word of God," he quoted from Isaiah, saying, "All flesh is like grass, and all its glory like the flower of grass. The grass withers, and the flower falls off, but the word of the Lord abides forever." It was the same saving truth, the same "word," he went on to say, "which was preached to you" (1 Peter 1:23–25; cf. Isa. 40:6–8).

Because Joseph and Mary genuinely trusted in God through His revelation in the Old Testament, they believed—even before Jesus' birth —that the Messiah and Savior, the very Son of God, would be miraculously born through Mary, just as the angels told them (Matt. 1:18–25; Luke 1:26–38). Because they genuinely trusted in God through His revelation in the Old Testament, both Simeon and Anna acknowledged and trusted in Jesus as the Christ, the prophesied Redeemer of Israel and Savior of the world, while He was still an infant (Luke 2:21–38).

It was because he trusted in God and was seeking to understand His revelation through the prophet Isaiah that the Ethiopian eunuch immediately believed Philip's testimony, placed his faith in Christ, and was saved (Acts 8:26–39). It was because they genuinely trusted in God and sought to understand His will that certain Jews in Berea "received the word [of Paul and Silas] with great eagerness, examining the Scriptures daily, to see whether these things were so, . . . [and] therefore believed, along with a number of prominent Greek women and men" (Acts 17:11–12).

To avoid the false trust against which Jesus warned—of trusting the knowledge of Scripture itself to give eternal life (John 5:39)—Paul, like his Lord, makes clear that the words in sacred writings do not in themselves have power to save but rather that **the wisdom** they impart **leads to salvation through faith which is in Christ Jesus.**

Like many Christians in the early church, Timothy and his mother and grandmother believed under both covenants. They had repented and sought the grace and mercy of forgiveness from the God of Abraham, Isaac, and Jacob, of Moses, David, and Elijah. And when they heard the gospel of Jesus Christ, then—like Joseph, Mary, Simeon, and Anna—they knew that God's great promise of the Messiah-Redeemer had been fulfilled, and they immediately believed in Him as Savior and Lord.

Just as were the men and women mentioned in Hebrews 11, every Old Testament saint was saved **through faith which is in Christ Jesus.** Although their spiritual understanding was limited, they were like their "father Abraham, [who] rejoiced to see [Christ's] day, and he saw it and was glad" (John 8:56), and like Moses, who considered "the reproach of Christ greater riches than the treasures of Egypt" (Heb. 11:26). Whatever they may have known or not known about the coming Messiah (cf. 1 Peter 1:10–12), they understood that He would come to suffer for their sins as the sacrifice that would satisfy God. John summed up godly Jewish anticipation when, upon first seeing Jesus, he exclaimed, "Behold, the Lamb of God who takes away the sin of the world!" (John 1:29).

SCRIPTURE PROVIDES
INSTRUCTION FOR SANCTIFICATION

All Scripture is inspired by God and profitable for teaching, for reproof, for correction, for training in righteousness; that the man of God may be adequate, equipped for every good work. (3:16–17)

Before we examine the sanctifying power of Scripture, this crucial statement by Paul must be considered. Some scholars suggest that **All Scripture is inspired** should be translated, "All Scripture inspired by God is . . ," which would leave open the possibility that *some* **Scripture** is *not* inspired by Him. But that rendering would make the Bible worthless as a reliable guide to divine truth, because we would then have no way to determine which part of it is inspired by God and which is not. Men would be left to their own finite and sinful devices and understanding to discover what part of the Bible may be true and which may not, what part is God's Word and what part is human conjecture. Paul's thought is that the Scripture that gives salvation must therefore be inspired by God. The words of men could never transform the inner person (Ps. 19:7).

In addition to the many other specific biblical references to the inspiration and authority of **Scripture**—some of which are mentioned below—it is important to note that similar Greek constructions in other parts of the New Testament (see, e.g., Rom. 7:12; 2 Cor. 10:10; 1 Tim. 1:15; 2:3; 4:4; Heb. 4:17) argue strongly from a grammatical perspective that **all Scripture is inspired** is the proper translation. Scripture is the revelation conveyed, inspiration is the means of that conveyance. In the words originally revealed and recorded, **all Scripture** is God's inerrant Word.

The first predicate adjective that describes **Scripture,** namely, its being **inspired by God,** focuses on the authority of His written Word. *Theopneustos* (**inspired by God**) literally means, "breathed out by God," or simply, "God-breathed." God sometimes breathed His words into the human writers to be recorded much as dictation. He said to Jeremiah: "Behold, I have put My words in your mouth" (Jer. 1:9). But, as clearly seen in Scripture itself, God's divine truth more often flowed through the minds, souls, hearts, and emotions of His chosen human instruments. Yet, by whatever means, God divinely superintended the accurate recording of His divinely breathed truth by His divinely chosen men. In a supernatural way, He has provided His divine Word in human words that any person, even a child, can be led by His Holy Spirit to understand sufficiently to be saved.

It is of utmost importance to understand that it is **Scripture** that is **inspired by God,** not the men divinely chosen to record it. When speaking or writing apart from God's revelation, their thoughts, wisdom, and understanding were human and fallible. They were not inspired in the sense that we commonly use that term of people with extraordinary artistic, literary, or musical genius. Nor were they inspired in the sense of being personal repositories of divine truth which they could dispense at will. Many human authors of Scripture penned other documents, but none of those writings exist today, and, even if discovered, they would not carry the weight of Scripture. We know, for instance, that Paul wrote at least two other letters to the church at Corinth (1 Cor. 5:9; 2 Cor. 2:4), but no copies of those letters have ever been found. The letters doubtless were godly, spiritually insightful, and blessed of the Lord, but they were not Scripture.

Many men who wrote **Scripture,** such as Moses and Paul, were highly trained in human knowledge and wisdom, but that learning was not the source of the divine truth they recorded. David was a highly gifted poet, and that gift doubtless is reflected in the beauty of his psalms, but it was not the source of the divine truths revealed in those psalms.

Scripture first of all and above all is from God and about God, His self-revelation to fallen mankind. From Genesis through Revelation, God reveals His truth, His character, His attributes, and His divine plan for the redemption of man, whom He made in His own image. He even foretells the eventual redemption of the rest of His creation, which "also will be set free from its slavery to corruption into the freedom of the glory of the children of God" and which "groans and suffers the pains of childbirth together until now" (Rom. 8:21–22).

The Bible is not a collection of the wisdom and insights of men, even of godly men. It is God's truth, His own Word in His own words. The psalmist declared, "Forever, O Lord, Thy word is settled in heaven" (Ps. 119:89). God's Word is divinely revealed to men on earth and divinely authenticated in heaven. Peter declares unequivocally, "Know this first of all, that no prophecy of Scripture is a matter of one's own interpretation, for no prophecy was ever made by an act of human will, but men moved by the Holy Spirit spoke from God" (2 Peter 1:20–21). Those God-given, humanly recorded words became God's written Word, inerrant and authoritative as originally given. *Prophēteia* ("prophecy") is not used here in the sense of prediction but in its basic and broader meaning of speaking forth, of proclaiming a message. It carries the same inclusive idea as "the oracles of God," with which ancient Israel had the marvelous privilege of being entrusted (Rom. 3:2). "Interpretation" (2 Peter 1:20b) translates *epilusis*, which refers to something that is released, sent out, or sent forth. In this verse the Greek noun is a genitive of source, indicating origin. In other words, no message of Scripture was originated and sent forth by men's own wisdom and will. Rather, the godly men through whom Scripture was revealed and recorded were divinely instructed and carried along by the Holy Spirit.

Within the Bible itself, "God" and "Scripture" are sometimes used almost interchangeably. Referring to words spoken directly by God to Abraham (Gen. 12:3), Paul wrote that "the Scripture, foreseeing that God would justify the Gentiles by faith, preached the gospel beforehand to Abraham, saying, 'All the nations shall be blessed in you'" (Gal. 3:8). Later in that same chapter the apostle again personifies Scripture as God, declaring that "Scripture has shut up all men under sin, that the promise by faith in Jesus Christ might be given to those who believe" (v. 22). In his letter to the church at Rome, Paul wrote, "For the Scripture says to Pharaoh, 'For this very purpose I raised you up, to demonstrate My power in you, and that My name might be proclaimed throughout the whole earth'" (Rom. 9:17).

When he first preached in Galatia, many years before he wrote his epistle to the churches there, the apostle had declared,

> And we preach to you the good news of the promise made to the fathers, that God has fulfilled this promise to our children in that He raised up Jesus, as it is also written in the second Psalm, "Thou art My Son; today I have begotten Thee." And as for the fact that He raised Him up from the dead, no more to return to decay, He has spoken in this way: "I will give you the holy and sure blessings of David." Therefore He also says in another Psalm, "Thou wilt not allow Thy Holy One to undergo decay." (Acts 13:32–35)

THE INSPIRED AND INERRANT SCRIPTURE

Scripture *is inspired and inerrant in both testaments.* **All Scripture** refers to the New as well as to the Old Testament. As noted above, the *hieros grammata* ("sacred writings") were the Hebrew Scriptures (the Old Testament), which Timothy had been taught from childhood

(v. 15). *Graphē* (Scripture), on the other hand, was commonly used in the early church not only of the Old Testament but also of God's newly revealed Word, in what came to be called the New Testament.

During His earthly ministry, Jesus gave powerful and unambiguous testimony to the divine authority of both testaments. The four gospels contain the first divine revelation after that of the Old Testament prophets, which had ceased some four hundred years earlier. Jesus' declaration that "Scripture [*graphē*] cannot be broken" (John 10:35) applied specifically to the Hebrew Scriptures but also, as will be seen, to the totality of Scripture, that is, to both testaments, which together compose God's written Word.

Early in His ministry, Jesus said of the Old Testament, "Do not think that I came to abolish the Law or the Prophets; I did not come to abolish, but to fulfill. For truly I say to you, until heaven and earth pass away, not the smallest letter or stroke shall pass away from the Law, until all is accomplished" (Matt. 5:17–18). Later He said, "It is easier for heaven and earth to pass away than for one stroke of a letter of the Law to fail" (Luke 16:17).

Jesus repeatedly used divinely revealed truths from the Old Testament to affirm His messiahship. He declared, "He who believes in Me, as the Scripture said, 'From his innermost being shall flow rivers of living water'" (John 7:38), and, "Has not the Scripture said that the Christ comes from the offspring of David, and from Bethlehem, the village where David was?" (John 7:42). As Jesus walked with the two disciples on the Emmaus road after His resurrection, "beginning with Moses and with all the prophets, He explained to them the things concerning Himself in all the Scriptures" (Luke 24:27).

In addition to His teaching that "Scripture [*graphē*] cannot be broken" (John 10:35), Jesus said that "He who rejects Me, and does not receive My sayings has one who judges him; the word I spoke is what will judge him at the last day. For I did not speak on My own initiative, but the Father Himself who sent Me has given Me commandment, what to say, and what to speak. And I know that His commandment is eternal life; therefore the things I speak, I speak just as the Father has told Me" (John 12:48–50). The words of the incarnate Christ are the words of God the Father; therefore, to reject Jesus' words is to reject God's Word.

The men whom God assigned to write the gospels would not have been able in their mere humanness to remember accurately everything Jesus said or did. For that reason Jesus promised that "the Helper, the Holy Spirit, whom the Father will send in My name, He will teach you all things, and bring to your remembrance all that I said to you" (John 14:26; cf. 15:26–27).

The Lord would reveal additional truth after He returned to heaven. "I have many more things to say to you," He said, "but you cannot bear them now. But when He, the Spirit of truth, comes, He will guide you into all the truth; for He will not speak on His own initiative, but whatever He hears, He will speak; and He will disclose to you what is to come. He shall glorify Me; for He shall take of Mine, and shall disclose it to you" (John 16:12–14).

In 1 Timothy, Paul wrote, "The Scripture [*graphē*] says, 'You shall not muzzle the ox while he is threshing,' and 'The laborer is worthy of his wages'" (1 Tim. 5:18). It is important to note that the first quotation is from the Old Testament (Deut. 25:4) and that the second is from Jesus' own lips (Luke 10:7), that is, from the New Testament.

The Pentateuch (the first five books of the Old Testament) contains at least 680 claims to divine inspiration. Such claims are found 418 times in the historical books, 195 times in the poetic books, and 1,307 times in the prophetic books. The New Testament contains more than 300 direct quotations and at least 1,000 indirect references from the Old Testament, almost all of them declaring or implying that they were God's own Word. The book of Hebrews opens with the declaration "God, after He spoke long ago to the fathers in the prophets in many portions and in many ways, in these last days has spoken to us in His Son" (Heb. 1:1–2). The writer was speaking of both testaments, God's speaking through "the prophets" representing the Old and His speaking through "His Son" representing the New.

Many New Testament writers directly testified that they knew they were writing God's Word. Paul reminded believers in Corinth of a truth he doubtless had taught them many times in person when he ministered there: "[These] things we also speak," he said, "not in words taught by human wisdom, but in those taught by the Spirit, combining spiritual thoughts with spiritual words" (1 Cor. 2:13; cf. 16). In his next letter to them he defended his earnestness as well as his authority, saying, "We are not like many, peddling the word of God, but as from sincerity, but as from God, we speak in Christ in the sight of God" (2 Cor. 2:17).

Paul assured the churches in Galatia: "I would have you know, brethren, that the gospel which was preached by me is not according to man. For I neither received it from man, nor was I taught it, but I received it through a revelation of Jesus Christ. . . . He who had set me apart, even from my mother's womb, . . . called me through His grace, [and] was pleased to reveal His Son in me, that I might preach Him among the Gentiles" (Gal. 1:11–12, 15–16). He told the church in Colossae, "Of this church I was made a minister according to the stewardship from God bestowed on me for your benefit, that I might fully carry out the preaching of the word of God, that is, the mystery which has been hidden from the past ages and generations; but has now been manifested to His saints, to whom God willed to make known what is the riches of the glory of this mystery among the Gentiles, which is Christ in you, the hope of glory" (Col. 1:25–27). And to the church at Thessalonica he wrote, "For this reason we also constantly thank God that when you received from us the word of God's message, you accepted it not as the word of men, but for what it really is, the word of God, which also performs its work in you who believe" (1 Thess. 2:13).

Peter recognized that Paul, a fellow apostle, had been used by the Lord to write His Word. Referring to Paul's letters, Peter wrote of "some things [in them that were] hard to understand, which the untaught and unstable distort, as they do also *the rest of the Scriptures,* to their own destruction" (2 Peter 3:16, emphasis added). Jude attests that "the words that were spoken beforehand by the apostles of our Lord Jesus Christ" carried the weight of Scripture, divinely warning that "in the last time there shall be mockers, following after their own ungodly lusts" (Jude 17–18).

No New Testament writer had a greater awareness that he was recording God's own Word than did the apostle John. That awareness is affirmed with particular certainty in the book of Revelation, which begins, "The Revelation of Jesus Christ, which God gave Him to show to His bond-servants, the things which must shortly take place; and He sent and communicated it by His angel to His bond-servant John, who bore witness to the word of God and to the testimony of Jesus Christ, even to all that he saw" (Rev. 1:1–2). A few verses later the apostle says, "I was in the Spirit on the Lord's day, and I heard behind me a loud voice like the sound of a trumpet, saying, 'Write in a book what you see, and send it to the seven churches'" (vv. 10–11). At or near the end of each message to those churches is the admonition "He who has an ear, let him hear what the Spirit says to the churches" (2:7, 11, 17, 29; 3:6, 13, 22). The apostle also makes clear in many other parts of that book that he is writing God's explicitly revealed truth (see, e.g., 19:9; 21:5; 22:6).

It is both remarkable and significant that, although most, if not all, of the human writers were aware they were recording **Scripture** and sometimes were overwhelmed by the truths God revealed to them, they exhibit a total lack of self-consciousness or apology, in the common sense of that word. Together, the biblical writers make some 4,000 claims to be writing God's Word, yet they offer no defense for being employed by God in such an elevated function. Despite their realization of their own sinfulness and fallibility, they wrote with the utter confidence that they spoke infallibly for God and that His revelation itself is its own best and irrefutable defense. "For as the rain and the snow come down from heaven," Isaiah proclaimed for God, "and do not return there without watering the earth, and making it bear and sprout, and furnishing seed to the sower and bread to the eater; so shall My word be which goes forth from My mouth; it shall not return to Me empty, without accomplishing what I desire, and without succeeding in the matter for which I sent it" (Isa. 55:10–11).

Scripture *is inspired and inerrant in its words.* To deny that all of the Bible is **inspired** obviously is to deny that all of the *words* of **Scripture** are **inspired.** Just as obviously, such denial places man as judge over God's Word, acknowledging as authentic and binding only those portions which correspond to one's personal predispositions. Whether the human judgment about inspiration is made by a church council, church tradition, or individual preference, it is based on subjective, sin-tainted, and imperfect knowledge and understanding. When men decide for themselves what to recognize as true and worthwhile, as meaningful and relevant, they vitiate all authority of Scripture. Even when they concur with **Scripture,** the agreement is based on their own human wisdom.

Unless the very *words* of **Scripture** are **inspired** and authoritative, man is left to his own resources to ferret out what *seem to be* underlying divine concepts and principles. But instead of discovering what has been called "the Word behind the words"—that is, the divine truth behind the human words—that approach leads to the very opposite. It presumptuously and self-deceptively "discovers" man's *word,* as it were, behind God's words, judging God's divine truth by the standards of man's sinful inclinations and distorted perceptions. As Paul said to Titus, the commandments of men turn people away from God's truth (Titus 1:14).

Even from a purely logical perspective, to discount the *words* of **Scripture** is to discount all meaning of Scripture. Not only is it impossible to write without using words but also is impossible, except in the most nebulous way, even to think without words. It is as meaningless to speak of thoughts and ideas without words as to speak of music without notes or mathematics without numbers. To repudiate the *words* of **Scripture** is to repudiate the *truths* of **Scripture.**

It is true, of course, that both testaments contain revelations whose bare words God intentionally made cryptic. In some cases, as with Jesus' parables, the purpose was to hide the meaning from willful unbelievers. When the disciples asked Jesus why He spoke to the multitudes in parables, "He answered and said to them, 'To you it has been granted to know the mysteries of the kingdom of heaven, but to them it has not been granted'" (Matt. 13:10–11). In other cases, as with predictive prophecies, even the most godly believers, including the men to whom God revealed the prophecies, could not discern the full meaning. Peter explains, for example, that, "as to this salvation [through Jesus Christ], the prophets who prophesied of the grace that would come to you made careful search and inquiry, seeking to know what person or time the Spirit of Christ within them was indicating as He predicted the sufferings of Christ and the glories to follow. It was revealed to them that they were not serving themselves, but you, in these things which now have been announced to you through those who preached the gospel to you by the Holy Spirit sent from heaven—things into which angels long to look" (1 Peter 1:10–12).

In other words, although **Scripture** never reveals truths apart from words, in some places it reveals words apart from their full truth. The point is this: The *words* of **Scripture** are always inerrant, whether or not they convey their full meaning to those who read them or can be fully understood by our limited comprehension.

When Moses protested to God that he was not qualified to lead Israel because he had "never been eloquent" and was "slow of speech and slow of tongue, . . . the Lord said to him, 'Who has made man's mouth? Or who makes him dumb or deaf, or seeing or blind? Is it not I, the Lord? Now then go, and I, even I, will be with your mouth, and teach you what you are to say'" (Ex. 4:10–12). When Moses continued to object, "the anger of the Lord burned against Moses, and He said, 'Is there not your brother Aaron the Levite? I know that he speaks fluently. . . . And you are to speak to him and put the *words* in his mouth; and I, even I, will be with your mouth and his mouth, and I will teach you what you are to do. Moreover, he shall speak for you to the people; and it shall come about that he shall be as a mouth for you, and you shall be as God to him'" (Ex. 4:14–16, emphasis added).

In Psalm 147, the inseparable relationship between God's Word and His words is clear. The Lord "sends forth His command to the earth; His *word* runs very swiftly. He gives snow like wool; He scatters the frost like ashes. He casts forth His ice as fragments; who can stand before His cold? He sends forth His *word* and melts them; He causes His wind to blow and the waters to flow. He declares His *words* to Jacob, His statutes and His ordinances to Israel" (Ps. 147:15–19, emphasis added). It is only through words that God has revealed His Word.

Jeremiah testified: "The Lord stretched out His hand and touched my mouth, and the Lord said to me, 'Behold, I have put My *words* in your mouth.' . . . Therefore, thus says the Lord, the God of hosts, 'Because you have spoken this word, behold, I am making My words in your mouth fire and this people wood, and it will consume them.' . . . Thy *words* were found and I ate them," the prophet responded, "and Thy *words* became for me a joy and the delight of my heart; for I have been called by Thy name, O Lord God of hosts" (Jer. 1:9; 15:14, 16, emphasis added). Ezekiel made a similar affirmation, saying, "Then [the Lord] said to me, 'Son of man, I am sending you to the sons of Israel, to a rebellious people who have rebelled against Me. . . . But you shall speak My *words* to them whether they listen or not, for they are rebellious.' . . . Moreover, He said to me, 'Son of man, take into your heart all

My *words* which I shall speak to you, and listen closely'" (Ezek. 2:3, 7; 3:10, emphasis added).

In reply to Satan's temptation to make bread from stones in order to satisfy His physical hunger, Jesus quoted from Deuteronomy 8:3, saying, "It is written, 'Man shall not live on bread alone, but on *every word* that proceeds out of the mouth of God'" (Matt. 4:4, emphasis added). Man is fed spiritually by God's "every word," and every revealed word of God is found in His written Word, the Bible. In His last major public discourse, Jesus said, "Heaven and earth will pass away, but My *words* shall not pass away" (Matt. 24:35, emphasis added).

Earlier in His ministry, Jesus proclaimed the essence of the gospel: "Truly, truly, I say to you, he who hears My *word*, and believes Him who sent Me, has eternal life, and does not come into judgment, but has passed out of death into life" (John 5:24, emphasis added). "It is the Spirit who gives life; the flesh profits nothing," He said on another occasion. "The *words* that I have spoken to you are spirit and are life" (John 6:63, emphasis added). "For I did not speak on My own initiative," our Lord again makes clear, "but the Father Himself who sent Me has given Me commandment, what to say, and what to speak. And I know that His commandment is eternal life; therefore the things I speak, I speak just as the Father has told Me" (12:49–50; cf. 14:24). Believing in the Father is believing in the Son, and the Son's words are the Father's words.

Scripture *is inspired and inerrant in everything it teaches and reports.* Some scholars maintain that, because the Bible is not a textbook on such subjects as history, geography, and science, it is inerrant only when it speaks on spiritual and moral matters. But like those who claim to accept the underlying divine concepts and principles of Scripture but not its words, these interpreters also determine by their own resources what is divine and infallible and what is human and fallible. Again, man becomes the judge of Scripture.

Through the centuries, some scholars have pointed to "mistakes" in the Bible, statements about people, places, and things that did not jibe with the accepted "facts" of history, archaeology, or modern science.

Until Copernicus's discovery in the sixteenth century, men assumed that the sun rotated around the earth, because that is how it appears from our earthly perspective. Because we now know that the earth rotates around the sun, many scholars charge the Bible with factual error in reporting that Joshua successfully commanded the sun to stand still and the moon to be stopped (Josh. 10:12–13), whereas it must have been the earth that stood still. But highly trained meteorologists still speak of sunrise and sunset, especially when communicating with the general public. Those phrases are firmly established figures of speech throughout the world, and no sensible person accuses someone of being inaccurate or unscientific for using them. Not only that, but if God created the universe, stopping the rotation of the earth, the sun, or the moon—or of all three—would have been equally simple. It is significant that most people who question the reality of such miraculous events also question many of the clear theological and moral teachings of Scripture as well.

For many years some scholars charged the book of 2 Kings with error for reporting that "the king of Assyria required of Hezekiah king of Judah three hundred talents of silver and thirty talents of gold" (2 Kings 18:14). They based that judgment on an ancient Assyrian record of the transaction that gives the amount of silver as being 800 talents. But later archaeological findings have revealed that, although the Assyrian standard for a talent of gold was the same as that used by Judah and Syria, the standard for silver was considerably different. When adjusted for that difference, the biblical figure was found to be accurate.

Not only is the Bible's *reporting* of history unerring but so is its *prediction* of history. Ezekiel foretold in amazing detail the destruction of Tyre, first by Nebuchadnezzar, later by Alexander the Great (Ezek. 26:1–21; 29:18), and then by Egypt (30:10–26). In similar detail, Nahum predicted the devastation of Nineveh (Nahum 1:15–3:19; cf. Zeph. 2:13, 15), which was conquered and destroyed in 612 B.C. by the Medes and Chaldeans. Both Isaiah (Isa. 13–14; 21:1–10) and Jeremiah (Jer. 50–51) accurately predicted the ultimate destruction of Babylon, which would "never be inhabited or lived in from generation to generation" (Isa. 13:20). That great city was conquered first by Cyrus, founder of the Persian empire and the man whom God prophesied would free His people Israel from Babylonian captivity (Isa. 44:28; 45:1–14). That noble king not only allowed the Jews to return to Jerusalem, but, with an amazing awareness of his divine mission under the true God, charged them to rebuild the temple there and returned to them all the sacred and valuable temple objects pilfered by Nebuchadnezzar (Ezra 1). Other Assyrian and Persian kings successively conquered and plundered Babylon. Its final conquest was by Alexander the Great, who intended to rebuild the city but was prevented by his untimely death at the age of thirty-two. When the capital of the Syrian empire was moved from Babylon to Seleucia by Seleucus Nicator in 312 B.C., Babylon gradually died. By the time of Christ, the city was inhabited primarily by a small group of scholars, and bricks from its rubble were carried away to build houses and walls in surrounding towns. Today the almost barren site of ancient Babylon, located in the southern part of modern Iraq, is valued only for its archaeological significance.

As noted in the first point, God's divine Word, revealed through His divine words, is not itself the means or the power of salvation, but is the agency of it. Near the end of his gospel account, John explained that "these [things] have been written that you may believe that Jesus is the Christ, the Son of God; and that believing you may have life in His name" (John 20:31).

As Peter declared to the Jewish leaders in Jerusalem soon after Pentecost, "Let it be known to all of you, and to all the people of Israel, that by the name of Jesus Christ the Nazarene, whom you crucified, . . . He is the stone which was rejected by you, the builders, but which became the very corner stone. And there is salvation in no one else; for there is no other name under heaven that has been given among men, by which we must be saved" (Acts 4:10–12).

In his letter to the church at Rome, Paul echoes the words of Jesus: "If you confess with your mouth Jesus as Lord, and believe in your heart that God raised Him from the dead, you shall be saved; for with the heart man believes, resulting in righteousness, and with the mouth he confesses, resulting in salvation. . . . So faith comes from hearing, and hearing by the *word of Christ*" (Rom. 10:9–10, 17, emphasis added; cf. James 1:18).

Christ also uses His Word to sanctify and cleanse His church from sin. In his letter to the church at Ephesus, Paul said: "Christ also loved the church and gave Himself up for her; that He might sanctify her, having cleansed her by the washing of water *with the word*" (Eph. 5:25–26, emphasis added). In his first letter to believers at Thessalonica he said, "And for this reason we also constantly thank God that when you received from us the *word of God's message,* you accepted it not as the word of men, but for what it really is, *the word of God,* which also performs its work in you who believe" (1 Thess. 2:13, emphasis added; cf. Phil. 2:16).

The second predicate adjective Paul uses to describe Scripture is **profitable,** which focuses on the sufficiency of God's written Word. **Profitable** translates *ōphelimos,* which includes the ideas of beneficial, productive, and sufficient.

Scripture is sufficient in being comprehensive. Paralleled in the Old Testament only by Psalm 119 and confirmed by Joshua 1:8, these verses supremely affirm the absolute sufficiency of Scripture to meet all the spiritual needs of God's people.

David understood the sufficiency of God's Word, and in one of his most uplifting psalms he exulted:

> The law of the Lord is perfect, restoring the soul; the testimony of the Lord is sure, making wise the simple. The precepts of the Lord are right, rejoicing the heart; the commandment of the Lord is pure, enlightening the eyes. The fear of the Lord is clean, enduring forever; the judgments of the Lord are true; they are righteous altogether. They are more desirable than gold, yes, than much fine gold; sweeter also than

honey and the drippings of the honeycomb. Moreover, by them Thy servant is warned; in keeping them there is great reward. Who can discern his errors? Acquit me of hidden faults. Also keep back Thy servant from presumptuous sins; let them not rule over me; then I shall be blameless, and I shall be acquitted of great transgression. (Ps. 19:7–13)

In verses 7–9 David refers to God's Word by six different titles: God's law, testimony, precepts, commandment, fear (referring to worship), and judgments. In those same verses, he mentions six characteristics of that divine Word: It is perfect, sure, right, pure, clean, and true. Also included are six blessings that the Word brings in the believer's life: It restores the soul, makes wise the simple, rejoices the heart, enlightens the eyes, endures forever, and produces complete righteousness. The remaining verses (10–13) extol the benefits of the work of the Word: It makes rich, delights, rewards, convicts, and protects. It is a marvelous mark of God's loving grace that He has given us every truth, every principle, every standard, and every warning that we will ever need for living out our salvation according to His will.

Scripture also is complete. Jude admonished his readers to "contend earnestly for the faith which was once for all delivered to the saints" (Jude 3). John closes the book of Revelation, as well as the entire Old and New Testaments, with this sobering warning from the Lord: "I testify to everyone who hears the words of the prophecy of this book: if anyone adds to them, God shall add to him the plagues which are written in this book; and if anyone takes away from the words of the book of this prophecy, God shall take away his part from the tree of life and from the holy city, which are written in this book" (Rev. 22:18–19).

False religious systems that claim to be Christian invariably expose their falsehood by their view of Scripture. Mormonism considers *The Book of Mormon* to be as divinely inspired and authoritative as the Bible, in fact more so, because they view that book as being a latter-day, updated revelation from God. Christian Science views *Science and Health, With a Key to the Scriptures* in the same way. Some charismatics claim to have received special revelations from God, which, if genuine, would carry the same divine authority as the Bible. For most of the twentieth century, a large percentage of members and a higher percentage of clergymen in most major Protestant denominations have not recognized the Bible as being wholly revealed by God and inerrant. Those views and many others like them share the common heresy of considering Scripture to be incomplete or inadequate.

It is because of such distorted and destructive views of Scripture within professing Christendom that biblical believers must, more than ever before, "contend earnestly for the faith which was once for all delivered to the saints" (Jude 3). As in the early church, the greatest danger to the church has always been from within. Paul warned the godly, mature church at Ephesus, pastored first by the apostle and then by Timothy, and led by godly elders, "I know that after my departure savage wolves will come in *among you,* not sparing the flock; and from *among your own selves men will arise,* speaking perverse things, to draw away the disciples after them" (Acts 20:29–30, emphasis added).

In the remainder of verse 16, Paul declares that Scripture is **profitable** for believers in four important ways: **for teaching, for reproof, for correction, for training in righteousness.**

THE TEACHING SCRIPTURE

for teaching, (3:16b)

As mentioned in chapter 8 of this commentary in regard to verse 10, *didaskalia* does not refer to the process or method of **teaching** but to its content. In this context, as in most others in the New Testament, *didaskalia* refers specifically and exclusively to divine instruction, or doctrine, given to believers through God's Word, which included not only the Hebrew Scriptures (Old Testament) and the **teaching** of Jesus during His incarnation but also the inspired **teaching** of the apostles and New Testament authors.

"A natural man," Paul explains, "does not accept the things of the Spirit of God; for they are foolishness to him, and he cannot understand them." It is not that the unsaved person is intellectually inferior, but that such truths "are spiritually appraised. But he who is spiritual appraises all things, yet he himself is appraised by no man. For who has known the mind of the Lord, that he should instruct Him? But we have the mind of Christ" (1 Cor. 2:14–16).

While warning believers about the dangerous teachings and work of antichrists, John assures his readers: "You have an anointing from the Holy One, and you all know. . . . As for you, let that abide in you which you heard from the beginning. If what you heard from the beginning abides in you, you also will abide in the Son and in the Father. . . . And as for you, the anointing which you received from Him abides in you, and you have no need for anyone to teach you; but as His anointing teaches you about all things, and is true and is not a lie, and just as it has taught you, you abide in Him" (1 John 2:20, 24, 27).

When it comes to godly living and godly service, to growing in "the discipline and instruction of the Lord" (Eph. 6:4), God-breathed Scripture provides for us the comprehensive and complete body of divine truth necessary to live as our heavenly Father desires for us to live. The wisdom and guidance for fulfilling everything He commands us to believe, think, say, and do is found in His inerrant, authoritative, comprehensive, and completed Word.

Even after conversion, trust in one's own wisdom is a severe hindrance to correct understanding of Scripture and to full usefulness in the Lord's service. The counsel to "trust in the Lord with all your heart, and do not lean on your own understanding" (Prov. 3:5) is every bit as valid for Christians as it was for Old Testament saints.

Throughout church history, the Lord has uniquely and wonderfully sustained and blessed the spiritual lives and influence of believers who, because of imprisonment, illiteracy, isolation, or other restrictions beyond their control, could not study His Word. But the teaching of Scripture is the divine body of truth without which no believer who has access to it can live, minister, or witness effectively. Tragically, some of the most biblically illiterate believers in our day live in lands where God's Word is readily available and where scriptural preaching, teaching, and literature are abundant.

It goes without saying that it is impossible to believe, understand, and follow what you do not even know. It is completely futile, as well as foolish, to expect to live a spiritual life without knowing spiritual truth. Biblically untaught believers, especially those in biblically untaught churches, are easy prey for false teachers. They are spiritual "children, tossed here and there by waves, and carried about by every wind of doctrine, by the trickery of men, by craftiness in deceitful scheming" (Eph. 4:14). Throughout most of redemptive history, God could have said what He said in Hosea's day: "My people are destroyed for lack of knowledge" (Hos. 4:6). It is for that reason, as well as for the even greater reason of honoring the Lord, that regular, systematic, and thorough study of the doctrine in God's Word is imperative for God's people.

We not only are to guard what we know but sincerely seek to learn more of God's inexhaustible truth. We should pray with Job, "Teach Thou me what I do not see" (Job 34:32). That dauntless man of God had lost his children, his servants, his flocks, his health, and even his reputation. He was wholly unable to see why God permitted those calamities to come upon him, and he therefore wanted the Lord to teach him whatever he needed to learn in order to endure his painful existence and to profit from it spiritually.

Just before Jehovah's covenant with Israel was ratified near Sinai, Moses "took the book of the covenant and read it in the hearing of the people; and they said, 'All that the Lord has spoken we will do, and we will be obedient!'" (Ex. 24:7). Unfortunately, the people of Israel seldom again demonstrated such reverence for God's Word. Shortly before they were to enter and take possession of the Promised Land, Moses reminded them again: "See, I have taught you statutes and judgments just as the Lord my God commanded me, that you should do thus in the land where you are entering to possess it. . . . And the Lord commanded me at that time to teach you statutes and judgments, that you might perform them in the land where you are going over to possess it" (Deut. 4:5, 14). God's command to Joshua, Moses' successor, applies to every believer: "Be strong and very courageous; be careful to do according to all the law which Moses My servant commanded you; do not turn from it to the right or to the left, so that you may have success wherever you go. This book of the law shall not depart from your mouth, but you shall meditate on it day and night, so that you may be careful to do according to all that is written in it; for then you will make your way prosperous, and then you will have success" (Josh. 1:7–8).

When the young but godly King Josiah heard read to him "the words of the book of the law," which had been discovered as the temple was being repaired, "he tore his clothes. Then the king commanded Hilkiah the priest, Ahikam the son of Shaphan, Achbor the son of Micaiah, Shaphan the scribe, and Asaiah the king's servant saying, 'Go, inquire of the Lord for me and the people and all Judah concerning the words of this book that has been found, for great is the wrath of the Lord that burns against us, because our fathers have not listened to the words of this book, to do according to all that is written concerning us'" (2 Kings 22:11–13).

Although they did not believe their own words, the unbelieving and hypocritical Pharisees were completely correct when they said of Jesus, "You are truthful and teach the way of God in truth, and defer to no one; for You are not partial to any" (Matt. 22:16). It was because of His utter truthfulness and righteousness and His refusal to defer to anyone that those men, and others like them, put Jesus to death. Contrary to their godly forefather Josiah, they would not accept the teaching of God.

On a trip from Greece back to Jerusalem, Paul reminded the Ephesian elders, many of whom had ministered both with him and with Timothy, "You yourselves know, from the first day that I set foot in Asia, . . . how I did not shrink from declaring to you anything that was profitable, and teaching you publicly and from house to house, solemnly testifying to both Jews and Greeks of repentance toward God and faith in our Lord Jesus Christ. . . . For I did not shrink from declaring to you the whole purpose of God" (Acts 20:18, 20–21, 27).

Both the first and last pieces of spiritual armor that Paul mentions in his letter to believers at Ephesus pertain to Scripture. "Stand firm therefore," he says, "having girded your loins with truth." Then, after putting on the "breastplate of righteousness," shodding our feet with "the gospel of peace, "taking up the shield of faith," and donning "the helmet of salvation," we are to equip ourselves with the only offensive implement mentioned here—"the sword of the Spirit, which is the word of God" (Eph. 6:14–17). *Machaira* ("sword") refers to a short sword, or dagger, a weapon used in close combat that required skillful use in order to be effective. "Word" translates *rhēma,* which refers to a specific statement or wording, not to general truth, as does the more commonly used *logos.*

Our "wielding" of Scripture, as it were, should be as precise, accurate, and appropriate as possible. No matter how good our intentions might be, to interpret or apply a passage thoughtlessly or to quote it out of context creates confusion and uncertainty. It does disservice to the Lord and to those we are attempting to instruct. In order to present ourselves "approved to God as a workman who does not need to be ashamed," we must handle "accurately the word of truth" (2 Tim. 2:15). Careless use of Scripture, even by the Lord's own people, can do great damage to the cause of Christ, as it often has done throughout church history.

During His wilderness ordeal, Jesus responded to each of Satan's temptations with an accurate and carefully chosen quotation from Scripture (see Matt. 4:3–10). Because He was the incarnate Son of God, anything He might have said would have carried the same divine weight as Scripture. But as an example for His followers, He chose to quote divine truth that already was recorded in the Hebrew Scriptures. Following the pattern of our gracious Lord, our weapon against the temptations and deceptions of the devil should always be a careful and precise use of God's revealed Word. It then goes without saying that, in order to use Scripture in that effective way, we must thoroughly know it and understand it. Empowered by the Holy Spirit, we must "let the word of Christ richly dwell within [us], with all wisdom" (Col. 3:16).

The truths of God's Word are spiritual wealth that we should continually be depositing into our minds and hearts. Like deposits of money in our bank account, those deposits of divine truth become spiritual assets that we can draw on readily when confronting temptation, when making moral choices and when seeking God's specific will and guidance for our lives.

THE REPROVING SCRIPTURE

for reproof, (3:16c)

A second work of the Word in the life of believers is that of **reproof.** *Elegmos* (**reproof**) carries the idea of rebuking in order to convict of misbehavior or false doctrine. As with teaching, Scripture's work of reproof has to do with content, with equipping believers with accurate knowledge and understanding of divine truth, in this context divine truth that exposes falsehood and sin, erroneous belief, and ungodly conduct.

Richard Trench, a noted nineteenth-century British theologian, comments that *elegmos* refers to rebuking "another with such effectual wielding of the victorious arm of the truth, as to bring him not always to a confession, yet at least to a conviction of his sin."

Regular and careful study of Scripture builds a foundation of truth that, among other things, exposes sin in a believer's life with the purpose of bringing correction, confession, renunciation, and obedience.

Using the same Greek word as Paul does in Ephesians 6:17, the writer of Hebrews speaks of the Bible as a divine sword that exposes sin in a believer's life. "The word of God is living and active and sharper than any two-edged sword [*machaira*], and piercing as far as the division of soul and spirit, of both joints and marrow, and able to judge the thoughts and intentions of the heart. And there is no creature hidden from His sight, but all things are open and laid bare to the eyes of Him with whom we have to do" (Heb. 4:12–13). Scripture precisely and thoroughly penetrates the believer's mind, soul, and heart.

Every Christian who has been saved for any length of time has experienced times of being sharply and deeply convicted by reading a particular Bible passage or hearing it preached or taught. Every experienced Christian also knows that during times of disobedience he is strongly tempted to forsake Bible study and worship and finds that fellowship with faithful believers becomes less attractive and comfortable. Looked at from the opposite side, decreased desire to study God's Word, to worship Him, and to be with His people is reliable evidence of unconfessed and unforsaken sin. It is for that reason that a Bible-teaching, Bible-believing, and Bible-obeying church is never a haven for persistent sinners. As Jesus explained the principle to Nicodemus, "Everyone who does evil hates the light, and does not come to the light, lest his deeds should be exposed" (John 3:20).

Scripture has the negative ministry of tearing down and destroying that which is sinful and false as well as of building up and improving that which is righteous and true. Just as in medicine, infection and contamination must be excised before healing can begin. Paul told the Ephesian elders, "I testify to you this day, that I am innocent of the blood of all men. . . . Therefore be on the alert, remembering that night and day for a period of three years I did not cease to admonish each one with tears" (Acts 20:26, 31).

Reproving the wrongdoing of his people is as much a pastor's responsibility as helping build them up in righteousness. At the beginning of the next chapter of this letter, Paul wrote, "I solemnly charge you in the presence of God and of Christ Jesus, who is to judge the living and the dead, and by His appearing and His kingdom: preach the word; be ready in season and out of season; reprove, rebuke, exhort, with great patience and instruction" (2 Tim. 4:1–2). The first two of those three admonitions are negative, the first one being the verb form of *elegmos* (**reproof**). God's minister, like God's Word, must reprove sin and falsehood.

Scripture is the divine plumb line by which every thought, principle, act, and belief is to be measured. Paul reminded the Corinthian church what he doubtless had taught them many times. "We are not like many," he said, "peddling the word of God, but as from sincerity, as from God, we speak in Christ in the sight of God. . . . We have renounced the things hidden because of shame, not walking in craftiness or adulterating the word of God, but by the manifestation of truth commending ourselves to every man's conscience in the sight of God" (2 Cor. 2:17; 4:2). Luke commended God-fearing Jews in Berea because they "were more noble-minded than those in Thessalonica, for they received the word with great eagerness, examining the Scriptures daily, to see whether these things were so" (Acts 17:11). As every preacher and teacher should be, Paul and Silas were not offended but were greatly pleased that everything they said was measured against God's Word.

"I have more insight than all my teachers," the psalmist testified before the Lord, "for Thy testimonies are my meditation. I understand more than the aged, because I have observed Thy precepts" (Ps. 119:99–100). "From Thy precepts I get understanding," he continues a few verses later; "therefore I hate every false way. Thy word is a lamp to my feet, and a light to my path" (vv. 104–105). God's Word steers us away from sin and toward righteousness.

Isaiah warned the people of Israel to "hate every false way." "And when they say to you, 'Consult the mediums and the spiritists who whisper and mutter,' should not a people consult their God? Should they consult the dead on behalf of the living? To the law and to the testimony! If they do not speak according to this word, it is because they have no dawn [light]" (Isa. 8:19–20).

When we are constrained by God's Word to reprove a sinning brother or sister, we should do so in humility and love. That always was Paul's practice. "I do not write these things to shame you," he told immature and disobedient believers in Corinth, "but to admonish you as my beloved children" (1 Cor. 4:14). If the holy Lord obligates Himself to reprove and discipline His disobedient children in love (Heb. 12:5–11), how much more are His children obligated to reprove each other in love.

It is just as important, although more difficult, to be gracious when we *receive* **reproof,** whether directly by God's Word or from other believers who call us to biblical account. "For the commandment is a lamp, and the teaching is light," an Old Testament saint professed, "and reproofs for discipline are the way of life" (Prov. 6:23). Like him, every believer should be as grateful for the reproving work of the Word as for its encouragement. It is impossible to genuinely seek righteousness and truth if we do not hate and renounce sin and falsehood.

THE CORRECTING SCRIPTURE

for correction, (3:16d)

Epanorthōsis (**correction**) is used only here in the New Testament and refers to the restoration of something to its original and proper condition. In secular Greek literature it was used of setting upright an object that had fallen down and of helping a person back on his feet after stumbling. After exposing and condemning false belief and sinful conduct in believers, Scripture then builds them up through its divine **correction.**

Correction is Scripture's positive provision for those who accept its negative reproof. "Therefore, putting aside all malice and all guile and hypocrisy and envy and all slander," Peter admonishes, "like newborn babes, long for the pure milk of the word, that by it you may grow in respect to salvation" (1 Peter 2:1–2).

Perhaps the most extensive praise of God's Word in all of Scripture is found in Psalm 119. Among the many well-known verses in that beautiful tribute to God and His Word, the unknown psalmist wrote, "How can a young man keep his way pure? By keeping it according to Thy word. With all my heart I have sought Thee; do not let me wander from Thy commandments. Thy word I have treasured in my heart, that I may not sin against Thee" (Ps. 119:9–11).

"If we confess our sins," the Lord assures us through John, "He is faithful and righteous to forgive us our sins and to cleanse us from all unrighteousness" (1 John 1:9). "And now I commend you to God and to the word of His grace," Paul told the Ephesian elders, "which is able to build you up and to give you the inheritance among all those who are sanctified" (Acts 20:32). When submitted to the Lord's marvelous grace, our areas of greatest weakness can, through correction, become areas of greatest strength.

Shortly before His arrest and crucifixion, Jesus told the disciples, "I am the true vine, and My Father is the vinedresser. Every branch in Me that does not bear fruit, He takes away; and every branch that bears fruit, He prunes it, that it may bear more fruit" (John 15:1–2). In order to make His people obedient, useful, and effective in His service, the Lord has to trim away not only things that are sinful but also things that are useless. He may take away things that are perfectly good in themselves, even things that seem necessary, but which He knows are a hindrance to our spiritual growth and service. They can sap time, attention, and effort from the work He has for us to do. Like His discipline, this process sometimes "for the moment seems not to be joyful, but sorrowful," but also like discipline, "to those who have been trained by it" the Lord's wise and gracious cropping of superfluous branches "afterwards . . . yields the peaceful fruit of righteousness" (Heb. 12:11).

As with reproof, godly believers, especially pastors and teachers, are often the channel through which the Word brings **correction.** Earlier in this letter, Paul reminded Timothy that "the Lord's bond-servant must not be quarrelsome, but be kind to all, able to teach, patient when wronged, with gentleness *correcting* those who are in opposition, if perhaps God may grant them repentance leading to the knowledge of the truth" (2 Tim. 2:25, emphasis added). In his letter to believers at Colossae, the apostle gives similar counsel: "Brethren, even if a man is caught in any trespass, you who are spiritual, restore such a one in a spirit of gentleness; each one looking to yourself, lest you too be tempted" (Gal. 6:1). Despite the dreadful calamities with which God allowed him to be afflicted, Job affirmed to his friend Eliphaz that "he who has clean hands shall grow stronger and stronger" (Job 17:9).

THE SCRIPTURE THAT TRAINS FOR RIGHTEOUSNESS

for training in righteousness; (3:16e)

Training translates *paideia,* which had the original meaning of bringing up and training a child (*paidion*), but it came to be used of any sort of **training.** It also is rendered "correcting" (2 Tim. 2:25) and "discipline" (Eph. 6:4; Heb. 12:5, 7, 11). In the context of verses 16–17, it clearly refers to **training** in the broader and probably more positive sense, since the negatives are covered by **reproof.** It is directed at the ideas of instruction and building up. Until the Lord takes us to be with Himself, His Word is to continue **training** us **in righteousness.**

As with teaching, reproof, and correction, godly believers—especially leaders in the church—are instruments through which Scripture provides **training** for God's people. After reminding Timothy that "everything created by God is good, and nothing is to be rejected, if it is received with gratitude; for it is sanctified by means of the word of God and prayer" (1 Tim. 4:4–5), Paul assured him that "in pointing out these things to the brethren, you will be a good servant of Christ Jesus, constantly nourished *on the words of the faith* and of *the sound doctrine* which you have been following" (v. 6, emphasis added).

Peter gives similar counsel to believers: "You have been born again not of seed which is perishable but imperishable, that is, through the living and abiding word of God. For, 'All flesh is like grass, and all its glory like the flower of grass. The grass withers, and the flower falls off, but the word of the Lord abides forever.' And this is the word which was preached to you" (1 Peter 1:23–25).

And just as milk nourishes a baby in ways it does not understand, so God's Word nourishes us in ways we often do not understand. No matter how deep our understanding of Scripture may be, we still should be able to affirm with the psalmist, "As the deer pants for the water brooks, so my soul pants for Thee, O God" (Ps. 42:1). We should rejoice with Paul that "we all, with unveiled face beholding as in a mirror the glory of the Lord, are being transformed into the same image from glory to glory, just as from the Lord, the Spirit" (2 Cor. 3:18).

THE ENABLING SCRIPTURE

that the man of God may be adequate, equipped for every good work. (3:17)

The Bible can be of great value to an unbeliever. Most important, as discussed in the previous chapter, it will lead to salvation those who come to trust in the Savior and Lord it proclaims. But Paul is speaking here of Scripture's special value for preachers, who are able, with the Spirit's guidance, to understand and to proclaim the truths of God's Word.

The apostle is addressing **the man of God,** a technical phrase used only of Timothy in the New Testament. In the Old Testament it is frequently used as a title for one who proclaimed the Word of God. In this context, **man of God** refers most directly to Timothy and, by extension, to all preachers.

Artios (**adequate**) refers to persons who are complete, capable, and proficient in everything they are called to be or do. In Christ "you have been made complete," Paul tells Colossian believers (Col. 2:10). The preacher who carefully studies and sincerely believes and obeys the truths of Scripture will stand strong in living and defending the faith.

Equipped for every good work could be paraphrased, "enabled to meet all demands of righteousness." By his life he will affirm the power of the Word to lead men to salvation and to equip them for righteous living and for faithful service to the Lord. When the **man of**

God is himself **equipped** by the Word, he can then equip the believers under his care. Just as "we are [the Lord's] workmanship," Paul explains, we also should be doing His work. We are "created in Christ Jesus for good works, which God prepared beforehand, that we should walk in them" (Eph. 2:10). Christ says to all those who belong to Him what He said to the Twelve: "We must work the works of Him who sent Me, as long as it is day; night is coming, when no man can work" (John 9:4).

Whether our purpose is to lead men and women to saving faith in Jesus Christ, to teach God's truth to believers, to refute error in the church, to correct and rebuild erring believers, or to train believers to live righteously, our supreme and sufficient resource is God's Word. It not only gives us the information to teach but also shapes us into living examples of that truth.

One cannot help wondering why so many evangelical pastors of our day, like many Christians throughout history, have lost sight of that foundational truth. Every church, everywhere and in every time, should be totally committed to preaching, teaching, and implementing the Word, thereby pleasing and exalting the gracious and sovereign God who has revealed it.

Through the convincing and convicting power of the Holy Spirit, Scripture is *God's own provision* for every spiritual truth and moral principle that men need to be saved, to be equipped to live righteously in this present life and to hear one day in the life to come, "Well done, good and faithful servant, . . . enter into the joy of your Master" (Matt. 25:21).

Marks of the Faithful Preacher

10

I solemnly charge you in the presence of God and of Christ Jesus, who is to judge the living and the dead, and by His appearing and His kingdom: preach the word; be ready in season and out of season; reprove, rebuke, exhort, with great patience and instruction. For the time will come when they will not endure sound doctrine; but wanting to have their ears tickled, they will accumulate for themselves teachers in accordance to their own desires; and will turn away their ears from the truth, and will turn aside to myths. But you, be sober in all things, endure hardship, do the work of an evangelist, fulfill your ministry. (4:1–5)

The final section of 2 Timothy, which begins with this passage, contains the last inspired words penned by Paul, who knew that his earthly life was nearing its end. "I am already being poured out as a drink offering," he wrote, "and the time of my departure has come" (v. 6). With that bittersweet prospect in mind (cf. Phil. 1:23), in his final charge he beseeched his beloved Timothy to be faithful in his ministry to the Lord Jesus Christ.

In what had been an exemplary church at Ephesus, some believers, including men in positions of leadership, had begun to defect, just as Paul predicted (Acts 20:28–31). Timothy had been placed by the apostle as defender of the faith in that congregation, where sound doctrine and godliness had lost their primacy.

Empire-wide persecution of the church was well under way and doubtless was responsible for much of the defection. Those who were loyal in easier times deserted when discipleship became costly.

In this second letter, Paul already has admonished Timothy "to kindle afresh the gift of God which is in you through the laying on of my hands" (1:6). As with every genuine preacher of the gospel, Timothy did not choose his ministry but was appointed to it by God. The Lord had set him apart for the preaching and teaching of His Word. He ministered under divine authority and divine obligation. Just as God had sovereignly called Timothy to salvation, He also had sovereignly appointed him to preach the gospel. Timothy could say with his mentor, "I am under compulsion; for woe is me if I do not preach the gospel" (1 Cor. 9:16).

Paul did not focus on the visible success of Timothy's ministry but on the excellence of his service. He focused not on Timothy's opportunities but on his commitment, not on his personal prominence but on his character. He expressed no concern for the young pastor's acceptance or reputation but great concern for his faithfulness and godliness. He did not emphasize the size, wealth, or influence of the church at Ephesus but rather its spiritual life and health under Timothy's care. He did not concentrate even on Timothy's spiritual gifts, important as those were, but on his spiritual life and his spiritual service. His advice to Timothy could be summarized in his charge to believers in Corinth: "Whether, then, you eat or drink or whatever you do, do all to the glory of God" (1 Cor. 10:31).

Regardless of how things may appear to the world, to the rest of the church, or even to ourselves, God's Word assures us that the best of life belongs to those who know Christ as Savior and Lord and who give themselves up for His service and His glory. The central truth of the Beatitudes could be condensed to "Blessed, happy, and satisfied are those who love and serve the Lord."

Unfortunately, many Christians, including some pastors and other leaders, seek for success rather than excellence. But success focuses on the external rather than the internal, on the temporal rather than the eternal, and is measured by human standards rather than by divine. Desire for success comes from pride, whereas genuine desire for excellence comes from humility.

In his book *Christian Excellence,* John Johnstone rightfully maintains that success and excellence are competing ideals and that everything a believer does, whether consciously or not, is devoted to one of those ideals or the other. It is not that excellence in a believer precludes every form of outward success but that any success that comes from the pursuit of excellence is incidental. Success is not to be sought or to be gloried in if it is achieved.

Success is attaining cultural goals that elevate one's importance in the eyes of society and generally is marked by power, prestige, wealth, and privilege, according to Johnstone. Excellence, on the other hand, is the pursuit of the highest quality in one's work and effort, whether others recognize and approve it or not. Success is measured in relation to others, whereas excellence is measured by one's own God-given potential and calling. Success seeks to please men; excellence seeks to please God. Success rewards only a few, whereas excellence is available to any believer who is willing to pay the price. Success pertains to possessions and reputation, whereas excellence pertains to character. Success can be cheap, attained by shortcuts, lying, and stealing. The price of excellence is never discounted, never available for anything less than full price. (This paragraph is adapted from Johnstone.)

Although directed first of all to Timothy, Paul's commission in 2 Timothy 4:1–5 applies to every minister of the gospel in every age, every place, and every circumstance. In a broader way it can be applied to every faithful believer, because it is essential for every congregation to know and understand this charge. Churches are responsible, under God and with God, to hold their pastors accountable to these divine precepts.

The role of the preacher in Christ's church is vital, and God has ordained that His people be taught and shepherded by Spirit-gifted, Spirit-led, and Spirit-empowered men. The spiritual life and faithfulness of a congregation always is closely related to the spiritual life and faithfulness of its pastor.

Scripture is not nebulous about what the Lord expects of those He calls to preach, teach, and pastor His people. Among the many other qualifications and standards for such men given in the New Testament, are the eight which Paul mentions in the present text: the seriousness (v. 1), content (v. 2a), scope (v. 2b), urgency (vv. 3–4), attitude (v. 5a), cost (v. 5b), extent (v. 5c), and goal (v. 5d).

THE SERIOUSNESS OF HIS COMMISSION

I solemnly charge you in the presence of God and of Christ Jesus, who is to judge the living and the dead, and by His appearing and His kingdom: (4:1)

Paul first points out the seriousness of Timothy's divine commission. **Solemnly charge** translates a form of the verb *diamarturomai*, which here carries the idea of giving a forceful order or directive. The apostle has twice before used the verb to admonish Timothy (1 Tim. 5:21; 2 Tim. 2:14; cf. 1 Tim. 6:13). The aged warrior of the faith, whose godly life was totally committed to the service of Christ, again seeks to capture Timothy's undivided attention for what he is about to say. The devotion of Paul himself was not unlike that of John Knox, who prayed, "Give me Scotland or I die," yet who, when later compelled to preach, locked himself in his room and wept for days because of the fearful seriousness of that calling. The apostle's deepest desire for Timothy was for him to share that seriousness and devotion.

The solemnity of Paul's **charge** is drawn from the fact that it is tied directly to the awesome majesty of the One who commissions men to divine service. Those who are called to proclaim and interpret the Word of God have the most profound responsibility that the Lord places on any man. It is for that reason that James warns, "Let not many of you become teachers, my brethren, knowing that as such we shall incur a stricter judgment. For we all stumble in many ways. If anyone does not stumble in what he says, he is a perfect man, able to bridle the whole body as well" (James 3:1–2). No human being apart from Jesus has ever spoken perfectly, not even the prophets or apostles, except when recording God's revealed Word. James readily included himself ("for we all stumble") among those who speak imperfectly and who therefore must take special care to prevent their imperfections from clouding their testimony and besmirching their Lord's name.

That responsibility is especially fearsome in that it is carried out **in the presence of God and of Christ Jesus.** The Greek construction also allows the rendering "in the presence of God, *even* Christ Jesus." That wording seems especially appropriate in this context because of Paul's following reference to Christ as Judge. Jesus said, "Not even the Father judges anyone, but He has given all judgment to the Son" (John 5:22; cf. vv. 26–27). It is not, of course, that a believer ever lives or ministers apart from the presence of the Father and the Holy Spirit. But Paul here emphasizes the believer's unique accountability to the Son—not as Savior and Lord but as Judge. The point of the first half of the sentence is that every minister who is called by **Christ Jesus,** the Son, constantly ministers under the omniscient scrutiny of His divine **presence.**

The phrase **in the presence of** parallels a common format used in Roman courts and legal documents and would have been familiar to Timothy and others of that day. A typical summons might have begun: "The case will be drawn up against you in the court at Hierapolis, in the presence of the honorable judge Festus, chief magistrate."

Service of **Christ Jesus** not only is done before His constant watchful eye but also will be subject to the judgment of this infinitely greater Magistrate, **who is to judge the living and the dead** (cf. Matt. 25:34–41; Acts 10:42; 17:30–31).

In the New Testament, *krinō* (**to judge**) has numerous shades of meaning, ranging from the broad and usually positive sense of forming an opinion or of resolving an issue (as in Luke 7:43; Acts 4:19) to the immeasurably more serious and negative sense of condemning or damning (as in John 12:48; Acts 13:27; 2 Thess. 2:12).

The New Testament reveals three distinct judgments of human beings that Christ will conduct: the bema seat judgment of believers only (1 Cor. 3:12–15; 2 Cor. 5:10); the sheep and goats judgment of the nations, in which believers will be separated from unbelievers (Matt. 25:31–33); and the great white throne judgment of unbelievers only (Rev. 20:11–15).

In the present text, Paul's focus is on the Lord's judgment of believers, all of whom one day will "appear before the judgment seat of Christ, that each one may be recompensed for his deeds in the body, according to what he has done, whether good or bad" (2 Cor. 5:10; cf. 1 Cor. 3:12–15). And the emphasis is not so much on the preacher's proclaiming that truth to others, although that idea is implied, as on the excellence of his own ministry in light of that judgment.

In marked contrast to human courts, in the bar of divine judgment—whether for reward, separation, or condemnation—there will be no argument, no new evidence to be revealed, no cross-examination, no witnesses to call, no excuses, no jury of peers, and no appeal. In the most absolute way, the Judge's decision will be final.

When we stand before our omniscient Lord, He already will know, far better than we ourselves can know even in our most honest moments, exactly how faithful and godly our life has been. Not a year or a month, not an hour, minute, or second escapes His notice or His judgment. Paul could say with complete honesty, "I am conscious of nothing against myself." Nevertheless, he went on to say, "Yet I am not by this acquitted; but the one who examines me is the Lord. Therefore do not go on passing judgment before the time, but wait until the Lord comes who will both bring to light the things hidden in the darkness and disclose the motives of men's hearts; and then each man's praise will come to him from God" (1 Cor. 4:4–5).

The grammatical construction of 2 Timothy 4:1 suggests the idea of imminency, that **Christ Jesus . . . is** *about* **to judge** momentarily, and gives a second reason for Paul's solemn charge to Timothy.

As already noted, this particular judgment will be the bema seat judgment of all believers, both **the living and the dead,** after **Christ Jesus** takes them to be with Himself at the Rapture (1 Thess. 4:13–8). The apostle exults a few verses later that "there is laid up for me the crown of righteousness, which the Lord, the righteous Judge, will award to me on that day; and not only to me, but also to all who have loved His appearing" (2 Tim. 4:8). It was in light of that same judgment and reward that, in his previous letter, Paul admonished Timothy to "keep the commandment without stain or reproach until the appearing of our Lord Jesus Christ" (1 Tim. 6:14). In his letter to Titus, written perhaps a year before 2 Timothy, the apostle wrote, "For the grace of God has appeared, bringing salvation to all men, instructing us to deny ungodliness and worldly desires and to live sensibly, righteously and godly in the present age, looking for the blessed hope and the appearing of the glory of our great God and Savior, Christ Jesus" (Titus 2:11–13).

A preacher's ultimate accountability is not to a board, a local church, a denomination, or any other human institution, no matter how doctrinally sound and godly it may be, but to the Lord, who has called and empowered him and who one day will judge him. Paul both preached and lived in the light of that truth. He could therefore ask Galatian believers rhetorically, "Am I now seeking the favor of men, or of God? Or am I striving to please men? If I were still trying to please men, I would not be a bond-servant of Christ" (Gal. 1:10). For the sake of example, a faithful minister is concerned about the things in his life and ministry that others can see. But he is supremely concerned about the things that only the Lord can see. And probably more often than not, the quality of the things that only God can see will eventually become evident in the quality of the things that men can see.

When the French sculptor created the magnificent Statue of Liberty as a gift from his own country to the United States, there were no airplanes or helicopters. Yet he made that statue in such complete detail that even the top of its head was perfectly sculpted. Little did the artist know that one day tens of thousands of people a year would fly over the statue and be able to appreciate the full excellency of his work. It was such concern for excellency that motivated Paul's ministry, a concern which he desired his beloved Timothy to share.

Epiphaneia (**appearing**) literally means "a shining forth" and was used by the ancient Greeks of the supposed appearance of a pagan god to men. William Barclay notes that it also was used of Roman emperors. "His accession to the throne of the Empire was his *epiphaneia;* and in particular—and this is the background of Paul's thought here—it was used of a visit by the Emperor to any province or town. The emperor's appearance in any place was his *epiphaneia.* Obviously when the Emperor was due to visit any place, everything was put in perfect order" (*The Letters to Timothy, Titus, and Philemon* [Philadelphia: Westminster, 1957], 233).

In the New Testament, the noun *epiphaneia* is found only in the letters of Paul. He uses it once of Christ's incarnation (2 Tim. 1:10) and once of His coming to destroy Antichrist at the end of the Great Tribulation (2 Thess. 2:8). In all four of the other instances, he uses it of Christ's taking His saints to be with Himself at the Rapture (here; in 1 Tim. 6:14; 2 Tim. 4:8; and Titus 2:13).

This particular judgment also will have a special relation to Christ's earthly **kingdom,** His thousand-year reign, which will begin after the Great Tribulation and the Battle of Armageddon and ultimately merge into the eternal state. At that time, the Lord's resurrected, raptured, and rewarded saints will return with Him to establish His millennial **kingdom.** "He who overcomes," He promises, "I will grant to him to sit down with Me on My throne, as I also overcame and sat down with My Father on His throne" (Rev. 3:21). When they stand before the Lamb on His heavenly throne, the four creatures and the twenty-four elders will sing, "And Thou hast made them to be a kingdom and priests to our God; and they will reign upon the earth" (Rev. 5:10).

THE CONTENT OF HIS COMMISSION

preach the word; (4:2a)

The faithful minister of Jesus Christ is commanded to **preach the word,** which focuses on the content of what is proclaimed. **Preach** translates the first of nine imperatives Paul uses in this passage, five of them in verse 2 (preach, be ready, reprove, rebuke, exhort) and four in verse 5 (be sober, endure, do, fulfill).

Preach is from *kērussō,* which means to herald, to proclaim publicly. In New Testament times, the herald, acting as imperial messenger, would go through the streets of a city to announce special events, such as the appearing of the emperor. His duties also included public announcement of new laws or government policies and actions.

Paul himself not only was appointed an apostle but also, like Timothy, was appointed a preacher (1 Tim. 2:7; cf. 2 Tim. 1:11). But because of Timothy's timid spirit, that task was especially challenging for him. He did not have the naturally strong and aggressive personality or constitution of his mentor. He also may not have had the formal training or intellectual skill to argue successfully on a human level with more sophisticated and experienced errorists in and around the church. He doubtless felt inadequate and intimidated when they presented arguments for which he had not yet developed a successful apologetic or polemic. And in the eyes of some believers in Ephesus, he also was handicapped because of his youthfulness, although Paul had earlier counseled him to disregard such criticism (1 Tim. 4:12). In addition to resistance within the church, Timothy faced growing hostility from unbelieving Jews and from the Roman government. It was persecution by those enemies that had put Paul in prison.

There were other reasons why Timothy might have been tempted to muffle his proclamation, especially that of evangelism, which Paul mentions in verse 5. Timothy realized that the idea of salvation solely through God's grace runs totally counter to the thinking of natural men and is often met with anger or indifference. But when preaching to unbelievers, whether Jew or Gentile, Timothy was to be like Noah, who "was a righteous man, blameless in his time; [and] walked with God" (Gen. 6:9; cf. Heb. 11:7). Timothy also was to be like Noah in being "a preacher of righteousness" (2 Peter 2:5). Long before God made His covenant with Abraham, before He made His covenant with Israel and gave them the law at Sinai, and still longer before He made the final and perfect covenant through His Son, Jesus Christ, Noah preached God's righteousness to the ever-more-wicked antediluvians. As far as we know, Noah was not persecuted, but we do know that his preaching for a hundred years while he was building the ark fell on completely indifferent ears, because not a single soul outside his immediate family trusted in God and was saved.

Like every preacher of God's truth to unbelievers, Timothy also was to be like Jonah, who declared to the wicked pagan city of Nineveh, "Yet forty days and Nineveh will be overthrown" (Jonah 3:4). In great contrast to that of Noah, however, Jonah's preaching produced an amazing response of repentance and faith in the true God. "The men of Nineveh shall stand up with this generation at the judgment," Jesus declared, "and shall condemn it because they repented at the preaching of Jonah" (Matt. 12:41).

Timothy was to be like "John the Baptist [who] came, preaching in the wilderness of Judea, saying, 'Repent, for the kingdom of heaven is at hand'" (Matt. 3:1–2), and who then proclaimed "the Lamb of God, who takes away the sin of the world!" (John 1:29).

By **the word,** Paul doubtless means the entire written Word of God, His complete revealed truth, which the apostle also calls "the whole purpose of God" (Acts 20:27) and which he has just referred to as "the sacred writings" and the "Scripture" (2 Tim. 3:15–16).

A preacher cannot continue to faithfully **preach** and teach God's **word** unless he carefully protects its truth. "O Timothy, guard what has been entrusted to you," Paul had warned in his previous letter, "avoiding worldly and empty chatter and the opposing arguments of what is falsely called 'knowledge'" (1 Tim. 6:20). Near the beginning of this second letter he admonished, "Retain the standard of sound words which you have heard from me, in the faith and love which are in Christ Jesus," and, "Guard, through the Holy Spirit who dwells in us, the treasure which has been entrusted to you" (2 Tim. 1:13–14). He also implored Timothy to handle "accurately the word of truth" (2 Tim. 2:15), because truth that is poorly retained, guarded, and handled inevitably will be poorly taught.

After declaring the marvelous truth first proclaimed by the prophet Joel (2:32) that "whoever will call upon the name of the Lord will be saved," Paul asks rhetorically in his letter to the church at Rome, "How then shall they [unbelievers] call upon Him in whom they have not believed? And how shall they believe in Him whom they have not heard? And how shall they hear without a preacher? And how shall they preach unless they are sent?" Again quoting from the Old Testament, this time from Isaiah 52:7, the apostle then exults, "How beautiful are the feet of those who bring glad tidings of good things!" (Rom. 10:13–15).

Of his own preaching Paul said,

> I was made a minister according to the stewardship from God bestowed on me for your benefit, that I might fully carry out the preaching of the word of God, that is, the mystery which has been hidden from the past ages and generations; but has now been manifested to His saints, to whom God willed to make known what is the riches of the glory of this mystery among the Gentiles, which is Christ in you, the hope of glory. And we proclaim Him, admonishing every man and teaching every man with all wisdom, that we may present every man complete in Christ. And for this purpose also I labor, striving according to His power, which mightily works within me. (Col. 1:25–29)

There are gifted orators who can sway an audience with the power of their persuasive rhetoric. There are men who are erudite, knowledgeable, well-trained, and worldly-wise, who can cause other men to change their minds about certain matters. There are men who can relate moving stories that tug at a hearer's heart and move him emotionally. Throughout the history of the church, including our own time, God has chosen to endow some ministers with such abilities. But God also has chosen not to bless every faithful preacher in those particular ways. Nevertheless, He charges them with the same task of preaching His Word, because the spiritual power and effectiveness of preaching does not rest in the skill of the speaker but in the truth.

Intellectually brilliant as he was, the apostle testified to believers at Corinth: "Brethren, I did not come with superiority of speech or of wisdom, proclaiming to you the testimony of God. For I determined to know nothing among you except Jesus Christ, and Him crucified. And I was with you in weakness and in fear and in much trembling. And my message and my preaching were not in persuasive words of wisdom, but in demonstration of the Spirit and of power, that your faith should not rest on the wisdom of men, but on the power of God" (1 Cor. 2:1–5).

In his next letter to that church, he said, "We do not preach ourselves but Christ Jesus as Lord, and ourselves as your bond-servants for Jesus' sake" (2 Cor. 4:5).

By far the most reliable and effective way to proclaim all of God's Word is to preach it expositorily. In his book *The Ministry of the Word*, the nineteenth-century Scotsman William Taylor writes,

> By expository preaching, I mean that method of pulpit discourse which consists in the consecutive interpretation, and practical enforcement, of a book of the sacred canon. . . . Exposition is the presentation to the people, in an intelligible and forcible manner, of the meaning of the sacred writer. . . . It is the honest answer which the preacher gives, after faithful study, to these questions, "What is the mind of the Holy Spirit in this passage?" and "What is its bearing on related Christian truths, or on the life and conversation of the Christian himself?" ([Grand Rapids: Baker, 1975], 155, 157, 159)

Like countless men before and after his time, Taylor preached expositorially because he wanted to know the mind of the Spirit, because he wanted to know how one Scripture truth bore upon another, and he had to carefully understand what God desired for his people.

For many reasons, faithful and full proclamation of **the word** is the only right way to **preach.** First of all, such preaching lets God speak rather than man, because it declares God's own Word. And it is an incredibly thrilling privilege to give voice to God!

Second, preaching **the word** is the only right way to **preach** because it brings the preacher into direct contact with the mind of the Holy Spirit, the author of Scripture. It is for that reason that the preacher of the Word finds the process of study and discovery to be even more rewarding than the preaching that results from it, gratifying as that can be.

It is tragic and puzzling that so many preachers who recognize Scripture to be God's own Word spend more time investigating and interacting with the limited and imperfect minds of other men than delving into the infinite and holy mind of God. Part of the reason, of course, is that many hearers do not really want to delve into the depths of God's righteousness and truth, because it exposes their own shallowness and sin. Paul already has warned Timothy about the danger of those who hold "to a form of godliness, although they have denied its power" (2 Tim. 3:5). Later in the present passage he will warn again that "the time will come when they will not endure sound doctrine; . . . and will turn away their ears from the truth, and will turn aside to myths" (2 Tim. 4:3–4; cf. Acts 20:29–30).

Third, preaching **the word** is the only right way to **preach** because it forces the preacher to proclaim all of God's revelation, including those truths that even many believers find hard to learn or accept.

Fourth, preaching **the word** is the only right way to **preach** because it promotes biblical literacy in a congregation, not only through what is learned from the sermon itself but also through the increased desire to study Scripture more carefully and consistently on their own. The faithful pastor, and all other faithful believers, love to learn God's Word because they love the God of the Word.

Fifth, preaching **the word** is the only right way to **preach** because it carries ultimate authority. It is the complete and perfect self-revelation of God Himself and of His divine will for mankind, which He has created in His own image.

Sixth, preaching **the word** is the only right way to **preach** because only that kind of preaching can transform both the preacher and the congregation.

The final and most compelling reason that preaching **the word** is the only right way to **preach** is simply that it is His own Word, and only His own Word, that the Lord calls and commissions His preachers to proclaim.

In the book mentioned above, William Taylor writes, "Let it never be forgotten, then, that he who would rise to eminence and usefulness in the pulpit, and become 'wise in winning souls,' must say of the work of the ministry, 'This one thing I do.' He must focus his whole heart and life upon the pulpit. He must give his days and his nights to the production of those addresses by which he seeks to convince the judgments and move the hearts and elevate the lives of his hearers" (p. 7).

THE SCOPE OF HIS COMMISSION

be ready in season and out of season; reprove, rebuke, exhort, with great patience and instruction. (4:2b)

In order to be effective, a faithful preacher must understand the scope of his commission, which Paul here summarizes.

Like any other effective worker, he must **be ready.** This is the second command Paul uses in verse 2 and translates *ephistēmi,* which has a broad range of meanings as determined by tense, mood, and voice. It often connotes suddenness, as in Luke 2:9 ("suddenly stood before") and Acts 12:7 ("suddenly appeared"; cf. 1 Thess. 5:3); or forcefulness, as in Luke 20:1 ("confronted") and Acts 4:1; 6:12; 23:27 ("came upon"). In the aorist active imperative, as here, the word carries the complementary ideas of urgency, preparedness, and readiness. It could be used of a soldier who is ready to go into battle on a moment's notice or of a guard who keeps continually alert for any threat of infiltration or attack by the enemy.

For the faithful preacher, **be ready** carries similar meanings of gravity and vigilance. He should feel like Jeremiah, who felt under divine compulsion to prophesy. "If I say, 'I will not remember Him or speak anymore in His name,'" he testified, "then in my heart it becomes like a burning fire shut up in my bones; and I am weary of holding it in, and I cannot endure it" (Jer. 20:9; cf. 5:14).

While Paul stayed in Caesarea for a few days on his way back to Jerusalem after his third missionary journey, the prophet Agabus "took Paul's belt and bound his own feet and hands, and said, 'This is what the Holy Spirit says: "In this way the Jews at Jerusalem will bind the man who owns this belt and deliver him into the hands of the Gentiles,"'" . . . the local residents began begging him not to go up to Jerusalem." But Paul's immediate reply was, "What are you doing, weeping and breaking my heart? For I am ready not only to be bound, but even to die at Jerusalem for the name of the Lord Jesus" (Acts 21:11–13).

Such a sense of readiness and willingness to serve the Lord at any cost and at any time not only should characterize every faithful preacher but also every faithful Christian. Peter exhorted his readers, most of whom were suffering severe persecution from Rome, "Sanctify Christ as Lord in your hearts, always being ready to make a defense to everyone who asks you to give an account for the hope that is in you, yet with gentleness and reverence" (1 Peter 3:15). Writing to believers in the church where Timothy now was ministering, Paul implored, "Be careful how you walk, not as unwise men, but as wise, making the most of your time, because the days are evil" (Eph. 5:15–16).

In his classic *Lectures to My Students,* Charles Spurgeon wrote, "What in a Christian minister is the most essential quality for securing success in winning souls for Christ? . . . earnestness. And if I were asked a second or third time, I should not vary the answer. . . . Success is proportionate to the preacher's earnestness" ([Grand Rapids: Zondervan, 1955], 305).

Only continual study of God's Word, fellowship with Him in prayer, and submission to His Holy Spirit can keep alive a sense of exhilarating eagerness to preach. Apart from the Word and from prayer, the most gifted and orthodox preaching will grow spiritually stale, for the preacher and for the hearers. In the book just cited, Spurgeon said, "He, who at the end of twenty years ministry among the same people is more alive than ever, is a great debtor to the quickening Spirit" (*Lectures,* 309).

The faithful preacher must be ready **in season and out of season,** when it is convenient and when it is not, when it is immediately satisfying and when it is not, when from a human perspective it seems suitable and when it does not. His proclaiming God's Word must not be dictated by popular culture and propriety, by tradition, by esteem in the community (or even in the church), but solely by the mandate of the Lord.

Of the next three commands—**reprove, rebuke,** and **exhort**—the first two are negative, and third is positive.

Reprove and **rebuke** are closely related in meaning and are the third and fourth imperatives in this passage. Paul has just declared that all Scripture is "profitable for . . . reproof" (3:16). As noted in the previous commentary chapter, *elegmos* (reproof) carries the idea of correcting misbehavior or false doctrine. Reproving may have more to do with affecting the mind, with helping a person understand that what he believes or is doing is wrong. **Rebuke,** on the other hand, may have to do with the heart, with bringing a person under conviction of guilt. To **reprove** is to refute error and misconduct with careful biblical argument; to **rebuke** is to bring the erring person to repentance. The first discloses the sinfulness of sin, whereas the second discloses the sinfulness of the sinner.

The first call of the gospel reflects this reproof by calling for men to repent from sin. In preparing the way for the Messiah, John the Baptist declared, "Repent, for the kingdom of heaven is at hand" (Matt. 3:2). He not only preached against sin in general but against particular sins of particular people. "When Herod the tetrarch was reproved by him [John the Baptist] on account of Herodias, his brother's wife, and on account of all the wicked things which Herod had done, he added this also to them all, that he locked John up in prison" (Luke 3:19–20).

Like John the Baptist, Jesus began His public ministry by calling sinners to repentance. After being baptized by John and spending forty days and nights in the wilderness being tempted by Satan, "from that time Jesus began to preach and say, 'Repent, for the kingdom of heaven is at hand'" (Matt. 4:17). Although Jesus mentioned God's love on several occasions, He never preached a message on that theme. But He preached countless messages on God's condemnation of sin, on His judgment of sinners, and on the sinner's need for repentance. The unrepentant sinner has no hope in the love of God, because God's love is inseparable from His holiness and justice. A person who refuses to be cleansed of his sin by God's grace has no prospect of being accepted into heaven by His love.

Immediately after Peter's sermon at Pentecost, his hearers "were pierced to the heart, and said to Peter and the rest of the apostles, 'Brethren, what shall we do?' And Peter said to them, 'Repent, and let each of you be baptized in the name of Jesus Christ for the forgiveness of your sins; and you shall receive the gift of the Holy Spirit'" (Acts 2:37–38).

The preacher's continuing responsibility is to expose, **reprove, and rebuke** sin. Sin is that which totally separates unbelievers from God and which temporarily separates believers from close fellowship with their Lord. Paul therefore counseled believers in Ephesus, "Do not participate in the unfruitful deeds of darkness, but instead even expose them" (Eph. 5:11).

He warned Titus about those sinners who infiltrate the church: "There are many rebellious men, empty talkers and deceivers, especially those of the circumcision, who must be silenced because they are upsetting whole families, teaching things they should not teach, for the sake of sordid gain. . . . For this cause reprove them severely that they may be sound in the faith" (Titus 1:10–11, 13).

Sin must be addressed among believers as well. In his first letter to Timothy, Paul commanded, "Those who continue in sin, rebuke in the presence of all, so that the rest also may be fearful of sinning" (1 Tim. 5:20).

Paul next gives Timothy the positive imperative to **exhort,** which is from *parakaleō,* a common New Testament word that can range in meaning from simply calling out to someone to admonishing, which is clearly the meaning in this context. It also carries the idea of encouragement. After having reproved and rebuked disobedient believers under his care, the faithful preacher is then to come alongside them in love and encourage them to spiritual change.

That is the spirit in which Paul himself pastored those under his care. He reminded believers in Thessalonica, "You know how we were exhorting and encouraging and imploring each one of you as a father would his own children, so that you may walk in a manner worthy of the God who calls you into His own kingdom and glory" (1 Thess. 2:11–12; cf. Col. 1:28). Later in the letter he counseled those believers to do as he had done, saying, "We urge you, brethren, admonish the unruly, encourage the fainthearted, help the weak, be patient with all men" (5:14).

Not only are the things a preacher says and does important but also the way he says them and does them. He is to reprove, rebuke, and exhort **with patience.** *Makrothumē* (**patience**) means literally to "abide under" and therefore is often translated "endurance" (see, e.g., Luke 21:19; 2 Cor. 6:4; James 1:3) or "perseverance" (see, e.g., James 1:12; 2 Cor. 12:12). But here Paul is speaking specifically of **patience** with people, with members of a flock who may have been persistently stubborn and were resisting their pastor's admonitions. But the shepherd is not to become exasperated or angry, remembering that he himself is firmly but lovingly and patiently held accountable by the Great Shepherd, our supreme example of **patience.** Paul cautioned believers in Rome, "Do you suppose this, O man, when you pass judgment upon those who practice such things and do the same yourself, that you will escape the judgment of God? Or do you think lightly of the riches of His kindness and forbearance and patience, not knowing that the kindness of God leads you to repentance?" (Rom. 2:3–4). If the perfect Son of God is so kind, forbearing, and patient with sinners, how much are His people obliged to have those attitudes?

Although mentioned at the end of the verse, *didachē* (**instruction**) is foundational to preaching, reproving, rebuking, and exhortation. It is only through careful teaching of the Word that those tasks can be successfully carried out by a pastor. An unbeliever will not be convicted of his sin and come to salvation apart from some **instruction** from God's Word about his lost condition and his need for saving faith in Jesus Christ. Nor will a believer be convicted of his sin and brought to repentance and restoration apart from the work of the Word in his heart.

It is not by a preacher's personal authority or persuasiveness— no matter how well he knows Scripture or how highly he is gifted—but solely by the authority and power of Scripture itself, illuminated and applied by the Holy Spirit, that any ministry or Christian service can be spiritually effective and pleasing to the Lord. In 4:2 Paul essentially reiterates what he has just declared, namely, that "all Scripture is inspired by God and profitable for teaching, for reproof, for correction, for training in righteousness; that the man of God may be adequate, equipped for every good work" (3:16–17).

THE URGENCY OF HIS COMMISSION

For the time will come when they will not endure sound doctrine; but wanting to have their ears tickled, they will accumulate for themselves teachers in accordance to their own desires; and will turn away their ears from the truth, and will turn aside to myths. (4:3–4)

After calling Timothy to excellence in preaching and teaching, Paul now informs him about the opposition he eventually will face because of that preaching and teaching. For the second time in this letter (see 3:1–5; cf. 1 Tim. 4:1–3), the apostle prophesies about the end times, saying, **For the time will come when they will not endure sound doctrine**.

Because there is no antecedent for **they,** this pronoun possibly could refer to the unbelieving world, which, of course, is opposed by nature to God's truth (cf. 1 Cor. 2:14; 2 Cor. 4:4). But Paul's reference to

the time will come implies a change of mind, from once enduring to not enduring, in which case **they** refers to unbelievers who become nominal believers in the church, whose profession of faith was only superficial. **They** are men and women whose hearts are rocky and in whom the seed of God's Word does not produce fruit. In the words of Jesus' parable, the seed immediately springs up in their lives, but because there is no depth of belief there is no spiritual root. Therefore when they are tested by the heat of the ungodly world, their superficial profession is "scorched" and quickly withers (Matt. 13:5–6). That describes the urgency of Timothy's commission: Many nominal believers (**they**) in the church at Ephesus eventually would come to reject his faithful preaching of the Word, a pattern repeated through the centuries.

Kairos does not refer to chronological but epochal **time,** a period or era of **time.** It is the same word Paul uses in the previous chapter in regard to "dangerous times" that would come "in the last days," and doubtless refers to the same period of time as here.

Jesus gave a similar warning early in His ministry:

> Behold, I send you out as sheep in the midst of wolves; therefore be shrewd as serpents, and innocent as doves. But beware of men; for they will deliver you up to the courts, and scourge you in their synagogues; and you shall even be brought before governors and kings for My sake, as a testimony to them and to the Gentiles. And brother will deliver up brother to death, and a father his child; and children will rise up against parents, and cause them to be put to death. . . . And you will be hated by all on account of My name, but it is the one who has endured to the end who will be saved. (Matt. 10:16–18, 21–22)

Near the end of His ministry, as He shared the Last Supper with His disciples, Jesus again warned, "If the world hates you, you know that it has hated Me before it hated you. If you were of the world, the world would love its own; but because you are not of the world, but I chose you out of the world, therefore the world hates you. Remember the word that I said to you, 'A slave is not greater than his master.' If they persecuted Me, they will also persecute you; if they kept My word, they will keep yours also. But all these things they will do to you for My name's sake, because they do not know the One who sent Me" (John 15:18–21; 16:1–2).

Because of what lay ahead for Timothy, the need for his fearless, uncompromising preaching of the Word became all the more compelling. The time would come, perhaps not long off, when he would have less and less opportunity to preach and less and less response to the truth he proclaimed.

Anechō (**endure**) has the basic idea of holding up or holding onto, especially in face of difficulty, and also can be rendered "tolerate." Many people in the church at Ephesus would become intolerant of the unadulterated word, of **sound doctrine,** and of Timothy's preaching of it. **Sound** translates a form of the verb *hugiainō,* which means to be healthy, and is the term from which we derive "hygiene." It is rendered "safe and sound" in the story of the prodigal son (Luke 15:27). Timothy would face increasing resistance to **doctrine** that was spiritually healthy and nourishing, that was true to God's Word—to "the sacred writings" (3:15), to God-breathed "Scripture" (v. 16).

In his first letter, Paul reminded Timothy that men and women who are "lawless and rebellious, . . . ungodly and sinners, . . . unholy and profane, . . . murderers and immoral men and homosexuals and kidnappers and liars and perjurers" live lives that are "contrary to sound teaching" (1 Tim. 1:9–10). It is because **sound doctrine** is a stinging rebuke to ungodly living that it is unacceptable and intolerable to those who persist in sin. Those who live contrary to **sound doctrine** resent and resist the teaching of **sound doctrine.**

Later in that letter, the apostle commanded, "If anyone advocates a different doctrine, and does not agree with sound words, those of our Lord Jesus Christ, and with the doctrine conforming to godliness, he is conceited and understands nothing; but he has a morbid interest in controversial questions and disputes about words, out of which arise envy, strife, abusive language, evil suspicions, and constant friction between men of depraved mind and deprived of the truth, who suppose that godliness is a means of gain" (1 Tim. 6:3–5). It was in face of that danger that, near the beginning of this second letter, Paul admonishes Timothy: "Retain the standard of sound words which you have heard from me, in the faith and love which are in Christ Jesus. Guard, through the Holy Spirit who dwells in us, the treasure which has been entrusted to you" (2 Tim. 1:13–14; cf. Titus 1:9, 13; 2:8).

After the Lord asked Isaiah, "Whom shall I send, and who will go for Us?" the prophet responded, "Here am I. Send me!" (Isa. 6:8). But God warned His willing messenger that the people, His own chosen people, would "keep on listening, but . . . not perceive; keep on looking, but . . . not understand," that "the hearts of this people [would be] insensitive, their ears dull, and their eyes dim, lest they see with their eyes, hear with their ears, understand with their hearts, and return and be healed" (Isa. 6:8–10).

Timothy soon would face a similar prospect. The more faithfully he proclaimed God's Word, the more faithless some people in the church would prove themselves to be.

That also is the situation in much of the church today. Even in churches that once were genuinely evangelical, where the Bible was the divine standard for belief and for living, God's Word is compromised. Sometimes it is stripped of its clear meaning or is relegated to a place of secondary authority behind personal "revelations" claimed to be from God. In many churches who once preached **sound doctrine,** evils that God's Word plainly and repeatedly condemns are touted as acceptable. Women are ordained to ministries the Bible restricts to men, and radical feminists even reject the idea of God as heavenly Father. Homosexuals not only are welcomed without reproof or repentance into church fellowship but also are welcomed into the pulpit.

Instead of receiving **sound doctrine,** such churches fiercely reject it, **wanting** rather **to have their ears tickled** with unbiblical notions that raise their comfort level, justify or overlook their sins. They also reject as unloving anyone who presumes to hold them accountable to doctrinal beliefs and moral standards they deem outmoded and irrelevant. Consequently the preacher whom they least like to hear brings the message they need most to hear.

Not surprisingly, therefore, such false Christians **will accumulate for themselves** ungodly **teachers in accordance to their own** ungodly **desires.** Noted Bible scholar Marvin R. Vincent wrote insightfully, "If people desire a calf to worship, a ministerial calf-maker is readily found" (*Word Studies in the New Testament*, vol. 4 [New York: Scribner's, 1904], 321).

That sad truth was verified repeatedly throughout the history of Israel. Through Jeremiah, the Lord lamented, "An appalling and horrible thing has happened in the land: The prophets prophesy falsely, and the priests rule on their own authority; and *My people love it so!*" (Jer. 5:30–31, emphasis added). Not many years later, the Lord told Ezekiel, "They come to you as people come, and sit before you as My people, and hear your words, but they do not do them, for *they do the lustful desires* expressed by their mouth, and their heart goes after their gain. And behold, you are to them like a sensual song by one who has a beautiful voice and plays well on an instrument; for they hear your words, but they do not practice them" (Ezek. 33:31–32, emphasis added). Apparently this prophet was a captivating speaker to whom the people liked to listen purely for his impressive oratory. But they totally rejected what he had to say, being determined instead to fulfill their "lustful desires" and pursue "their gain." They were not interested in learning the truth but were much like "all the Athenians and the strangers" whom Paul confronted with the gospel in Athens, who "used to spend their time in nothing other than telling or hearing something new" (Acts 17:21).

It was the self-will of Adam and Eve, **their own desires,** that led to the Fall, and it is that naturally transmitted self-will that has driven their descendants ever since. It is to please their own desires that so many people today flock to preachers who proffer God's blessings apart from His forgiveness, His salvation apart from their repentance, His acceptance as their Savior but not as their Lord. Because they love the "ungodliness and unrighteousness" that manifest **their own desires,** the unsaved "suppress the truth in unrighteousness" (Rom. 1:18). In doing so, they **turn away their ears from the truth.**

The compound verb **will turn away** is from *apostrephō,* meaning "to cause to turn away" and is active. **Will turn aside** is from the closely related *ektrepō,* meaning "to cause to turn aside" but is passive. The verse therefore can be literally rendered, "And *will cause themselves* to turn away their ears from the truth, and *will be caused* to turn aside to myths." *Ektrepō* sometimes was used medically to refer to a dislocated joint. The minds and hearts of those who reject God's truth become spiritually dislocated, knocked out of joint, as it were. Paul used the same verb in his first letter to Timothy of those who had "already *turned aside* to follow Satan" (1 Tim. 5:15, emphasis added).

"If our gospel is veiled," Paul explained to the church at Corinth, "it is veiled to those who are perishing, in whose case the god of this world has blinded the minds of the unbelieving, that they might not see the light of the gospel of the glory of Christ, who is the image of God" (2 Cor. 4:4). When God's **truth** is knowingly rejected, Satan's falsehood is inevitably, though often unknowingly, embraced. In other words, deliberate rejection of God's **truth** makes a person vulnerable to Satan's **myths.**

Many churches today are filled to overflowing with those who want their ears tickled with the **myths** of easy-believism and the many variations of selfism and so-called positive thinking. They come to have their egos fed and their sins approved, not to have their hearts cleansed and their souls saved. They want only to feel good, not to be made good. Tragically, such **myths** serve to religiously insulate people from the true gospel and drive them still further from the Lord.

THE ATTITUDE OF HIS COMMISSION

But you, be sober in all things, (4:5a)

The faithful preacher is to **be sober in all things. Be sober,** the sixth imperative in this passage, is from *nephō,* which literally means to be free of intoxicants. Here, however, it is used metaphorically like its English counterpart, of being level-headed, well-balanced, and in control of one's faculties. By extension it includes the ideas of being stable, unwavering, steadfast.

The **sober** preacher is like the diligent athlete, who "exercises self-control in all things," who, like Paul himself, runs "in such a way, as not without aim," boxes "in such a way, as not beating the air," and buffets his body to make it his slave, lest, after having "preached to others, [he himself] should be disqualified" (1 Cor. 9:25–27). In the midst of a changing world, a changing church, and even a changing gospel— which is not really the gospel but a distortion of "the gospel of Christ" (Gal. 1:7; cf. 2 Cor. 11:4)—he remains committed to the changeless truth of God's Word.

The faithful preacher refuses to be trendy or compromising, to be an ear-tickler and men-pleaser rather than a God-pleaser. He can declare with Paul, "For our exhortation does not come from error or impurity or by way of deceit; but just as we have been approved by God to be entrusted with the gospel, so we speak, not as pleasing men but God, who examines our hearts. For we never came with flattering speech, as you know, nor with a pretext for greed" (1 Thess. 2:3–5). He also could say with the apostle, "For am I now seeking the favor of men, or of God? Or am I striving to please men? If I were still trying to please men, I would not be a bond-servant of Christ. For I would have you know, brethren, that the gospel which was preached by me is not according to man" (Gal. 1:10–11), "for we do not preach ourselves but Christ Jesus as Lord" (2 Cor. 4:5).

THE COST OF HIS COMMISSION

endure hardship, (4:5b)

Paul's seventh command to Timothy was to **endure hardship.** The verb *kakopatheō* (**endure hardship**) literally means to suffer evil and was used by Paul earlier in this letter to describe his own suffering for the Lord (2:9). A few verses earlier, the apostle had used a closely related verb in asking Timothy to "suffer hardship with me, as a good soldier of Christ Jesus" (v. 3). At the time he wrote these words, he was "already being poured out as a drink offering" (4:6). For many years he had suffered countless hardships. "[I was] beaten times without number," he said,

> often in danger of death. Five times I received from the Jews thirty-nine lashes. Three times I was beaten with rods, once I was stoned, three times I was shipwrecked, a night and a day I have spent in the deep. I have been on frequent journeys, in dangers from rivers, dangers from robbers, dangers from my countrymen, dangers from the Gentiles, dangers in the city, dangers in the wilderness, dangers on the sea, dangers among false brethren; I have been in labor and hardship,

through many sleepless nights, in hunger and thirst, often without food, in cold and exposure. (2 Cor. 11:23–27)

Not only that, but, "apart from such external things," he also suffered "the daily pressure upon [him] of concern for all the churches" (v. 28).

There is no such thing as a faithful ministry that is not costly. A painless ministry is a shallow and fruitless ministry.

Although Paul probably did not write the letter to the Hebrews, the author of that epistle also knew and loved Timothy. He rejoiced "that our brother Timothy has been released [from prison], with whom, if he comes soon, I shall see you" (Heb. 13:23). Because Hebrews likely was written soon after 2 Timothy, this young pastor must have been arrested and jailed while he ministered in Ephesus, soon after he received the letter. The time quickly came (see v. 3) for him to **endure hardship** in service of His Lord.

THE EXTENT OF HIS COMMISSION

do the work of an evangelist, (4:5c)

Poieō (**do the work**), is the eighth imperative that Paul here gives to Timothy. The noun *euangelistēs* (**evangelist**) is used only three times in the New Testament, always in reference to a specific office of ministry. In his letter to the church at Ephesus, Paul tells us that Christ "gave some as apostles, and some as prophets, and some as evangelists, and some as pastors and teachers" (Eph. 4:11). The only person specifically called an evangelist is Philip (Acts 21:8), who was among the first deacons chosen in the church (6:5) and was used by the Lord to bring to salvation the Ethiopian official as he returned from worshiping in Jerusalem (8:26–38).

But the related verb *euangelizō* (to evangelize) and its compounds are used 54 times, and the noun *euangelion* (gospel, good news) is used 76 times. Both words are used not only in relation to evangelists but also in relation to the call of every Christian to witness for Christ and of the responsibility of every preacher and teacher to proclaim the gospel of salvation.

It is important to note, therefore, that Paul does not call Timothy an evangelist but rather calls him to **do the work of an evangelist.** In other words, proclaiming the gospel of salvation was an important part of, but was not all of, Timothy's ministry. As he preached, taught, and pastored those who already belonged to the Lord, he also was to confront the lost—in particular, nominal Christians within the church—with their need of a Savior.

It is also important to note that the purpose of evangelization—whether by an ordinary Christian to a neighbor, by a pastor to the unsaved in his congregation, or by an evangelist to the general public—is to carefully but simply help unbelievers become aware of their sinfulness and lostness and to proclaim Jesus Christ as the only Savior and Lord. Any human manipulation in that process, no matter how well intentioned, always becomes a barrier to genuine belief.

THE GOAL OF HIS COMMISSION

fulfill your ministry. (4:5d)

Finally, Timothy was to **fulfill** the unique **ministry** given to him by the Lord. *Plērophoreō* (**fulfill**) is the ninth and final imperative and carries the basic idea of giving full measure or bringing to completion. In relation to a person's work, it also carries the ideas of eagerness and wholeheartedness.

That was the way Paul sought to fulfill his own ministry. He assured the congregation at Colossae,

> Of this church I was made a minister according to the stewardship from God bestowed on me for your benefit, *that I might fully carry out the preaching of the word of God,* that is, the mystery which has been hidden from the past ages and generations; but has now been manifested to His saints, to whom God willed to make known what is the riches of the glory of this mystery among the Gentiles, which is Christ in you, the hope of glory. And we proclaim Him, admonishing every man and teaching every man with all wisdom, that we may present every man complete in Christ. *And for this purpose also I labor, striving according to His power,* which mightily works within me. (Col. 1:25–29, emphasis added; cf. 1 Cor. 9:24–27)

The apostle wanted Timothy also one day to be able say what he himself was about to say: "I have fought the good fight, I have finished the course, I have kept the faith" (2 Tim. 4:7).

The Triumphant Epitaph of Paul

11

For I am already being poured out as a drink offering, and the time of my departure has come. I have fought the good fight, I have finished the course, I have kept the faith; in the future there is laid up for me the crown of righteousness, which the Lord, the righteous Judge, will award to me on that day; and not only to me, but also to all who have loved His appearing. (4:6–8)

The final words of dying men and women usually are stripped of hypocrisy and reflect accurately their true beliefs and feelings. On his deathbed, Napoleon said, "I die before my time; and my body will be given back to earth, to become the food of worms. Such is the fate which so soon awaits the great Napoleon." Not long before he died, Gandhi, the world-renowned Hindu religious leader, confessed, "My days are numbered. I am not likely to live very long—perhaps a year or a little more. For the first time in fifty years I find myself in a slough of despond. All about me is darkness. I am praying for light." The nineteenth-century French statesman Talleyrand wrote the following words on a piece of paper and laid it on a nightstand near his bed: "Behold, eighty-three years passed away! What cares! What agitation! What anxieties! What ill-will! What sad complications! And all without other results, except great fatigue of mind and body, and a profound sentiment of discouragement with regard to the future, and of disquiet with regard to the past!"

How different are the words of Paul as he neared the end of his earthly life. They are a triumphant epitaph. Some thirty years after his encounter with Christ on the Damascus Road, in every regard that matters he was without regret or remorse. With an economy of words known only to a Holy Spirit–inspired writer, he not only affirms his own spiritual triumph but also offers forceful motivation for every believer to live a life of faithful service to Christ.

As noted several times previously, when Paul wrote this letter the pure gospel was being contaminated in many churches by compromise and falsehood. Ungodly teachers were distorting the truth and causing many nominal Christians to "fall away from the faith [and to pay] attention to deceitful spirits and doctrines of demons" (1 Tim. 4:1). Many true believers tolerated ungodliness in the body of Christ and in their own lives, being more concerned about pleasing themselves and other men than about pleasing God.

Paul knew that his present imprisonment would be his final one, from which he would escape only by martyrdom. It was a difficult time for him, not because of his own physical predicament but because of the spiritual predicament of so many of the believers for whom he had poured out his heart and his life. He had special concern for Timothy, for the problems of false teaching and false living he faced in the church at Ephesus and for the problems of timidity and apprehension he faced in his personal life. Again and again in his two letters to Timothy, he challenged him to have courage, consistency, and faithfulness, and to resist the onslaught of evil and error with the power of God's Word. In the words of a sixteenth-century theologian, Paul was "laying down his arms that Timothy might take them up." He wanted his son in the Lord to be able one day to write a similar epitaph for himself.

Yet despite his deep concerns for the church and for Timothy, the apostle's final words reflect the eloquent calmness that comes only from settled confidence in the Lord.

Although he was not of Paul's spiritual stature, Timothy nevertheless was in a wonderfully select group among the saints of God. He was Paul's successor in somewhat the way in which Joshua was the successor of Moses. "Now it came about after the death of Moses the servant of the Lord that the Lord spoke to Joshua the son of Nun, Moses' servant, saying, 'Moses My servant is dead; now therefore arise, cross this Jordan, you and all this people, to the land which I am giving to them, to the sons of Israel'" (Josh. 1:2). He also was similarly blessed as Elisha, on whom was placed not only Elijah's mantle but also his spirit (2 Kings 2:12–15).

In this passage, Paul examines his life from three perspectives. In verse 6, he looks at the close of his earthly life and ministry and declares he is ready. In verse 7, he looks at the past and declares he was faithful. In verse 8, he looks at the future and anticipates heavenly honor and reward.

THE PRESENT: THE CLOSE, FOR WHICH HE IS READY

For I am already being poured out as a drink offering, and the time of my departure has come. (4:6)

Like "but you" at the beginning of the previous verse, **For I** is emphatic. There was a special urgency for Timothy to perform his ministry with steadfastness, because Paul's ministry was about to end.

Being poured out as a drink offering is a figure taken from the Old Testament sacrificial system. As commanded in the book of Numbers, the people of Israel, as well as Gentiles who lived among them, were first to give a burnt offering of one of the prescribed animals, then a grain offering, and finally a drink offering (15:1–10). While writing Timothy, Paul **already** was **being poured out as a drink offering,** his final offering to the Lord who had sacrificed Himself for the apostle and for all people in all ages. And just as he had offered himself to the Lord as "a living and holy sacrifice, acceptable to God" (Rom. 12:1) while he was alive, he now offered himself to the Lord in his death. He was "ministering as a priest the gospel of God, that [his] offering of the Gentiles might become acceptable, sanctified by the Holy Spirit" (15:16).

Paul's speaking of his death **as a drink offering** also may have referred to the type of execution he expected to suffer. Because Roman citizens could not be crucified, he knew that he likely would be beheaded, literally pouring out his own blood for the Lord. Some five years earlier he had written believers in Philippi, "But even if I am being poured out as a drink offering upon the sacrifice and service of your faith, I rejoice and share my joy with you all" (Phil. 2:17).

Battle scars are the mark of the faithful soldier, and Paul had them in abundance. He had been "beaten times without number, . . . received from the Jews thirty-nine lashes, . . . [and been] beaten with rods." At least once he had been stoned, three times he was shipwrecked. He had spent "a night and a day . . . in the deep," and had "been in labor and hardship, through many sleepless nights, in hunger and thirst, often without food, in cold and exposure" (2 Cor. 11:23–27). But the supreme mark of the faithful soldier is to give his life in battle; and that mark the apostle was now willingly prepared to receive.

He always had been ready to make the ultimate sacrifice, but now the possibility was about to become reality: **the time of my departure has come.** As in verse 3, *kairos* does not here refer to chronological but epochal **time.** Paul was speaking of the final *period* of his life and ministry, not the final hours or days. He obviously expected to live a few more months before his **departure,** because he asked Timothy to "bring the cloak which I left at Troas with Carpus, and the books, especially the parchments" (v. 13), and to "make every effort to come before winter" (v. 21). He had the comforting hope of once more seeing Timothy face-to-face before he died.

When the apostle was first brought to trial in Rome, none of his fellow believers stood by him (v. 16). This great man of God was the spiritual progenitor, directly or indirectly, of perhaps most of the redeemed souls in the Gentile world. But during his time of greatest personal need, he sat friendless in a dark, filthy prison, facing Nero's certain sentence of death. He was not bitter but, like his Lord, prayed for his persecutors that the injustice might "not be counted against them" (v. 16). "The Lord stood with me, and strengthened me," he affirmed, "in order that through me the proclamation might be fully accomplished, and that all the Gentiles might hear; and I was delivered out of the lion's mouth. The Lord will deliver me from every evil deed, and will bring me safely to His heavenly kingdom" (vv. 17–18).

Has come translates an intensive perfect of *ephistēmi,* indicating that **the time** of Paul's **departure** had arrived but had a continuing effect. The clouds of death had come and still hovered over him.

But for Paul, they were not dark clouds, because death held no peril for him. Like Peter, he viewed death simply as "the laying aside of [his] earthly dwelling" (2 Peter 1:14). It was a move from his demanding and painful life on earth to the infinitely glorious life of peace and rest to come, when he would forever be with the Lord.

Departure is from *analusis,* which has a variety of meanings. William Barclay explains four of those meanings, each of which gives a vivid picture of the way in which the apostle viewed his last days.

(a) It is the word for unyoking an animal from the shafts of the cart or the plough. Death to Paul was rest from toil. He would be glad to lay the burden down. . . . (b) It is the word for loosening bonds or fetters. Death for Paul was a liberation and a release. He was to exchange the confines of a Roman prison for the glorious liberty of the courts of heaven. (c) It is the word for loosening the ropes of a tent. For Paul it was time to strike camp again. Many a journey he had made across the roads of Asia Minor and of Europe. Now he was setting out on his last and his greatest journey: he was taking the road that led to God. (d) It is the word for loosening the mooring ropes of a ship. Many a time

Paul had sailed the Mediterranean, and had felt the ship leave the harbour for the deep waters. Now he is to launch out into the greatest deep of all; he is setting sail to cross the waters of death to arrive in the haven of eternity. (*The Letters to Timothy, Titus and Philemon* [Philadelphia: Westminster, 1957], 209)

For a Christian, death is exchanging the burden of earthly life for the eternal joy of heaven (cf. Phil. 1:21).

Paul did not die like Napoleon, Gandhi, Talleyrand, or any other person—no matter how successful and acclaimed—who does not know Christ. The apostle faced his **departure** with no feeling of futility or hopelessness or despair but with the divine assurance that his real life was only about to begin. Just as he had faced earthly living without fear, he faced earthly dying without fear. Because he abode so faithfully in the will of his sovereign God, he could echo the words of Jesus, who said, "No one has taken [my life] away from Me, but I lay it down on My own initiative" (John 10:18). As the Lord Jesus had commanded, Paul took up his own cross and never laid it down, in the certain knowledge that "this perishable must put on the imperishable, and this mortal must put on immortality. But when this perishable will have put on the imperishable, and this mortal will have put on immortality," he would exult with Isaiah that "Death is swallowed up in victory," and cry out with Hosea, "O death, where is your victory? O death, where is your sting?'" (1 Cor. 15:53–55; cf. Isa. 25:8; Hos. 13:14).

THE PAST: THE COURSE, IN WHICH HE WAS FAITHFUL

I have fought the good fight, I have finished the course, I have kept the faith; (4:7)

Paul next reflects on his life and service since salvation. It was a life in which he breathed every breath and lived every moment in service of his Lord, a life in which no sacrifice was too great and no commitment too demanding.

Perhaps Theodore Roosevelt had that verse in mind when he wrote,

It is not the critic who counts; not the man who points out how the strong man stumbled or where the doer of deeds could have done better. The credit belongs to the man who is actually in the arena, whose face is marred by dust and sweat and blood, who strives valiantly; who errs, and comes short again and again, because there is no effort without error and shortcoming; who does actually try to do the deed; who knows the great enthusiasm, the great devotion, and spends himself in a worthy cause; who, at the worst, if he fails, at least fails while daring greatly.

Far better is it to dare mighty things, to win glorious triumphs, even though checked by failure, than to rank with those poor spirits who neither enjoy nor suffer much because they live in a gray twilight that knows neither victory nor defeat. (From speech on the strenuous life, Hamilton Club, Chicago, April 10, 1899)

Paul lived his life doing great things in the power of God. As reflected in the English, **have fought, have finished,** and **have kept** (like "has come" at the end of v. 6) translate intensive perfect verbs, indicating completed action that has continuing results. Paul had no regret, no sense of unfulfillment or incompleteness. After the Lord took control, he truly had lived life to the fullest. Everything God had called and enabled him to do, he did. He left no unfinished symphony. There can be no greater satisfaction—and certainly no more glorious way to end the Christian life—than to know, as he did, that you have fully accomplished all that the Lord has called you to do. That is precisely what he was asking Timothy to do: "fulfill your ministry" (v. 5).

We cannot help wondering how we too can live our lives in that way. How was Paul able to make such a claim? What was the motive of his astounding spiritual faithfulness and achievement? He himself gives the answer in the three short clauses of verse 7.

Five principles are expressed or implied in this verse that were foundational to Paul's life and service. First, he recognized that he was in a spiritual struggle. **Have fought** is from the verb *agōnizomai* and **fight** is from the related noun *agōn*. As one would guess, they are the source of our English "agonizing" and "agony." In New Testament times, both words were commonly used in reference to athletic contests, in particular public games such as the famous Greek olympics, which had originated several centuries earlier. The words also were used of other types of struggles that involve great effort and energy, whether physical or spiritual.

Paul had used the same basic phrase in his first letter to Timothy, admonishing him to "fight the good fight of faith" (6:12). He reminded Corinthian believers that "everyone who competes [*agōnizomai*] in the games exercises self-control in all things. They then do it to receive a perishable wreath, but we an imperishable" (1 Cor. 9:25). The same verb (italicized in the following references) was used by Jesus in calling men to "*strive* to enter by the narrow door" (Luke 13:24). In his letter to the church at Colossae, Paul testified that "for this purpose also I labor, *striving* according to His power, which mightily works within me" (1:29) and praised Epaphras, "one of your number, a bondslave of Jesus Christ, [who] sends you his greetings, always *laboring earnestly* for you in his prayers, that you may stand perfect and fully assured in all the will of God" (4:12). We are to "labor and *strive*," he says, "because we have fixed our hope on the living God, who is the Savior of all men, especially of believers" (1 Tim. 4:10).

The faithful and productive Christian life is nothing less than a fierce and relentless struggle "against the rulers, against the powers, against the world forces of this darkness, against the spiritual forces of wickedness in the heavenly places" (Eph. 6:12). Commenting on that verse, William Hendricksen writes,

> It had been a fight against Satan; against the principalities and powers, the world-rulers of this darkness in the heavenlies; against Jewish and pagan vice and violence; against Judaism among the Galatians; against fanaticism among the Thessalonians; against contention, fornication, and litigation among the Corinthians; against incipient Gnosticism among the Ephesians and Colossians; against fightings without and fears within; and last but not least, against the law of sin and death operating within his own heart. (*New Testament Commentary: Expositions of the Pastoral Epistles* [Grand Rapids: Baker, 1965], 315)

The faithful Christian constantly battles his own flesh, his own sin, his own ignorance and laziness. He even has to battle temptation to do things that are perfectly good in themselves in place of other things that are immeasurably more important. Every day there are new fronts on which the struggle continues.

Second, Paul recognized that the cause he pursued was noble. He had a tremendously elevated sense of dedication to the divine cause in which he was engaged. He was fighting **the good fight.** *Kalos* (**good**) refers to that which is intrinsically good, good in itself, without any qualification. It also was used of that which is inherently and genuinely beautiful and of things that fully conform to their basic nature and purpose. Elsewhere in the New Testament it is used of many such things. In Matthew it is used of good fruit (3:10), of a good tree (12:33), of good ground (13:8), and of good fish (13:48). Paul uses it of God's law (Rom. 7:16) and of all His creatures (1 Tim. 4:4).

The apostle was extremely perplexed that so many believers were seeking "after their own interests, not those of Christ Jesus" (Phil. 2:21). To the complete contrary, he considered his own impressive religious credentials to be rubbish (Phil. 3:4–7) and, in fact, counted "all things to be loss in view of the surpassing value of knowing Christ Jesus my Lord, for whom I have suffered the loss of all things, and count them but rubbish in order that I may gain Christ" (v. 8). Nothing mattered but the cause of Christ.

It was a great satisfaction for the apostle to be able to say that Timothy "is doing the Lord's work, as I also am" (1 Cor. 16:10). Despite his limitations, this younger co-laborer was following in the apostle's footsteps, selflessly serving, expending himself in the cause of Christ, faithfully proclaiming the divine "word of reconciliation" (2 Cor. 5:19).

Christians are not saved simply or even primarily for their own sakes. We are first of all saved for the glory of God and to fulfill His holy calling to be His witnesses to an unsaved world (Matt. 28:19–20; 2 Tim. 1:9; Heb. 3:1). That noblest of all callings to the noblest of all causes should inspire every believer to "seek first His kingdom and His righteousness" (Matt. 6:33). It should motivate us to yield every gift and talent, every hour and opportunity, every resource and all of our energy to lifelong service in the will and power of our Lord.

Third, Paul recognized the need to avoid wandering, to have the self-discipline to stay on his divinely appointed **course** until it was finished. From spiritual birth until the time God calls us into His divine presence, that is our divine mission.

Ted Williams, the famed baseball player, reportedly had such powers of concentration that, when he was standing at bat, he could not be distracted even by firecrackers thrown at his feet. He allowed nothing to interfere with his unusual concentration at that moment. That is the degree of self-discipline for which every child of God should yearn in serving Him. The writer of Proverbs wisely admonishes: "Let your eyes look directly ahead, and let your gaze be fixed straight in front of you. Watch the path of your feet, and all your ways will be established. Do not turn to the right nor to the left; turn your foot from evil" (Prov. 4:25–27).

Course is from *dromos,* which literally refers to the running of a race and metaphorically was used of fulfilling a lifetime career, occupation, or military service. During his first sermon in the synagogue at Antioch of Pisidia, Paul spoke of John the Baptist, saying, "And while John was completing his course [*dromos*], he kept saying, 'What do you suppose that I am? I am not He. But behold, one is coming after me the sandals of whose feet I am not worthy to untie'" (Acts 13:25). Using the same word to describe his own calling, the apostle some years later assured the elders from Ephesus, "I do not consider my life of any account as dear to myself, in order that I may finish my course [*dromos*], and the ministry which I received from the Lord Jesus, to testify solemnly of the gospel of the grace of God" (Acts 20:24).

The writer of Hebrews warns of the two major hindrances that relentlessly threaten to deflect believers from their God-given **course.** "Therefore, since we have so great a cloud of witnesses surrounding us," he says, "let us also lay aside every *encumbrance,* and the *sin* which so easily entangles us, and let us run with endurance the race that is set before us" (Heb. 12:1, emphasis added).

Because the writer distinguishes encumbrances from sin, they obviously are not the same thing. An encumbrance is not evil in itself. Normally, it may be harmless or even worthwhile. The danger and harm come when such things hinder our service to Christ. They weigh us down as we are running, they distract our attention when we should be concentrating, they move our focus from the Lord's work to something else, and they sap energy that should be dedicated entirely to Him. Anything unnecessary that we allow in our lives becomes a spiritual encumbrance. Paul called such things "wood, hay, straw" (1 Cor. 3:12). They are not bad but have very limited value.

The second hindrance mentioned in Hebrews 12:1 is more obvious and much worse. Sin does not merely deflect us from the Lord's work but often robs us of headway already gained. If the sin is unusually serious, the Lord Himself may pull us from the race, because our testimony and effectiveness have been undermined (cf. 1 Cor. 11:30; 1 John 5:16). The great apostle was very much aware of that potential threat to his own ministry. He had no fear of such things as "bonds and afflictions," as long as he could "finish [his] course, and the ministry which [he] received from the Lord Jesus, to testify solemnly of the gospel of the grace of God" (Acts 20:23–24). But he had great concern that he might somehow do something or fail to do something for which the Lord would find him unworthy of his calling. "Therefore I run in such a way, as not without aim," he said. "I box in such a way, as not beating the air; but I buffet my body and make it my slave, lest possibly, after I have preached to others, I myself should be disqualified" (1 Cor. 9:26–27).

The writer of Hebrews goes on to point us to the only protection against encumbrances and sin, namely, fixing "our eyes on Jesus, the author and perfecter of faith, who for the joy set before Him endured the cross, despising the shame, and has sat down at the right hand of the throne of God" (12:2).

Even after Jesus questioned Peter's love and warned of his coming afflictions for the sake of the gospel, the disciple still did not have his eyes fixed on the Master. Instead he became curious about John, saying, "Lord, . . . what about this man?" and received another rebuke: "Jesus said to him, 'If I want him to remain until I come, what is that to you? You follow Me!'" (John 21:22). In other words, if the Lord allowed John to live until the Second Coming, that was none of Peter's concern. Peter's concern should have been about his own faithfulness.

Rudyard Kipling's famous poem "If" is not Christian, but it captures the essence of the mature life, the life that keeps everything in its right perspective and priority.

If you can keep your head when all about you
    Are losing theirs and blaming it on you;
If you can trust yourself when all men doubt you,
    But make allowance for their doubting too;
If you can wait and not be tired by waiting,
    Or being lied about, don't deal in lies,
Or being hated don't give way to hating,
    And yet don't look too good, nor talk too wise;

If you can dream—and not make dreams your master;
    If you can think—and not make thoughts your aim;
If you can meet with Triumph and Disaster
    And treat those two impostors just the same;
If you can bear to hear the truth you've spoken
    Twisted by knaves to make a trap for fools,
Or watch the things you gave your life to, broken,
    And stoop and build 'em up with worn-out tools; . . .

If you can talk with crowds and keep your virtue,
    Or walk with Kings—nor lose the common touch;
If neither foes nor loving friends can hurt you;
    If all men count with you, but none too much;
If you can fill the unforgiving minute
    With sixty seconds' worth of distance run—
Yours is the Earth and everything that's in it,
    And—which is more—you'll be a Man, my son!

A fourth foundational principle of Paul's life was recognizing the need to treasure time. We have only the time allotted by God, and none of us knows when it will run out. Every Christian life runs by His divine timetable and against His divine clock. We do not know how long He will hold open the door of a given opportunity or of our entire time of service. "Be careful how you walk," Paul therefore counsels, "not as unwise men, but as wise, making the most of your time, because the days are evil" (Eph. 5:16). God gives us many things without limit—His love, His grace, and many others. But His gift of time is strictly measured.

In 490 B.C., the Athenians won a crucial and decisive battle over the forces of King Darius I of Persia on a plain near the small Greek coastal village of Marathon. One of the Greek soldiers ran nonstop from the battlefield to Athens to carry the news of victory. But he ran with such unreserved effort that he fell dead at the feet of those to whom he delivered the message. The marathon races that are so popular today are named for that battlefield. They also are a tribute to that soldier, the length of the run being based on the approximate distance (just over 26 miles) he ran in his last maximum effort for his country. He had completed his course, and there is no nobler way for a man to die.

A fifth foundational principle of Paul's life and ministry was recognizing his sacred trust regarding the Word of God, the controlling element of everything he said and did. We should all want to be able to say with the apostle's truthfulness and sincerity, **I have kept the faith.**

Have kept is from *tēreō,* which carries the various ideas of watching over, heeding, or preserving. Jesus used the verb three times in His high priestly prayer. He lovingly asked His Father to *"keep* them [His people] in Thy name, the name which Thou hast given Me, that they may be one, even as We are," remembering that "while I was with them, I was *keeping* them in Thy name which Thou hast given Me; and I guarded them, and not one of them perished." A few verses later, He asked that the Father would *"keep* them from the evil one" (John 17:11–12, 15, emphasis added; cf. 1 John 5:18). Jude speaks of believers as those "who are the called, beloved in God the Father, and *kept* for Jesus Christ" (Jude 1:1, emphasis added).

On our part, keeping **the faith** involves "being diligent to *preserve* the unity of the Spirit in the bond of peace" (Eph. 4:3; emphasis added) and *keeping* ourselves "free from sin" (1 Tim. 5:22). Using a different verb but giving the same admonition, Paul charged Timothy to guard the Word of God, which had been entrusted to him (1 Tim. 6:20; 2 Tim. 1:14). Regardless of the obstacles or cost, we are to preserve and proclaim the immeasurable treasure of the Word.

The first requirement for keeping that treasure is to recognize that it *is* a treasure. A beautiful and touching story is told of a young French girl who had been born blind. After she learned to read by touch, a friend gave her a Braille copy of Mark's gospel. She read it so much that her fingers became calloused and insensitive. In an effort to regain her feeling, she cut the skin from the ends of her fingers. Tragically, however, her callouses were replaced by permanent and even more insensitive scars. She sobbingly gave the book a good-bye kiss, saying, "Farewell, farewell, sweet word of my heavenly Father." In doing so, she discovered that her lips were even more sensitive than her fingers had been, and she spent the rest of her life reading her great treasure with her lips. Would that every Christian had such an appetite for the Word of God!

In 1904, William Borden, a member of the Borden dairy family, finished high school in Chicago and was given a world cruise as a graduation present. Particularly while traveling through the Near East and Far East, he became heavily burdened for the lost. After returning home, he spent seven years at Princeton University, the first four in undergraduate work and the last three in seminary. While in school, he penned these words in the back of his Bible: "No reserves." Although his family pleaded with him to take control of the business, which was foundering, he insisted that God's call to the mission field had priority. After disposing of his wealth, he added "No retreat" after "No reserves." On his way to China to witness to Muslims there, he contracted cerebral meningitis in Egypt and died within a month. After his death, someone looking through his Bible discovered these final words: "No regrets." He knew that the Lord does not require success, only faithfulness.

We should be constantly aware that our lives are a spiritual struggle, because that is what God's Word repeatedly teaches. We know we are engaged in the most noble of causes, because that is how the Word defines it. We are to labor with self-discipline, because that is what the Word requires. We know our time is precious and limited and we know our calling is a sacred trust, because that is what the Word declares to be true.

THE FUTURE: THE CROWN, WITH WHICH HE WILL BE REWARDED

in the future there is laid up for me the crown of righteousness, which the Lord, the righteous Judge, will award to me on that day; and not only to me, but also to all who have loved His appearing. (4:8)

Loipos, translated **in the future,** refers generally to what remains, that which is left to come. What yet remained for Paul, after the past and present were finished, would be by far the most glorious part of his life in Christ.

Paul had the certain, Spirit-inspired assurance that **in the future there [was] laid up for [him] the crown of righteousness.** After he had fought the good fight, finished the course, and kept the faith, he would be given the victor's reward.

Laid up carries the idea of being safely stored and carefully guarded. A certain part of their heavenly treasure is stored up in advance by believers themselves. "Lay up for yourselves treasures in heaven," Jesus commands, "where neither moth nor rust destroys, and where thieves do not break in or steal" (Matt. 6:20). In his first letter to Timothy, Paul counsels him to instruct the people in his congregation "to do good, to be rich in good works, to be generous and ready to share, storing up for themselves the treasure of a good foundation for the future, so that they may take hold of that which is life indeed" (1 Tim. 6:18–19).

Although he had not met Jesus during His earthly ministry, Paul doubtless had heard of his Lord's promise "Blessed are you when men cast insults at you, and persecute you, and say all kinds of evil against you falsely, on account of Me. Rejoice, and be glad, for your reward in heaven is great" (Matt. 5:11–12). Christ also said that His Father will reward those who give, pray, and fast in secret—that is, sincerely rather than for the notice and praise of men (Matt. 6:4, 6, 18). Christ will, in fact, join His Father in dispensing those rewards, "for the Son of Man is going to come in the glory of His Father with His angels; and will then recompense every man according to his deeds" (Matt. 16:27). Jesus' promise was not a new revelation but was a quotation from Psalm 62:12—"And lovingkindness is Thine, O Lord, for Thou dost recompense a man according to his work." The writer of Hebrews tells us that "he who comes to God [not only] must believe that He is, [but also must believe] that He is a rewarder of those who seek Him" (Heb. 11:6).

No writer of Scripture more forcefully proclaimed the truth that salvation is entirely by God's grace working through our faith than did the apostle Paul. Yet no other writer of Scripture more joyously anticipated the reward he one day would receive from the hand of the Lord who had saved and sustained him by grace. He continually pressed "on toward the goal for the prize of the upward call of God in Christ Jesus" (Phil. 3:14).

This reward will be based more on our motives than our accomplishments. The writer of Proverbs asks rhetorically, "Does He not consider it who weighs the hearts? And does He not know it who keeps your soul? And will He not render to man according to his work?" (Prov. 24:12). Selfishly motivated good deeds may be of great help to other people and may be used by God for His glory, but they will merit no reward for the doer.

On the other hand, good work that is sincerely intended but not completed through no fault of the doer will merit a sincere doer's reward, because it is the heart that God weighs. William Borden accomplished virtually none of the ministry he had envisioned, having been cut off by death even before he reached his field of service. But his final declaration of "No regrets" was well founded in the assurance that he had genuinely sought and faithfully obeyed the Lord's will.

Paul had no regrets. He did not claim perfection. "I am conscious of nothing against myself," he said, "yet I am not by this acquitted" (1 Cor. 4:4). Nevertheless, he had absolute confidence that God had **laid up for [him] the crown of righteousness.**

Crown is from *stephanos,* which has the literal meaning of surrounding and was used of plaited wreaths or garlands that were placed on the heads of dignitaries, military victors, and winners of athletic contests as a mark of great honor. It was a *stephanos* of thorns that Pilate's soldiers placed on Jesus' head as they mockingly hailed Him as "King of the Jews!" (Matt. 29).

Stephanos perhaps most commonly was used of the wreath placed on the heads of winning athletes, much as medals are placed around the necks of Olympic champions today. It was the only prize (cf.

2 Tim. 2:5) ancient athletes received but was cherished as a great treasure. Yet, they run "to receive a perishable wreath [*stephanos*]," Paul said, "but we an imperishable" (1 Cor. 9:25).

Of righteousness translates the single Greek noun *dikaiosunē*, which is here a genitive. Linguistically, it could be either a genitive of source, meaning that **righteousness** is the source of the crown, or a genitive of apposition, in which case **righteousness** describes the nature of the crown. As noted above, a believer's heavenly reward is based to some extent on his faithfulness, making possible a genitive of source. But in this context it seems more appropriate to take **righteousness** as an appositive, describing the crown. It is the crown of eternal righteousness—the very righteousness of the Redeemer granted in full perfection to the glorified believer.

Certain rewards that believers will receive or not receive will be individual, based on their own faithfulness. Summarizing the truths of the parable of the talents, Jesus said, "To everyone who has shall more be given, and he shall have an abundance; but from the one who does not have, even what he does have shall be taken away" (Matt. 25:29). Paul teaches that "we must all appear before the judgment seat of Christ, that each one may be recompensed for his deeds in the body, according to what he has done, whether good or bad" (2 Cor. 5:10). In his previous letter to believers at Corinth, he had explained that "each man's work will become evident; for the day will show it, because it is to be revealed with fire; and the fire itself will test the quality of each man's work. If any man's work which he has built upon it remains, he shall receive a reward. If any man's work is burned up, he shall suffer loss; but he himself shall be saved, yet so as through fire" (1 Cor. 3:13–15).

But Paul is here speaking of the **crown of righteousness** with which *every* believer will be crowned. James speaks of it as a "crown of life" (James 1:12), and Peter as "the unfading crown of glory" (1 Peter 5:4). In the parable of the landowner who hired men at different times throughout the day and paid them all the same wage (Matt. 20:1–16), Jesus explains that every believer will share equally in eternal life and eternal righteousness.

He also assures us that "blessed are those who hunger and thirst for righteousness, for they shall be satisfied" (Matt. 5:6). Our satisfaction will come from the very thing for which we seek, **righteousness** itself being the reward of those who seek it. It is "the hope of righteousness" for which believers eagerly wait "through the Spirit, by faith" (Gal. 5:5), as we look "for new heavens and a new earth, in which righteousness dwells" (2 Peter 3:13). "The kingdom of God *is* . . . righteousness and peace and joy in the Holy Spirit" (Rom. 14:17, emphasis added). **Righteousness** is that which, by the Lord's gracious provision, will one day be our harvest (2 Cor. 9:10) and our clothing (Rev. 19:8). It could not be otherwise, because "we know that, when [Christ] appears, we shall be like Him" (1 John 3:2).

When we believed in Christ as Savior and Lord, He imputed His righteousness to us (Rom. 4:6, 11); and as we live out our lives in Christ, His Holy Spirit works practical righteousness in us and through us (Rom. 6:13, 19; 8:4; Eph. 5:9; 1 Peter 2:24). Yet because of sin, which clings to us like an old dirty garment, we must battle against unrighteousness. It is only at the completion of that battle that His righteousness will be perfected in us, when we receive the very **crown of righteousness** from the Lord's own hands. It is the victor's wreath, Paul says, **which the Lord** Himself, **the righteous Judge, will award . . . on that day.**

Paul has referred to **that day** two other times in this letter. He said, "For this reason I also suffer these things, but I am not ashamed; for I know whom I have believed and I am convinced that He is able to guard what I have entrusted to Him until that day" (1:12). A few verses later he prayed that his beloved Onesiphorus would "find mercy from the Lord on that day" (v. 18).

He is speaking, of course, of the **day** of Christ's return in particular, the **day** of resurrection and rapture, when "the Lord Himself will descend from heaven with a shout, with the voice of the archangel, and with the trumpet of God; and the dead in Christ shall rise first. Then we who are alive and remain shall be caught up together with them in the clouds to meet the Lord in the air, and thus we shall always be with the Lord" (1 Thess. 4:16–17). In that glorious **day,** "we shall all be changed, in a moment, in the twinkling of an eye, at the last trumpet; for the trumpet will sound, and the dead will be raised imperishable, and we shall be changed. For this perishable must put on the imperishable, and this mortal must put on immortality. But when this perishable will have put on the imperishable, and this mortal will have put on immortality, then will come about the saying that is written, 'Death is swallowed up in victory'" (1 Cor. 15:51–54).

The apostle admonished the church in Philippi, "Do all things without grumbling or disputing; that you may prove yourselves to be blameless and innocent, children of God above reproach in the midst of a crooked and perverse generation, among whom you appear as lights in the world, holding fast the word of life, so that *in the day of Christ* I may have cause to glory because I did not run in vain nor toil in vain" (Phil. 2:14–16, emphasis added).

The glorious prospect of receiving God's crown of righteousness not only belongs to Paul **but also** belongs **to all who have loved His appearing.** Again the apostle uses a perfect tense (**have loved**), indicating the accomplishment of something in the past that has continuing effects.

"Love is from God," John says, "and everyone who loves is born of God and knows God" (1 John 4:7). Conversely, he goes on to explain, "The one who does not love does not know God, for God is love" (v. 8). Love of God is so absolutely essential that "if anyone does not love the Lord," Paul says, "let him be accursed" (1 Cor. 16:22).

In other words, a person who does not love God has no claim on God, either for salvation or for reward. And every true believer *will* love God and the things of God, because love is the supreme and necessary mark of salvation. When people become Christians, they come to love God. The regenerated believer is given a new heart, a new will, and a new spiritual attitude, all of which will be expressed in love, because "the love of God has been poured out within our hearts through the Holy Spirit who was given to us" (Rom. 5:5). There are no exceptions.

Likewise, all believers will love **His [Christ's] appearing,** because they look forward to coming into His divine presence, where they will live and serve throughout eternity. Because our true "citizenship is in heaven, . . . we eagerly wait for a Savior, the Lord Jesus Christ" (Phil. 3:20).

Paul was not speaking from pride. As much as any saint who has ever lived, he knew that every good thing he had and did came by the grace of God. "For this purpose also I labor," he explained to the church at Colossae, "striving according to His power, which mightily works within me" (Col. 1:29). He was not taking credit for himself but was acknowledging that by the grace and power of God, working through the human faithfulness that the Lord requires, his life was coming to a victorious end. On the basis of the Lord's own promise, he expected one day soon to hear, "Well done, good and faithful servant" (Matt. 25:21).

Friends and Foes

12

Make every effort to come to me soon; for Demas, having loved this present world, has deserted me and gone to Thessalonica; Crescens has gone to Galatia, Titus to Dalmatia. Only Luke is with me. Pick up Mark and bring him with you, for he is useful to me for service. But Tychicus I have sent to Ephesus. When you come bring the cloak which I left at Troas with Carpus, and the books, especially the parchments. Alexander the coppersmith did me much harm; the Lord will repay him according to his deeds. Be on guard against him yourself, for he vigorously opposed our teaching. At my first defense no one supported me, but all deserted me; may it not be counted against them. But the Lord stood with me, and strengthened me, in order that through me the proclamation might be fully accomplished, and that all the Gentiles might hear; and I was delivered out of the lion's mouth. The Lord will deliver me from every evil deed, and will bring me safely to His heavenly kingdom; to Him be the glory forever and ever. Amen.

Greet Prisca and Aquila, and the household of Onesiphorus. Erastus remained at Corinth, but Trophimus I left sick at Mi-

letus. Make every effort to come before winter. Eubulus greets you, also Pudens and Linus and Claudia and all the brethren. The Lord be with your spirit. Grace be with you. (4:9–22)

A business, government, or large organization cannot function properly or survive without networking. Suppliers, customers, employees, stockholders, and many others are necessarily involved. There is no better illustration of this principle than the human body with its wonderfully varied and intricately related parts. Paul used that figure in his first letter to the immature and disunified church at Corinth to teach them what unity and harmony in the body of Christ must be like (1 Cor. 12:14–27).

It is therefore no surprise that the last part of Paul's last letter focuses on other people, the many friends and a few foes, who influenced his ministry in one way or another. The great apostle knew they were involved in everything he did, and in these closing verses he recognizes and remembers this network of people. Even he could not effectively minister alone. He was fully aware of his distinctive calling and authority as an apostle of the Lord Jesus Christ (see, e.g., Rom. 1:1; 1 Cor. 1:1; 1 Tim. 1:1; 2 Tim. 1:1). But he did not presume to work for the Lord independent of other believers or try to meet every need and accomplish every task himself. He had teams of fellow workers, fellow servants, fellow preachers and teachers in whom he placed great trust for mutual ministry. Most of them were faithful co-laborers, "valiant men [and women] whose hearts God had touched" (1 Sam. 10:26).

Some of the people were old friends and some were new, some were consistent in their service and some were not, some were always ready to volunteer and some were never to be found, some were willing to make any sacrifice for the Lord, and others were not willing. Quite a few were unbelievers, some of them being within the church and others being outside. But all were a part of Paul's life, and all played a role in his ministry.

As he faced the executioner's ax, many of these people were on his mind. In passing on the mantle of ministry to Timothy, he brought the young pastor up to date on the spiritual condition, activities, and whereabouts of certain men and women. Some of them, including Timothy, he hoped would visit him before he died. Others he simply greeted or extended greetings from. Some are named, and others are nameless. Some of them he was sending out or had already sent out to strategic places to build up faltering congregations. Others he mentioned because of the special harm they had brought to him and to the cause of Christ.

Paul did not write this section as an afterthought; it was not incidental but vital to the Spirit-inspired message. The Lord wanted the rest of His church to know about these people in Paul's life and to learn from their faithfulness or their failure.

TIMOTHY, THE FAITHFUL SON

Make every effort to come to me soon; (4:9)

At the beginning of his first letter to Timothy, the apostle addresses him as "my true child in the faith" (1:2) and in this second letter as "my beloved son" (1:2). He had no other earthly friend who was so dear to him.

Nor did he have a co-worker who was more dependable. He tells the church at Corinth, "I exhort you therefore, be imitators of me. For this reason I have sent to you Timothy, who is my beloved and faithful child in the Lord, and he will remind you of my ways which are in Christ, just as I teach everywhere in every church" (1 Cor. 4:16–17). In the same spirit of confidence, the apostle told the church at Philippi, "I hope in the Lord Jesus to send Timothy to you shortly, so that I also may be encouraged when I learn of your condition. For I have no one else of kindred spirit who will genuinely be concerned for your welfare" (Phil. 2:19–20). Timothy not only followed Paul's doctrine but also his example.

The love was mutual. At the beginning of the second letter, the apostle says to Timothy, "I thank God, whom I serve with a clear conscience the way my forefathers did, as I constantly remember you in my prayers night and day, longing to see you, even as I recall your tears, so that I may be filled with joy" (2 Tim. 1:3–4).

Although the faithful and beloved Luke was with Paul in Rome at the time, the apostle longed to see Timothy with the longing of a father, especially because he knew the possibility of seeing him again in this life would soon be gone. It was therefore imperative that Timothy **make every effort to come** to Paul **soon.**

Many great Christian leaders have had a spiritual mentor, someone who has taken special care in teaching them the Word and in setting a high example. For Timothy, of course, that person was Paul. Like him, such mentors doubtless have no greater satisfaction than seeing someone under their guidance turn into an effective servant of Christ.

The writer of Hebrews told his readers to "take notice that our brother Timothy has been released" (Heb. 13:23). This young minister was following in Paul's footsteps, even to the point of being put in prison for boldly proclaiming and refusing to compromise the gospel.

DEMAS, THE UNFAITHFUL DESERTER

for Demas, having loved this present world, has deserted me and gone to Thessalonica; (4:10a)

Paul moves from the most faithful to the most unfaithful. It is possible that **Demas** in some way had been valuable to Paul and to the ministry in Rome and that the apostle wanted Timothy to come soon in order to pick up the work that **Demas** had abandoned.

Demas is first mentioned by Paul in Colossians, which was written shortly after 1 Timothy and some five years before 2 Timothy, during Paul's first imprisonment in Rome. At that time, **Demas,** along with Luke and Epaphras, was one of the apostle's closest associates (Col. 4:12–14). In the book of Philemon, written about the same time and from the same place, Paul sent greetings in behalf of **Demas,** one of his "fellow workers" (Philem. 24). We can be sure that Paul had invested much time and effort in the careful teaching, counseling, and encouraging of **Demas** and expected him to help carry on the ministry.

At that time any friend of Paul, especially a co-worker, risked sharing persecution and prison with him. As the risk increased, Demas's resolve decreased, because he **loved this present world** more than he loved the Lord, the Lord's people, or the Lord's work. He may not have been a true believer at all. "If anyone loves the world," John says, "the love of the Father is not in him" (1 John 2:15). Demas's heart may have been a rocky place, covered by just enough soil to superficially accept the seed of the gospel but not enough to bring full salvation. When the heat of the world's "affliction or persecution" became too fierce, he withered and fell away (Matt. 13:5–6, 20–21). Or perhaps his heart was thorn infested; and when "the worry of the world, and the deceitfulness of riches [choked] the word, . . . it [proved to be] unfruitful" (Matt. 13:7, 22). His reaction to the deprivations faced in his physical life eventually exposed the depravation of his spiritual life.

In any case, his cowardice was greater than his commitment, and he **deserted** Paul. **Deserted** is from *enkataleipo,* a strong verb that means to utterly abandon and leave someone helpless in a dire situation. Perhaps the sacrifice of many comforts, including the probable loss of his own freedom, became too high a price for Demas. He was a fair-weather disciple, who had never considered the cost of genuine commitment to Christ. He may have been caught up emotionally with the idea of a noble cause, which he did his part to serve when the demands were not great. But when the cause became costly, he was nowhere to be found.

His reason for fleeing **to Thessalonica** is not given, but he must have considered it to be a safe haven. Perhaps that was his home (see Philem. 4), in which case he may not have been known there as a Christian, or believers there were not yet persecuted. He may have renounced Christ altogether and rejoined the world. Whatever the case, he brought great disappointment and anguish to Paul.

CRESCENS, THE FAITHFUL UNKNOWN

Crescens has gone to Galatia, (10b)

Except for what little can be inferred from this brief mention, we know nothing about **Crescens.** Because he was sent **to Galatia** by Paul and did not flee, as did Demas, he obviously was a faithful and dependable servant of Christ. There were many churches in that region, most of which were strong and had been founded by the apostle himself. Paul had ministered in **Galatia** on each of his three missionary journeys, and believers there held a dear place in his heart. He would not have sent them a man in whom he had less than full confidence.

Crescens was a dedicated leader sent to dedicated churches. He is among the myriads of faithful men and women who, for the most part, were known in the early church but have been unknown in church history and are unknown in the church today. Yet his life and work were an open book to the Lord, and we can be sure that he will receive a full divine reward in addition to the deep gratitude of Paul.

TITUS, THE FAITHFUL KNOWN

Titus to Dalmatia. (4:10c)

Titus, on the other hand, was both known and faithful. Paul's letter to him was written several years after 1 Timothy and about a year before 2 Timothy. Besides here and in the book that carries his name, **Titus** is mentioned by the apostle nine times in 2 Corinthians and twice in Galatians.

Paul apparently had preached in Crete during a brief layover there on his way to Rome under guard (see Acts 27:12). At that time, he left **Titus,** his "true child in a common faith, . . . in Crete, that [he] might set in order what remains, and appoint elders in every city as [Paul] directed" (Titus 1:5).

Titus was a builder and equipper, a man the apostle fully trusted to teach and pastor struggling churches. Sometime after release from his two-year house arrest in Rome (Acts 28:30), Paul probably went to Macedonia. From there he went to Dalmatia (also known as Illyricum; see Rom. 15:19), which was located just north of Macedonia on the east side of the Adriatic Sea. He then traveled south to Nicopolis, a town in the province of Achaia near the Macedonian border. It was here that he asked **Titus** to meet him (Titus 3:12). It may have been from Nicopolis that **Titus** went **to Dalmatia,** probably at the request of Paul, in order to strengthen the church there and build up its leaders.

Luke, the Faithful Companion

Only Luke is with me. (4:11a)

Some interpreters take Paul's mention of **only** to indicate disappointment with **Luke,** as if the apostle were saying with regret, "I have no real friend or helper left, just **Luke.**" But that view is unfair to this man and flies in the face of everything else we know of him from the New Testament. It was rather that this devoted friend could not alone carry the burden of ministry in Rome while the apostle languished in a dungeon with no prospect of release. Because of Nero's brutal persecution, many believers had fled the capital. Those who remained were in constant danger and needed spiritual guidance and encouragement more than ever.

Luke is mentioned by name only three times in the New Testament, of which he is the only Gentile author. Yet he wrote the longest of the four gospels as well as the lengthy book of Acts. Paul himself refers to this man as "Luke, the beloved physician" (Col. 4:14) and as one of his "fellow workers" (Philem. 24). Because of his literary skills, it seems probable that he acted sometimes as Paul's amanuensis.

Although **Luke** was a physician by profession, we are told nothing of any medical work he may have done after his conversion, though he doubtless treated Paul and his other companions as their "beloved physician." From his gospel we know him as an evangelist, and from the book of Acts as a capable historian. He was used uniquely by the Holy Spirit to chronicle both the life of Christ and the early life of the body of Christ. Yet, as a humble servant of the Lord and of his fellow saints, he carefully kept himself in the background.

Luke had been a longtime companion of Paul, accompanying the apostle for many years and over hundreds, perhaps thousands, of miles. It is easy to trace his direct association with the apostle through his use of plural first-person pronouns in Acts (we, us, our, etc.). He was with Paul at Troas and Philippi during the second missionary journey, joined him again at the end of the third, and went with him to Jerusalem to face arrest and imprisonment. He accompanied Paul on the trip to Rome, was shipwrecked with him off the shores of Malta, ministered in Rome with him during the first imprisonment, and comforted him during the second and last. At the writing of this letter, the apostle is not sad but glad that Luke still **is with me.**

MARK, THE UNFAITHFUL RESTORED

Pick up Mark and bring him with you, for he is useful to me for service. (4:11b)

We do not know where **Mark** was at this time, but it seems evident that he lived somewhere on the route Timothy would take from Ephesus to Rome. He probably would have traveled by land to Troas (see v. 13) and from there taken a ship to Macedonia. After crossing Macedonia, he may have taken another ship to Brundisium on Italy's east coast and continued on to Rome.

Mark, who sometimes was called John, was a native of Jerusalem, and one of the first congregations of new believers met in his house (Acts 12:12). Because of his promise as a Christian leader, he was chosen to go with Paul and Barnabas as they set out with other companions on the first missionary journey. But when they "came to Perga in Pamphylia, . . . John [Mark] left them and returned to Jerusalem" (Acts 13:13). Whatever Mark's specific reason for leaving, Paul did not think it was adequate or excusable. Some years later, Paul and Barnabas set out again from Antioch to "return and visit the brethren in every city in which we proclaimed the word of the Lord, and see how they are." Barnabas wanted to give Mark a second chance, "but Paul kept insisting that they should not take him along who had deserted them in Pamphylia and had not gone with them to the work. And there arose such a sharp disagreement that they separated from one another, and Barnabas took Mark with him and sailed away to Cyprus" (Acts 15:36–39). Paul had no stomach for men who were lazy, cowardly, or uncommitted. He especially did not want fellow workers who would not carry their share of the load and who bailed out when things became too uncomfortable or demanding.

We do not know if **Mark** changed before or during his ministry with Barnabas, his older cousin (Col 4:10). From all New Testament accounts, Barnabas fully lived up to his name, which means "Son of Encouragement" (Acts 4:36) and probably was a descriptive and loving appellation given to him by the church. Whenever and however the change in **Mark** occurred, Barnabas must have been involved. By the time of Paul's first imprisonment in Rome—perhaps twenty years after the two had parted company—this young man had proved himself not only to Barnabas but also to Paul. During that incarceration, the apostle asked the church at Colossae to welcome the now-faithful **Mark** if he visited them (Col. 4:10) and counted him among his devoted "fellow workers" (Philem. 24).

Mark also spent time with Peter (1 Peter 5:13), from whom he may have received insight into the revelation he records in his gospel. In many ways and to many people, he had become a faithful and valued leader in the early church, and Paul asked Timothy to **bring him [Mark] with you, for he is useful to me for service.**

It is a great disappointment to see gifted servants of the Lord become disinterested in His work and shirk the demands and hardships of ministry. But it is a great satisfaction to see such a person turn from his fears and selfish pursuits and wholeheartedly return to the work of the kingdom.

TYCHICUS, THE FAITHFUL MESSENGER

Tychicus I have sent to Ephesus. (4:12)

Perhaps Paul had earlier sent **Tychicus . . . to Ephesus,** which was located in that man's home province of Asia (Acts 20:4). Or it may be that Paul was sending him there to deliver this second letter to Timothy, just as he had used him to deliver his letters to the churches at Ephesus (Eph. 6:12) and Colossae (Col. 4:7) and perhaps to deliver the letter to Titus (see Titus 3:12).

We do not know what abilities **Tychicus** had, but it seems likely that the Holy Spirit had given him the gift of service (Rom. 12:7). There is no evidence that he was a teacher or pastor, but he was a valuable asset to Paul and a trusted friend.

CARPUS, THE FAITHFUL HOST

When you come bring the cloak which I left at Troas with Carpus, and the books, especially the parchments. (4:13)

Along with his other personal requests of Timothy, Paul asked that he **bring the cloak which I left at Troas with Carpus. Troas** may have been the hometown of **Carpus;** he obviously lived there now. From the context it seems probable that Paul stayed with Carpus there and had entrusted him with the care of several valuable possessions. It also may be that the church in **Troas** met in Carpus's house.

A **cloak** was a large, heavy wool garment that served as both coat and blanket in cold weather, which Paul would soon face (v. 21). In the economy of that day, especially for Christians under Roman persecution, such clothing was extremely expensive.

Books and **parchments** also were expensive. Unlike the cloak, they could provide Paul with no physical comfort or protection, but they were invaluable to him for the sake of the ministry. **Books** probably refers to papyrus scrolls, possibly of Old Testament books. **Parchments** were vellum sheets, made of specially treated animal hides. They were extremely expensive and therefore used for only the most important of documents. These particular **parchments** may have contained copies of Paul's own letters or may have been blank sheets on which he planned to write other letters. He had no plans to finish studying or to finish writing.

One wonders why Paul would not have taken such costly possessions with him wherever he went. It is hard to believe he would have parted with them voluntarily, because the risk of never seeing them again was high. The trouble of taking them along when they were not needed would have paled in light of the trouble, physical and otherwise, of being without them when they *were* needed. For that reason, some scholars suggest that he was summarily arrested in Troas and had no opportunity, or was not allowed, to take these things with him.

ALEXANDER, THE FAITHLESS ENEMY

Alexander the coppersmith did me much harm; the Lord will repay him according to his deeds. Be on guard against him yourself, for he vigorously opposed our teaching. (4:14–15)

Paul devotes almost as many words to **Alexander the coppersmith** as he does to all the other men combined whom he has mentioned in the previous four verses. And for good reason.

This **Alexander** could hardly have been the person who risked his freedom, and possibly his life, by defending Paul in Ephesus (Acts 19:33). He may have been the man whom, along with Hymenaeus, the apostle had "delivered over to Satan, so that they may be taught not to blaspheme" (1 Tim. 1:20).

But Paul's identifying him as **the coppersmith** probably indicates he was neither of those men. Alexander was a common name in that day, and Ephesus was a large city. Like "Demetrius, a silversmith, who made silver shrines of Artemis" (Acts 19:24), this **Alexander** may have been an idolmaker who fiercely resented the apostle and did him **much harm.** For that, as well as for his false teaching, **the Lord will**

repay him according to his deeds, Paul said. Faithful to God's Word (Deut. 32:35), including his own teaching of it (Rom. 12:19), he left vengeance in the hands of God.

Because the apostle tells Timothy to **be on guard against him yourself,** this enemy may have lived in Rome and caused Paul trouble during one or both of his imprisonments. In that case, he was warning Timothy to be on the lookout for him when he arrived there to see Paul.

Even worse than the harm Alexander caused Paul personally was the harm he had done to the cause of Christ by being **vigorously opposed** to Paul's **teaching.** More than an enemy of Paul, he was the enemy of God.

THE UNFAITHFUL ANONYMOUS

At my first defense no one supported me, but all deserted me; may it not be counted against them. (4:16)

Defense translates *apologia,* from which we derive the English "apology" and "apologetics." It referred to a verbal defense and frequently was used as a legal term. In the Roman court system, an accused person had two hearings, the *prima actio,* to clearly establish the charge, and the *secunda actio,* to determine guilt or innocence. Paul's **first defense** would therefore have been a *prima actio.*

Whatever kind of trial it was, not one of Paul's friends and fellow believers had **supported** him. As with the noun **defense,** the Greek verb behind **supported** may have been a legal term, referring to official testimony in court. **No one** stood by Paul or testified on his behalf; instead they **all deserted him.**

It seems certain that Onesiphorus, who "often refreshed [Paul], and was not ashamed of [his] my chains" (1:16), and the faithful Luke (4:11) had not yet arrived in Rome. Had they been there at that time, they would have stood by Paul and gladly shared his fate.

The price for such a stand could have been high. Because Paul was such a well-known leader among the Christians, and because Nero was so vehemently anti-Christian, some scholars believe the emperor himself may have presided over this hearing. Only a few years earlier, Nero had set Rome ablaze, blaming the unbelievably callous and evil deed on the Christians. While still alive, some Christians were sewn into the skins of freshly killed animals and released into the arena among wild dogs, who tore them to pieces. Others were coated with pitch and set afire to light Nero's garden parties. That would be no excuse, of course, for those whom Jesus called not to take up their own crosses and follow Him (Matt. 10:38; 16:24; 27:40).

And although their actions were indefensible, perhaps some of them only rejected Paul, not Christ. Some may have been weak-hearted but not false-hearted. In any case, Paul prayed that their desertion might **not be counted against them.** Like Stephen (Acts 7:60) and the Lord Himself (Luke 23:24), the apostle had a supremely forgiving spirit.

CHRIST, THE FAITHFUL LORD

But the Lord stood with me, and strengthened me, in order that through me the proclamation might be fully accomplished, and that all the Gentiles might hear; and I was delivered out of the lion's mouth. The Lord will deliver me from every evil deed, and will bring me safely to His heavenly kingdom; to Him be the glory forever and ever. Amen. (4:17–18)

Empire-wide persecution of the church had begun and Paul was on trial for his life. He stood before the dreadful Roman tribunal, perhaps before Nero himself. The court would have been jammed with spectators, much as in the trials of famous people in our own day, except that none of the spectators in Rome was on Paul's side (cf. Acts 23:11).

Verses 17–18 form the apex of this passage, testifying to the faithfulness of Christ, **the Lord [who] stood with [Paul] and strengthened [him].** He **stood** there not only or even primarily for Paul's sake but **that through** the apostle **the proclamation** of the gospel **might be fully accomplished, and that all the Gentiles might hear.** Paul was the unique and divinely appointed apostle to the **Gentiles** (Rom. 11:13), and it was above all for their salvation and for the Lord's glory that the apostle himself ministered (cf. Acts 9:15; 22:21; 26:17).

Paul often had been **delivered out of the lion's mouth,** a common figure of mortal danger (see Ps. 22:21; 35:17). It also was the specific danger into which the Lord allowed Daniel to be placed and from which He miraculously delivered the prophet (Dan. 6:16–23). An immeasurably greater threat—for Paul and for every believer—comes from Satan himself, our "adversary, the devil, [who] prowls about like a roaring lion, seeking someone to devour" (1 Peter 5:8). Yet even the devil has no ultimate power over those who belong to Christ.

Paul did not fear physical danger. Many times he had faced death, and at least once was left for dead (see Acts 14:19). "Whatever I face," he declared, **the Lord will deliver me from every evil deed, and will bring me safely to His heavenly kingdom.** He knew that the completion of his own salvation was nearer than when he first believed (cf. Rom. 13:11) and preferred "rather to be absent from the body

and to be at home with the Lord" (2 Cor. 5:8). For Paul, as for every believer, "to live is Christ, and to die is gain" (Phil. 1:21). And although the
apostle would not give up the battle until the Lord took him home, his
loneliness, pain, deprivation, and desertion made the prospect of heaven
all the more appealing.

For that and for everything the Lord had done, was doing, and
was yet to do, Paul exulted, **To Him be the glory forever and ever.
Amen.**

THE FAITHFUL OLD FRIENDS

**Greet Prisca and Aquila, and the household of Onesiphorus.
Erastus remained at Corinth, but Trophimus I left sick at Miletus.
(4:19–20)**

Paul did not fail to remember old friends. He had met **Prisca
and Aquila** at Corinth on his second missionary journey. They had fled
Italy when the Emperor Claudius ordered all Jews expelled from Rome
(Acts 18:2). Because they were fellow tentmakers, Paul stayed at their
house while "reasoning in the synagogue every Sabbath and trying to
persuade Jews and Greeks" (v. 4). When he and his party left Corinth,
he took along this devoted couple and left them to minister in Ephesus
(vv. 18–19). While there, Priscilla (the longer form of **Prisca**) and **Aquila**
met a fellow "Jew named Apollos, an Alexandrian by birth, an eloquent
man, [who] . . . was mighty in the Scriptures" (v. 24). When they realized Apollos's understanding of the gospel was incomplete, they lovingly
took him aside "and explained to him the way of God more accurately"
(v. 26). In his letter to the Roman church, the apostle greeted "Prisca
and Aquila, [his] fellow workers in Christ Jesus" (Rom. 16:3), indicating
that these two special friends were again living and ministering in Corinth, the city from which the epistle was written.

Earlier in this letter, Paul expressed appreciation **for the household of Onesiphorus,** who "often refreshed me, and was not ashamed
of my chains" (1:16). Because the **household** is mentioned in both
places, it is obvious that everyone in it was a Christian, perhaps led to
Christ by **Onesiphorus** himself. Such a **household** would have included
not only family members but also servants and friends who lived with
Onesiphorus.

The **Erastus [who] remained at Corinth** probably was "the
city treasurer" of Corinth, who sent greetings through Paul to the church
at Rome (Rom. 16:23). He also may have been the man whom the apostle sent with Timothy to minister in Macedonia (Acts 19:22).

Trophimus was a native of the province of Asia, specifically the city of Ephesus, and had accompanied Paul from Greece to Troas (Acts 20:1–6). He probably helped carry the offering to the church in Jerusalem, where he was the unintentional cause of Paul's arrest for presumably bringing a Gentile into the temple (Acts 21:29). On his trip to Rome, Paul sadly had to leave him **sick at Miletus.**

It is important to note that Paul made no effort himself to heal **Trophimus,** who, incidentally, was present at the late-night service in Troas when the apostle miraculously restored life to Eutychus, a young man who went to sleep during the sermon and fell out a window to his death (Acts 20:9–10; cf. v.4). The sign gifts were coming to an end. There is no evidence that any of the apostles, including Paul, performed miracles of any sort during their later years. As more and more of the New Testament was revealed and made available to the church, God's Word no longer needed the verification of miracles.

THE FAITHFUL NEW FRIENDS

Make every effort to come before winter. Eubulus greets you, also Pudens and Linus and Claudia and all the brethren. (4:21b)

Before he extends greetings on behalf of fellow believers who now ministered with him and to him in Rome, Paul expands an earlier request (v. 9), asking Timothy to **make every effort to come before winter.** He would desperately need the cloak for warmth. As for the books and parchments, Paul realized that what little light he now had for reading and writing would decrease still more as the days became shorter.

Final greetings are extended on behalf of **Eubulus, . . . Pudens and Linus.** All three names were Latin, perhaps indicating that the men were from Italy and had been members of the church in Rome.

Claudia was a faithful believer and close friend of Paul about whom we know nothing else. Conjecture and legend have suggested she was the wife or mother of **Linus,** but no firm evidence supports those views.

THE BENEDICTION

The Lord be with your spirit. Grace be with you. (4:22)

All of the people Paul mentions in this passage were part of the network in which he was involved. The network included both men and women, close friends and avowed enemies, the faithful and the deserter, the true believer and the unbeliever. In one way or another, they all affected the ministry and outreach of the early church, especially the ministry and outreach of this great apostle.

As always, Paul's focus was on **the Lord,** whom he now asks to be with those special friends and co-workers in **spirit.** Most of them he would never see or hear from again. He left them in the Lord's hands and in His **grace.**

Bibliography

Barclay, William. *The Letter to the Romans.* Philadelphia: Westminster, 1957.

_____. *The Letters to Timothy, Titus and Philemon.* Philadelphia: Westminster, 1960.

Harvey, H. *Commentary on the Pastoral Epistles, I & II Timothy and Titus, and the Epistle to Philemon.* Philadelphia: American Baptist Pub. Soc., 1890.

Hendriksen, William. *New Testament Commentary: Expositions of the Pastoral Epistles.* Grand Rapids: Baker, 1965.

Kent, Homer A., Jr. *The Pastoral Epistles: Studies in I & II Timothy and Titus.* Chicago: Moody, 1958.

Montgomery, John Warwick. *Damned Through the Church.* Minneapolis: Bethany, 1970.

Spurgeon, Charles Haddon. *Lectures to My Students.* Grand Rapids: Zondervan, 1955.

Taylor, William. *The Ministry of the Word.* Grand Rapids: Baker, 1975.

Trench, Richard C. *Synonyms of the New Testament.* Grand Rapids: Eerdmans, 1960.

Vincent, Marvin R. *Word Studies in the New Testament.* Vols. 3, 4. New York: Scribner's, 1904.

Westcott, B. F., and F. J. A. Hort. *The New Testament in the Original Greek.* New York: Macmillan, 1929.

Wuest, Kenneth S. *Philippians, Hebrews, the Pastoral Epistles, First Peter.* Vol. 2 of *Word Studies from the Greek New Testament.* Grand Rapids: Eerdmans, 1966.

Indexes

Index of Greek Words

Index of Scripture

Index of Subjects

Moody Press, a ministry of the Moody Bible Institute,
is designed for education, evangelization, and edification.
If we may assist you in knowing more about Christ
and the Christian life, please write us without obligation:
Moody Press, c/o MLM, Chicago, Illinois 60610.